CHILDREN'S ENCYCLOPEDIA

SCIENCE | SPACE
INVENTIONS & DISCOVERIES

© Wonder House Books 2024

All rights reserved. No part of this book may be reproduced or transmitted in any form by any means, electronic or mechanical, including photocopying and recording, or by any information storage and retrieval system except as may be expressly permitted in writing by the publisher.

(An imprint of Prakash Books)

contact@wonderhousebooks.com

Disclaimer: The information contained in this encyclopedia has been collated with inputs from subject experts. All information contained herein is true to the best of the Publisher's knowledge.

ISBN : 9789358564686

Table of Contents

Inventions & Discoveries	6–7
Material Progress	8
All That Glitters	10–11
Exploration and Invention	12–13
Blocks of Civilisation	14
Cementing Success	15
To Spin a Yarn	16
Which Way is North?	17
Mightier than the Sword	18–19
Creating Surplus	20–21
The Adventures of Marco Polo	22–23
A Passage to India	24
The New World	25
Exploring North America	26
The Lands Down Under	27
The Evolution Revolution	28–29
Discovering Africa	30
Undercover Adventures	31
Around the World in 72 Days	32
The Lost City of the Incas	32
Cool Conquests	33
Vacuum Tubes	34
Semiconductors and Microchips	35
Batteries	36
Telegraph	37
Radio	38
Who Invented the Telephone?	39
Television: Moving Pictures Sent on Radio Waves	40
Computers: A Fruit of the Loom	41–42
The Development of Computers	43
Networking	44–45

A Balancing Act	46–47
Ingenious Engines	48
What is Internal Combustion?	49
The First Cars	50–51
A World on Track	52
To Keep the Wheels Turning	53
Ships Ahoy!	54–55
Flights of Fantasy	56
Soaring High	57
The Rocket Launch	58
Reaching for the Stars	59
A Peek Inside the Body	60–61
Photography for Physicians	62–63
Preventing Infections	64–65
An Infectious Theory	66–67
Indispensable Medicine	68
What is a Transplant?	69
Sussing out Surgery	70–71
Genetics	72
Royal Rarities	73
Cosmology: From Ancient Times to the 19th Century	74–75
The Space Race	76–77
Kicking off Space Exploration	78–79
To the Moon and Back	80–81
Artificial Satellites	82
Telescopes: A Distant Look	83

Science

	84–85
Space Stations: Stellar Base Camps	86
Living in Space	87
What Makes Up Matter	88–89
The Periodic Table	90–91
States of Matter	92
Metals	93

Purification Methods	94
Acids, Bases, and pH	95
Electricity: The Basics	96–97
Current and Resistance	98–99
Making Electricity	100–101
Electric Circuits	102–103
Magnetism	104
Semiconductors	105
Renewable Energy	106–107
Force: Making Things Move	108–109
What Makes Us Move	110–111
When Things Move in a Straight Line	112–113
When Things Don't Move in a Straight Line	114–115
Why Things Fall Down	116–117
Forces of Resistance	118
Engines	119
Machines	120–121
Density and Buoyancy	122–123
Nanotechnology	124–125
Artificial Intelligence	126
3D Printing	127
Robotics	128–129
Genetic Engineering	130–131
Photons	132–133
Electromagnetism	134–135
Energy	136–137
Optics	138–139
Lenses and Prisms	140–141
Heat Transfer	142–143
Space	144–145
Creation of the Universe	146–147
All about Galaxies	148–149

Amazing Celestial Oddities: Black Holes & Auroras	150
Amazing Asteroids	151
Meteoroids, Meteors, & Meteorites	152–153
Satellites: Natural & Artificial	154
Matter & Antimatter	155
The Life Cycle of Stars	156–157
Nebulas: The Birthplace of Stars	158–159
What's a Supernova?	160–161
Stargazers	162–163
Constellations in the Sky	164
Spotting Constellations	165
Constellations in the Northern Hemisphere	166–167
Constellations in the Southern Hemisphere	168–169
A Brief History	170–171
Renaissance and Astronomy	172–173
Modern Astronomy	174–175
The International Space Station	176
The Hubble Space Telescope	177
Satellites	178
The Future of Space Exploration	179
All about Astronauts	180–181
The First Humans in Space	182
The First Human Beings to Reach the Moon	183
Milestones in Space Exploration	184–185
Word Check	**186–189**
Image Credits	**190–192**

INVENTIONS & DISCOVERIES

This encyclopedia is an intriguing exploration of human evolution and the remarkable inventions that have shaped history. Beginning around six to three million years ago, our early ancestors transitioned from walking on all fours to walking upright, unlocking the potential of their arms and opening new avenues of achievement.

As their arms became free, early humans harnessed their creativity and curiosity, leading to groundbreaking discoveries and inventions. The field of electronics and communication witnessed remarkable progress during the wars of the previous century, resulting in the gadgets and technologies that now dominate our lives.

Astronomers, mapping the sky through the ages, unveiled the secrets of planets, stars, and galaxies. The study of the universe, known as cosmology, and its physical laws, astrophysics, allow us to delve into the mysteries of the cosmos and explore alien worlds.

In the realm of medicine, ancient beliefs in supernatural causes gave way to a search for physical explanations. Major advancements during the Middle Ages led to identifying microorganisms as agents of disease, revolutionizing healthcare and saving countless lives.

The Industrial Age transformed labor and transportation with the invention of locomotive engines. From simple steam engines to modern electric power, these innovations enabled humanity to conquer new frontiers and facilitate ease of travel.

Join us on a captivating journey through time as we delve into the story of the evolution of our species. Discover the pivotal inventions that have shaped our world and marvel at the wonders of the cosmos. This is an exploration of human achievement, where past discoveries lay the foundation for our present and inspire future progress.

▼ *Neanderthals were some of the first human beings to walk on two feet*

Material Progress

Look at any timeline of human history and you will notice that historians track human progress in terms of when certain materials were invented and used. Glass, paper, mortar, metals, and cloth are all a part of this timeline. Some materials are so important to us that historical periods have been named after them. The Stone Age, the Bronze Age and the Iron Age are classified according to when stone, bronze, and iron were used to create tools and technologies.

⭐ Incredible Individuals

Over 3 million years ago, the ancestors of humans began making stone tools. Among these early inventors was East Africa's *Australopithecus afarensis*. The most popular member of this species is Lucy. She was discovered by Donald Johanson and Tom Gray in 1974 in Hadar, Ethiopia. While Lucy was not the first to be discovered, her discovery revolutionised our understanding of human evolution; most importantly, that our brain size increased after we became **bipedal**

◀ Bone fragments of Lucy, who lived some 3.2 million years ago

2.58 MILLION YEARS AGO

This marked the start of the Palaeolithic Period, or the Old Stone Age. However, the world's earliest stone tools were even older. They belonged to **proto humans** who lived 3.3 million years ago, near Lake Turkana in East Africa.

C. 1.5 MILLION YEARS AGO

Evidence shows that humans used fire for light, warmth, and to keep insects and predators away.

600,000 YEARS AGO

The earliest known man-made hearth or fireplace lay inside the Qesem Cave in Israel. About 15–20 people may have lived there and used fire for cooking. In fact, cooking food regularly may have played a role in expanding the brain!

500,000 YEARS AGO

In England, a Stone Age horse was discovered with a hole in its shoulder bone, made by a wooden spear.

The oldest stone-tipped spears were seen in South Africa.

C. 170,000 YEARS AGO

Humans began covering their bodies with clothes at this point. The first lice belongs to the same time. Do you think there is a connection between the invention of clothes and the evolution of lice?

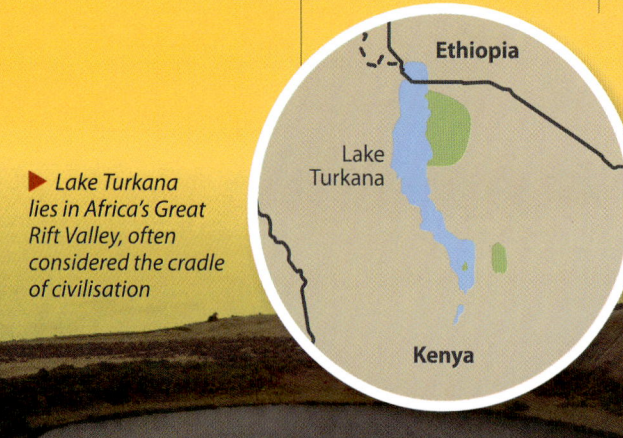

▶ Lake Turkana lies in Africa's Great Rift Valley, often considered the cradle of civilisation

▶ *Australopithecus afarensis* looked part-ape and part-human

INVENTIONS & DISCOVERIES | ANCIENT CIVILISATIONS

Breakthroughs by Early Humans

Learning human history is not easy. Time, climate, and changing circumstances have destroyed many ancient artefacts. The Stone Age is regarded as the period in history when—across the world—early human tribes were using tools of wood, bone, and stone. Over time, humans have used many types of amazing materials to invent complex structures that made their lives comfortable, efficient, and sophisticated.

In Real Life

Do you think that only humans hunted animals with spears? Then you will be amazed by the videos of a group of chimpanzees in Africa that use spears to hunt galagos. Researchers have been able to spot the chimps hunting them about 22 times!

▶ *Galagos, also called bush babies, are smaller primates hunted by chimps in Africa*

c. 26,000 BCE

Clay was used to make figurines, such as the Venus of Dolni Vestonice. She even bore the fingerprints of an ancient human child who held her!

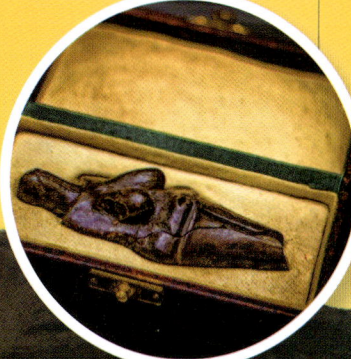

◀ *The Venus of Dolni Vestonice, the oldest known clay figurine*

18,000 BCE

Clay vessels were made by early humans. Some of the oldest clay pots were found in Xianrendong Cave in China.

c. 6,000 BCE

Bricks were used to make the world's first cities. The ruins at Jericho, Turkey, belong to the oldest known city in our knowledge.

◀ *Sun-dried bricks were made in Ur, an ancient city in Mesopotamia in c. 4,000 BCE*

5,550–5,000 BCE

Ancient Egyptians invented linen cloth, spindles, and looms. Ancient Indians discovered the uses of cotton. Metal daggers were created.

All That Glitters

The Copper Age, also called the Chalcolithic Age, began 9,000–11,000 years ago. It is dated from around 4,000–2,000 BCE. It was the first time that humans began using metals. Early humans found that by heating copper, you could make it less hard and more malleable. This meant that they could beat it, melt it, mould it, and even mix it with other metals to make it stronger. Copper was easily mined and more durable than stone-made objects. Experimentation with copper led to the first metalwork technologies and the first smiths in the world.

▲ A bell beaker from Central Europe dating back to the Copper Age

▲ Copper in its natural form

The Bronze Rush

The Copper Age melts into the Bronze Age around 3,000 . The Bronze Age began in Greece and China with the discovery of **alloys**. As different cultures learned the science of melting metals together, so the age spread across the globe. For instance, the Bronze Age in some parts of Africa began as late as the 1st millennium .

Bronze is a yellowish alloy of copper and tin. It was used to make weapons, vessels, jewellery, statues, and heaps of other things. As demand for bronze grew, people looked far and wide for new sources of tin, leading to various explorations!

In Real Life

It is generally agreed that gold was the first metal to be discovered by humans. But it turned out to be too soft, too rare, and too expensive for practical daily use. Soon, the knowledge and skill of purifying and fashioning gold also became greatly valued. This is especially seen in ancient Egypt. Discovered in 1922, the tomb of the late Bronze Age pharaoh **Tutankhamun** is a hoard of golden treasures. His expressive funeral mask in particular is an example of the Egyptians' unparalleled craftsmanship.

▶ Necklaces, plates, and rings from a Bronze Age hoard in Denmark

INVENTIONS & DISCOVERIES | ANCIENT CIVILISATIONS

Bronze Age Leaps

▲ Gold bull-headed bracelet from Bronze Age, Transylvania

After the invention of the wheel and the sailing ship, the first chariots appeared. Trading began, as metals were exchanged for wines and oils. Mathematics became more complex, leading to breakthroughs in astronomy and to improved weights and measures. People could now build spectacular structures like pyramids, temples, and ziggurats. Knowledge poured in from far-off regions. This included different ways of cooking and preserving foods.

▲ A carving of a Sumerian war chariot

▲ An iron dagger from Anatolia, possibly the first country ever to use iron weapons beginning from around 2,000 BCE

▶ Bronze and Iron Age weapons from Romania

▼ The Ziggurat of Ur in Iraq, originally a temple

Iron Man

Over 1,200–300 , iron replaced bronze as the metal of choice. Around 900 , the Egyptians were the first to alloy iron with carbon to create the much lighter and stronger steel. Iron and steel weapons gave civilisations in Greece and Rome a huge advantage. This caused large-scale wars and migrations. Several kingdoms rose and faded during the Iron Age.

▶ The secret of smelting iron ore to fashion tools was a technological breakthrough of the Hittite people of Anatolia

Exploration and Invention

The Bronze Age saw an explosion of action across the globe. This was largely inspired by the need for metals such as tin, which was needed to make bronze. In the process, people travelled to and explored faraway lands. As they travelled, new trade routes were established. In addition, the means for journeying abroad were created, with inventions such as the wheel and the sailboat. As knowledge passed between cultures, human civilisation profited and progressed.

◀ An ancient sailboat on the wall of the Temple of Edfu in Egypt

◀ The Sun Chariot (c. 1,400 BCE) shows the Bronze Age belief that a divine horse pulled the Sun along its path for eternity

c. 4,000–3,000 BCE — The wheel, later used for pottery and for transport; early sailboats; the gnomon—an early form of the sundial; and the first writing system are invented. The oldest engineered roadway—the Sweet Track—is built using wood in England.

c. 3,500 BCE — Earliest evidence of man-made glass is seen in **Mesopotamia** and Egypt.

c. 2,200–1,550 BCE — The spoked-wheel and chariot are invented.

c. 1,600 BCE — The Nebra Sky Disc is the earliest known map of the sky. It is made of bronze and gold. The disc served as a reminder to insert a leap month and has been traced back to Central Europe.

👤 In Real Life

Glass is made of a material called silicon, which lends its name to the age in which we live. The Silicon Age is dependent on electronic devices such as computers, TVs, cell phones, smart appliances, and so forth. These inventions are powered by silicon chips.

◀ A Greek amphora (c. 550 BCE) showing a pair of horses harnessed to a chariot with spoked-wheels

INVENTIONS & DISCOVERIES | ANCIENT CIVILISATIONS | 13

Breakthroughs of the Bronze Age

As trade and knowledge grew, record-keeping became necessary. Thus, scripts were invented in the Bronze Age. Cuneiform, the earliest known form of writing, developed in ancient Sumeria. It was considered a gift from the god, Enlil. The Chinese developed their script around 1,600–1,046 by throwing oracle bones. The cracks in the bones were considered the word of god and set down by writers.

▲ The world's oldest coin, the Lydian Lion, is made of electrum, a mix of gold and silver. The Lydians may have been the first people to use gold and silver coins

The first paved trackway called diolkos is built in ancient Greece. It is a line of grooved paving stones connecting two seaports. Goods 'trains' are hauled across it to save shipping costs. Light warships are also transported over the diolkos.

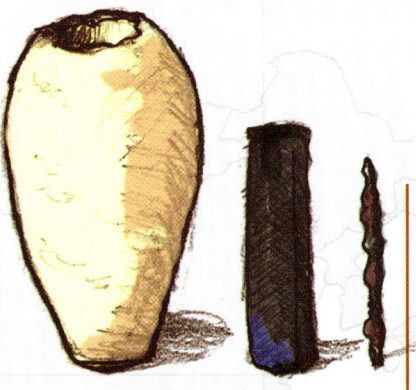

The first battery is made by Parthians in an area that lies in present-day Baghdad. It is made of clay jars filled with vinegar. Inside each jar is a copper cylinder with an iron rod on top. This early type of battery is most likely used to electroplate silver, which stops it from going black.

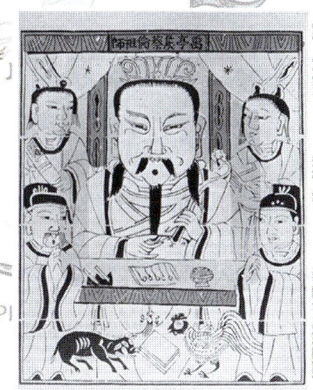

Cai Lun invents paper.

600 BCE | **500–400 BCE** | **250 BCE** | **105 BCE**

◀ The Nebra Sky Disc shows the Sun, Moon, and the Pleiades constellation of stars

▶ An old gnomon—the projecting piece on a sundial—from the 7th century Sui dynasty in China

Blocks of Civilisation

Around 4,000 BCE, the Sumerians were the first civilisation to build cities across their land. With names like Kish, Lagash, Umma, Eridu, and Uruk, these urban centres had temples, schools, and the tallest buildings ever seen. As with other forms of human progress, cities would have been impossible without the invention of certain material technologies.

Moulding the Earth

Clay is one of the earliest materials exploited by humans. Different communities invented their own methods of using clay to advance civilisation. As a result, the remains of unique styles of earthenware can help us identify changing civilisations, even in the same region.

All forms of long-lasting pottery require the clay to be baked in an oven. If a vessel is made with only sun-dried clay, it cannot hold any liquid. But if it is heated (fired) in a kiln, to at least 500°C, irreversible chemical changes will occur within the clay to make the material stronger.

▲ *Aqueducts are ancient structures that carried water to fields and cities. Many of them required brick and clay*

The Appearance of Clay

Variations in the kiln and in firing give amazingly different kinds of pottery. Some ancient inventions in clay-based technologies include terracotta, ceramic, stoneware, porcelain, and china. Even in modern times, clay arts require much knowledge and skill, and the best clay pieces can be identified by region and artist. Clay was also used as an ingredient to make stronger building materials.

▶ *The Greek god of grapes and wine, Dionysus, in a ship sailing among dolphins; black-figure pottery from Mycenaean Greece, c. 530 BCE*

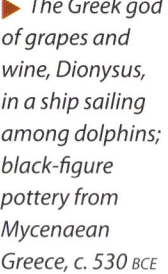 Brick by Brick

The invention of bricks allowed humans to build the first cities. The earliest bricks were sun-dried blocks of clay mixed with things like straw and shale. In the Mesopotamian city of Ur—roughly modern-day Iraq—sun-baked bricks were used to build the first true arch. This happened during 4,000 . Eventually, people discovered the right mix of earthy ingredients to make the strongest bricks. They also fired bricks in kilns to make them more long-lasting.

In 210 , engineers used both fired and sun-dried bricks to build the Great Wall of China. By 600 , the Babylonians and Assyrians were adding a glaze or enamel to make coloured bricks. It is unfortunate that some of this ancient technology, the creation of certain blue glazes in particular, has been lost and cannot be recreated today.

▶ *Brick ruins of a reservoir in Gujarat, India, which was part of the Indus Valley Civilisation*

Cementing Success

Mortar is a slushy mix that is layered into the gaps between bricks or stones. It hardens in the air and holds the construction together more securely. Mortar is made of sand, water, and some kind of binder, such as lime. Ancient Egyptians developed the earliest known mortar in about 4,000 BCE. This was a soft paste of gypsum (plaster) and sand. The Romans used a slightly more advanced method to create lime mortars.

▲ Many experts believe that the spectacular pyramids of Egypt had some type of mortar that held the stones together

🔍 Roman Cement

About 2,000 years ago, the ancient Greeks and Romans invented a type of cement that used lime and volcanic ash. These two compounds reacted in the presence of water to form a hard mass. The mix set very slowly and took centuries to harden completely. As a result, many Roman structures are still standing today, though they were built way back in the Iron Age. In comparison, some of our modern mortars used in bridges, roads, and buildings crumble in 50–100 years.

▲ In 79 CE, a volcanic eruption covered the ancient Roman city of Pompeii in lava. The cooling rock preserved the streets and buildings, including signs on shop fronts and Iron Age graffiti

🔍 Monument for the Ages

The word cement comes from the Latin word 'caementum', which referred to stone chips, like the ones used to make Roman mortar. It did not refer to the cement mixture itself. Most buildings in Rome made use of multiple materials to create comfortable homes and striking landmarks. For instance, the famous Pantheon of Rome was constructed in 123 using brick, but had an amazing dome of concrete that stretched across 43 m.

▲ The Basilica of Maxentius is a marvel of Roman engineering and would have been impossible without mortar

▲ Bathing was a social activity in Roman times. Ancient Roman baths were large constructions that required mortar

To Spin a Yarn

Clothes were first worn by proto humans called Neanderthals. They used animal hides to cover themselves and to show off their status! Then came the **Cro-Magnons**, who used needle-like tools to punch holes into hides and lace them up again.

▶ *Prehistoric clothes of Otzi, the Iceman*

Otzi the Iceman

Otzi the Iceman is a 5,300-year-old human who showed us what prehistoric fashion was like. His clothes were made from the skins, bones, horns, and feathers of six types of animals. His attire also had leaves, wood, and fibre from 17 different trees.

A New Set of Threads

Felt is the name given to the first man-made cloth; that is, not leather or fur, but real fabric. Felt is made by matting, condensing, and pressing natural fibres together. It was invented well before spinning, weaving, and knitting. You have most likely seen felt in your arts and crafts classes.

The Sumerians believed that it was Urnamman of Lagash, who discovered the secret of felt-making.

◀ *A felt hat from the Loulan kingdom of Iron Age China*

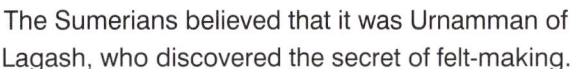 The Silk Road

This was a cross-continental east-west network that allowed merchants to exchange luxury goods. It brought great wealth to civilisations across China, India, Egypt, Central Asia, and Rome.

 Weaving

The oldest bit of woven cloth dates to the 7th millennium . It was used for wrapping the dead in Anatolia (present-day Turkey). Nalbinding, an early type of knitting, was seen soon after, around 6,500 .

In Japan, weaving was well established by 5,500 . Painted pottery from this time shows people wearing clothes. As civilisations discovered new fibres, they invented more ways of creating textiles.

▲ *A bundle of silkworm cocoons*

Loose Ends

Spinning is the word for pulling and twisting raw fibre into thread. Surprisingly though, spinning seems to have been invented after weaving. Around the time the Egyptians were producing linen, they invented the drop spindle, hand-to-hand spinning, and rolling the yarn on the thigh. They also knew of the horizontal ground loom and the vertical two-beam loom, both of which came from Asia.

◀ *The Egyptian drop spindle*

💡 Isn't It Amazing!

A 50,000-year-old needle is the oldest sewing tool in existence. It is made from the bone of a large bird and has a bit of twine still attached to it.

Which Way is North?

Did you know that Earth has two poles? What we think of as the top and bottom points of the planet are the geographic north and south poles, respectively. But, Earth also has magnetic north and south poles, which are hundreds of miles away from the true or geographic north and south. The compass, which is a magnetic device, will always point to the magnetic north pole. But when was it invented?

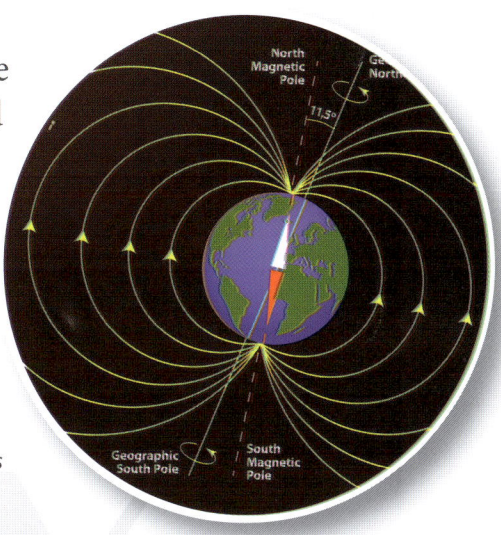

▶ *Earth is a giant spinning magnet with moving magnetic poles and fixed geographic poles*

Incredible Individuals

Chinese inventor Ma Jun (200–265) built a chariot with a small statue atop that always pointed south. This clever contraption did not use magnets. It had a system of gears that turned the statue in the direction opposite to the chariot, but at the same angles. Thus, one could never be lost in a chaotic battlefield with such a tool.

Legend has it that the Qin dynasty (221–206) invented a south-pointing ship along similar lines. But it is more likely that the ship used magnets, which were well known to the Qin engineers.

Compass

Some scholars believe that the magnetic compass was invented by the Chinese during the 2nd–1st century . Early magnetized needles were set on wood and floated in a basin of water. When the needle came to a standstill, its marked tip would point North-South. Records show a spoon-shaped compass dating from the ancient Han Dynasty. The magnetic spoon rested on a square bronze plate—representing Earth—that bore a circle—symbolizing heaven. The board was marked with constellations and astrological signs. The first Chinese emperor is said to have used such a divining board and compass in court to affirm his right to the throne! It would be several centuries more before the compass was put to practical use by travellers.

◀ *Ma Jun's south-pointing chariot*

Isn't It Amazing!

If you had a compass 800,000 years ago, its needle would have pointed towards the southern hemisphere! Since its discovery in the early 19th century, the magnetic north has drifted over 966 kms and continues to move every year. Scientists worry that the next pole swap could destroy our entire electric grid!

◀ *This south-pointing spoon is a compass of the Chinese Han dynasty (202 BCE–220 CE)*

Mightier than the Sword

Though speaking comes naturally to all of us, writing has to be formally learned. But when did writing systems evolve? In the 4th millennium BCE, trade and wealth were expanding rapidly. People needed a way to track their bargains, monies, properties, and other details. Kings also needed such information, so they could exact taxes for making roads and war. The first scripts were most likely invented as memory aids and bookkeeping tools. But they soon flourished to express larger, bolder, newer ideas that would change the world over and over again.

▼ This giant cuneiform 'page' was inscribed into the side of a hill by order of the Persian King Xerxes in praise of the God Ahuramazda

▶ Sumerian cuneiform is the earliest writing we know of. This cone from 1,850 BCE records, 'Sin-kashid, mighty man, king of Uruk, king of the Amnanum, provider of the temple Eanna, built his royal palace'

▲ Ancient Egyptian scripts are called hieroglyphics, meaning 'sacred carvings'. You often see them on amazing murals accompanying gods and pharaohs

▼ Evidence of Chinese writing exists from 1,500 BCE, but it likely developed well before that. This tortoise shell shows a divination from the time of King Wu Ding (1,200 BCE)

▼ Hieroglyphic carvings at an ancient Egyptian temple

▼ One of the 12 clay tablets of the earliest known poem, 'The Epic of Gilgamesh', 2,003–1,595 BCE

INVENTIONS & DISCOVERIES | ANCIENT CIVILISATIONS

Carved in Stone

The scripts of the 4th millennium were etched on to clay tablets with a reed stylus. Sometimes, they were drawn with ink made of ground charcoal, powdered insects, plants, or natural pigments. People also wrote on bone, stone, wax tablets, animal skins, tanned leather, bark, and silk. Around 3,100–2,900 , Egypt invented papyrus from reeds that grew by the River Nile. This was used in the form of washable, reusable scrolls, and to wrap mummies!

Around 104–105 , the imperial official Cai Lun showed his invention of paper to the Han emperor of China. It rapidly became the writing material of choice for the entire world.

▲ *In ancient India, sacred and political texts would be recorded on strips of palm leaves tied together to form manuscripts*

In Real Life

The invention of the alphabet powered most modern written languages. Most Western, Arabic, and Indian alphabets come from a system of writings popular in Syria in the 11th century . The Greeks were the first to adapt it to their language, around 1,000–900 .

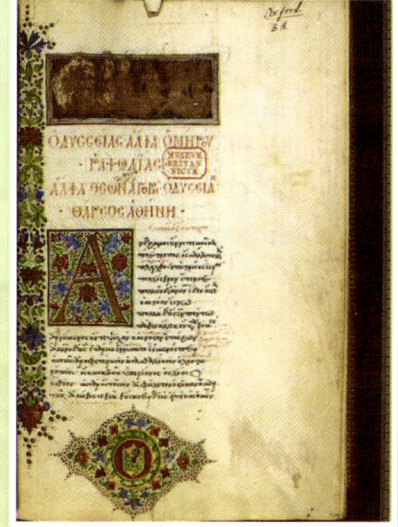 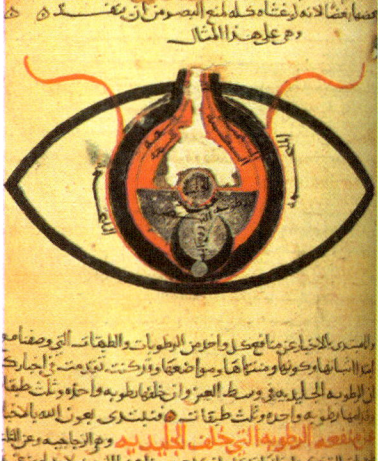

▲ *Ancient alphabets: a Greek page from 'The Odyssey'; an Arabic medical book page about the eye*

◀ *The Code of Hammurabi is a stone tablet from 2nd millennium BCE recording the laws and punishments of its Babylonian king*

▼ *Some of the Dead Sea Scrolls (300 BCE– 200 CE), manuscripts of great importance to Christianity and Judaism, were written on thin, whitish leather*

Creating Surplus

▲ The Fertile Crescent was a sickle-shaped land that was the birthplace of a number of technological innovations

Historians often mark the beginning of civilisation as that crucial time when hunter-gatherers gave up wandering and began farming. Agricultural technologies allowed humans to literally reap the wealth of the earth. To farm successfully, we tamed rivers, mountains, and, of course, plants and animals. The farmers' labour and ingenuity created so much surplus that populations grew rapidly. With more people came specialised occupations and about 11,000 years of the most amazing advances in civilisation.

◀ The first large network of dams and channels was created by Egypt's First Dynasty. It began in 3,100 BCE under King Menes and led to the formation of Lake Moeris, which is still around

▲ The Egyptians invented the Nilometer in the 3rd century BCE. It is a measuring column that sunk into the river to check flood levels

9,500 BCE
The eight founding crops of agriculture—emmer and einkorn wheat, barley, peas, lentils, bitter vetch, chickpeas, and flax—are cultivated in the Fertile Crescent.

8,000 BCE
Agriculture begins in parts of the Americas as hunter-gatherers grow wild crops to broaden their food sources. Squash is one of these early crops.

6,000 BCE
Irrigation begins: the floodwaters of the Nile (in Egypt) and the rivers Tigris and Euphrates (in Mesopotamia) are diverted to the fields over July–December and then drained back into the rivers.

2,800 BCE
The first evidence of a ploughed field is seen at Kalibangan. The area was part of the Indus Valley Civilisation.

INVENTIONS & DISCOVERIES | ANCIENT CIVILISATIONS

In Real Life

The fertile Indian subcontinent was ideal for ancient farmers. Oranges, wheat, and legumes were easily cultivated. Dates and mangoes appeared by 4,000 . By 2,000 , teas, bananas, rice, and apples were being grown. Over the next millennium, coconuts were being exported to Africa and eggplants were in cultivation.

▲ Three water wheels in front of the Azem Palace, Syria

▶ Modern rice farms in mountainous China

◀ The counter-weighted Shadoof raising water up from a low river with steep banks

1,700 BCE
When the river is not in flood, an invention called the Shadoof allows farmers to lift water for irrigating fields using a bucket. By 700 , this is further eased by the invention of the water wheel, which required little human effort.

500 BCE
Greece uses crop rotation methods on large estates.

▶ A hydraulic-powered trip hammer

100 BCE
The Chinese invent the hydraulic-powered trip hammer to pound and polish grain.

100 CE
The Chinese invent the square-pallet chain pump. It is powered by a water-wheel or pulled by oxen. It raises water up into channels that irrigate farmland on high ground.

The Adventures of Marco Polo

Italian merchant Marco Polo (1254–1324) introduced the fabled worlds of China and Asia to medieval Europe. Marco belonged to a family of jewel merchants who traded with Eastern nations. In 1271, he journeyed with his father and uncle (Niccolo and Maffeo Polo) to the powerful Mongol kingdom. Marco Polo was just 17 years old. Over the next 24 years, he would acquire incredible knowledge of Asia and Europe through his fantastic travels.

▲ *An 1867 mosaic of Marco Polo at the Palazzo Grimaldi Doria-Tursi (the Municipal Palace of Genoa)*

🔍 The Legendary Silk Road

Carrying letters from the Pope to the Mongol Emperor Kublai Khan, Marco and his relatives journeyed through the wealthy city of Acre into south-eastern Turkey and northern Iran. They crossed hostile bandit-infested deserts and rested at Hormuz, a city on the Persian **Gulf**. The Polos then continued into Asia using the Silk Road.

The legendary Silk Road was a string of valuable trade routes across China, India, and the Mediterranean. Large convoys of wealth-laden caravans were a common sight here. They were often accompanied by armed cohorts to guard the riches. The Polos visited fabulous places like Khorasan, Badakhshan, Pamir, Kota, and even the Gobi Desert. Finally, in 1275, they reached Chengdu, where they met Kublai Khan at his summer palace.

▼ *Marco Polo's route from Venice (Italy) to Mongol China, then known as Cathay to the West*

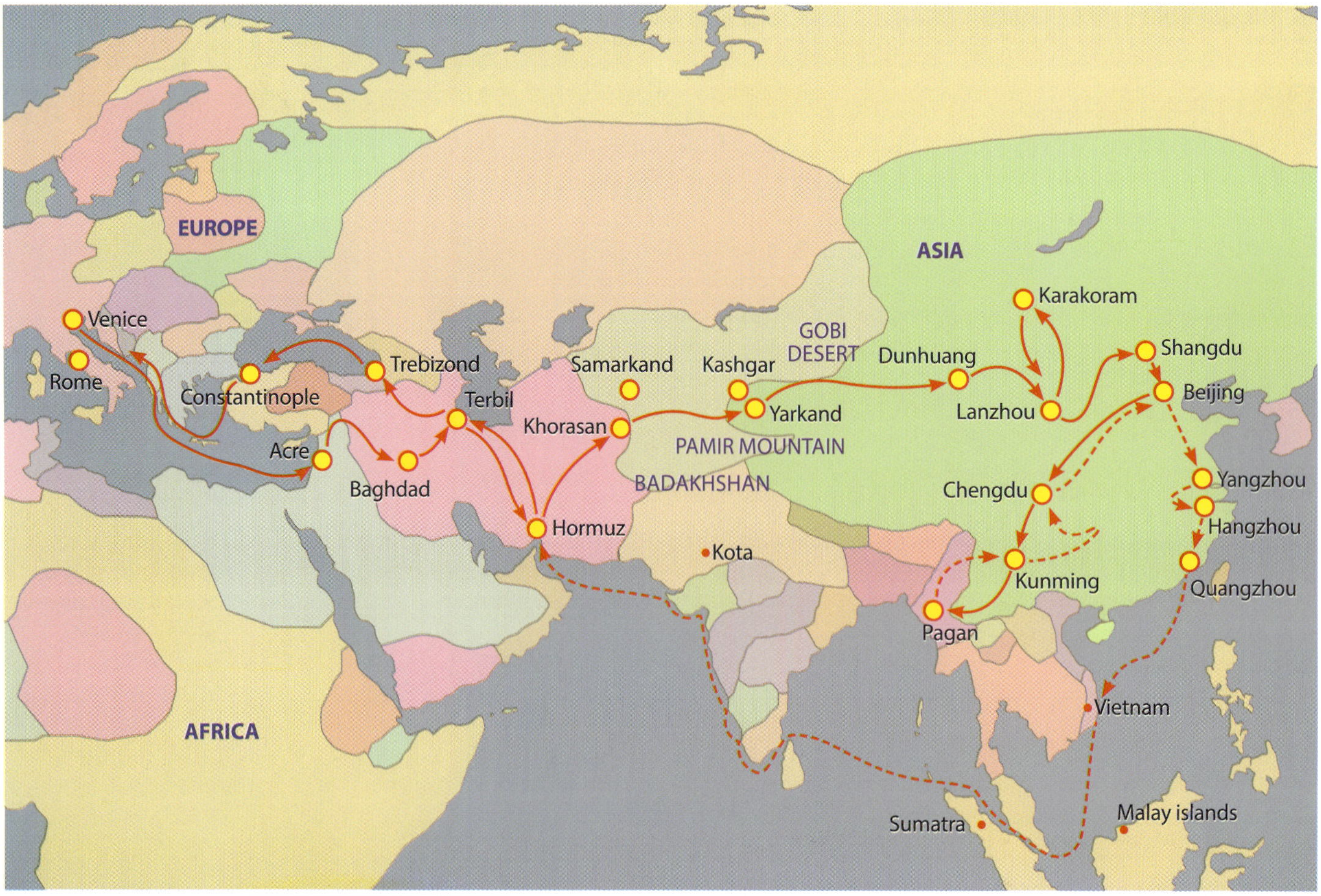

INVENTIONS & DISCOVERIES | EARTH DISCOVERIES

⭐ Incredible Individuals

Young Marco was amazed by the opulence of Mongol China. Nothing in Europe quite compared to it. The Khan's capital city, **Kinsay**, was large, clean, and organised. It had wide roads and extraordinary infrastructure—like the Grand Canal, which is, even today, the largest man-made waterway.

The food, the clothes, the people, and the animals were all new and fascinating to Marco. In his book, he wrote of rhinoceroses and crocodiles, which he thought were unicorns and giant, toothed serpents with "eyes bigger than a four penny loaf!"

▶ An engraving of Marco Polo

🔍 The Khan's Favourite

Marco was about 20 years old when he reached China. He would live there for another 17 years. He became a favourite of Kublai Khan, who loved listening to his stories of far-off lands. In fact, the emperor sent Marco to explore different parts of his own empire. Eventually, Marco held official posts at court. He even claimed to be the governor of Yangzhou for about three years.

🔍 Journey Home

Around 1290–1292, Kublai Khan sent a princess-bride to Argun Khan of Persia. She was accompanied by 600 courtiers and 14 ships. Reluctantly, he also allowed the Polos to leave in her train. They visited Vietnam, the Malay islands, and Sumatra, before reaching Persia. From there, the Polos travelled on to Trebizond (where they were badly robbed) and Constantinople. They reached home in Venice, in 1295.

▲ Soon after his death in 1294, Kublai Khan was painted (as a younger man) by the Nepalese artist and astronomer Anige. This silk painting can be seen at the National Palace Museum in Taiwan

🔍 Il Milione

In 1298, Marco Polo became a prisoner of war. That year, he narrated his stories to a fellow prisoner, Rustichello. The tales were published and became hugely popular. For the first time in centuries, Europeans learned what the East was really like. The amazing book, *Il Milione* is more commonly known as *The Travels of Marco Polo* in English.

👤 In Real Life

The maps that Marco Polo brought back from his journey influenced the development of **cartography** and are still used as a guide for undiscovered archaeological sites.

▲ The 15th century monk Fra Mauro's map of the world—the most accurate map of that time—owed a great deal to a nautical map and a world map that Polo brought back from his travels

▲ Marco Polo passed away at the age of 70 in Venice. He lies buried at the Campo San Lorenzo

A Passage to India

The infamous Portuguese navigator Vasco da Gama (1460–1524) opened up a new sea route from Europe to India. This took him around the Cape of Good Hope, which is located in the south of the continent of Africa. Its name comes from a belief of ancient travellers that India could be reached by sea from Europe. Vasco da Gama sailed for King Manuel I of Portugal, who wanted to control the riches of India.

▲ *King Manuel I directs a kneeling Vasco da Gama to sail to India*

The First Voyage: 1497–1499

Da Gama left Lisbon with four ships on 8 July 1497. After battling storms and scurvy, they sailed into Calicut on 20 May 1498. Calicut was then a wealthy port-city on India's western coast. Its powerful ruler, the Zamorin, courteously received the Portuguese sailors. But in return, da Gama offered cheap gifts. He even tried selling poor-quality items to the savvy city merchants. Naturally, people refused his offers and looked down upon him. A sulking da Gama left by the end of August, vowing revenge.

Isn't It Amazing!

On his first voyage, da Gama was away for over two years. He spent 300 days at sea and travelled about 39,000 km.

▲ *An 1850 engraving shows da Gama greeting the Zamorin, the king of Calicut*

In Real Life

Da Gama's ships carried stone pillars meant to mark 'discovered' territories, even though the regions were already inhabited by **indigenous** populations.

▲ *Arriving from Lisbon, Portugal to Kochi, India*

The Second Voyage: 1502–1503

Da Gama returned to India with an armed fleet, intent on wreaking havoc. He began by stealing the cargo of an Arab ship and setting its 200–400 passengers—men, women, and children—on fire! With the help of Cannore (now Kannur) and Cochin (now Kochi)—enemies of Calicut—he forced the Zamorin to agree to his terms. Da Gama sailed back to Portugal with shiploads of ill-gotten gains.

The Last Voyage: 1524 CE

In 1524, da Gama returned as the Portuguese Viceroy of India. However, he fell ill and died in Kochi. In 1538, his body was sent back to Portugal.

◀ *Vasco da Gama's pillar in Kenya, to commemorate his 'discovery' of the land*

The New World

The 15th century Italian explorer Christopher Columbus is often credited with **discovering the Americas.** However, many others were there before him—notably the Native Americans and the Vikings. Columbus's achievement was bringing the Americas into wider public consciousness. His ambition kicked off global territorial battles. In the same century, a Spanish **conquistador** named Vasco Nunez de Balboa established the first stable settlement in the New World and 'discovered' its eastern shores of the Pacific Ocean.

▲ *In the 16th century, Italian explorer Amerigo Vespucci first realised that South America was a proper continent and not an extension of Asia. He thus called it the New World. He also discovered present-day Brazil*

A Permanent Settlement

In 1510, Balboa, a failing planter and pig farmer in Haiti, escaped his creditors by hiding in a ship's barrel, along with his dog Leoncico! The ship brought him to the Spanish settlement of Uraba in modern Colombia. The settlement eventually moved to the **Isthmus** of Panama. There, they defeated 500 Native Americans led by chief Cemaco and established Santa Maria la Antigua del Darien, the first permanent settlement of Europeans on the American mainland.

◀ *Columbus lands in the West Indies and claims the territory for imperial Spain, while ignoring the fact that the land was already home to many indigenous people*

Panama and the Pacific

In 1515, Balboa sailed from Santa Maria to Acla, the narrowest part of the Isthmus of Panama. He was hunting for a rumoured gold-rich province. Balboa brought along 190 Spaniards and hundreds of porters. They travelled southwards through deep forests, crossing rivers and swamps, and ascending a mountain range. On 25 September 1513—though part of the travel record also states 27 September as the date—standing "silent, upon a peak in Darien", Balboa found himself looking at the Pacific Ocean.

▲ *The modern Port of Balboa on the Panama Canal, built over the 19th and 20th centuries*

The South Sea

A group led by Alonso Martin became the first to actually reach the Pacific shore. Balboa himself arrived on 29 September. He walked into the sea with a holy flag and a sword. Taking possession of the new sea for the King of Castille, he named it the Mar del Sur, or South Sea.

▶ *A statue showing Vasco Nunez de Balboa claiming the South Sea*

Exploring North America

English explorer Henry Hudson (1565–1611) is famous for his discoveries of the region around present-day New York. Hudson's journeys began as a search for an ice-free shortcut to Japan and China, by way of the North Pole. He set off in 1607 with his son John and ten others. On this voyage, he explored the polar ice front as far east as the Svalbard archipelago. He set out again on 22 April 1608, exploring the area between Svalbard and Novaya Zemlya islands, east of the Barents Sea. Unfortunately, he was forced to return after finding his path blocked by ice.

▲ Aerial view of New York City and the Hudson River

🔍 The Hudson River

In 1609, Hudson embarked on his third voyage on the ship *Half Moon*. While navigating the Atlantic shores, he encountered a vast river that had already been discovered in 1524 by Florentine navigator Giovanni da Verrazzano. However, this would eventually be called the Hudson River. By September, Hudson had passed Cape Cod, Chesapeake **Bay**, and Delaware Bay and reached the river's **estuary** without discovering any route to the Pacific.

▲ A replica of the Dutch ship Halve Maen (Half Moon)

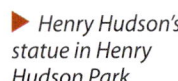
▶ Henry Hudson's statue in Henry Hudson Park

🔍 Hudson Bay

Hudson's next journey led him to an inlet of water that would later be known as Hudson Strait. Sailing on the ship *Discovery* on 17 April 1610, Hudson stopped briefly in Iceland, then passed through the straits to Hudson Bay. Exploring it thoroughly, he landed in James Bay, the southern end of Hudson Bay, still finding no outlet to the Pacific.

Hudson eventually got stranded there for the winter. Quarrels arose among his people. On 22 June 1611, mutineers set Hudson and his son adrift on a small open boat. Neither of them were seen again. The ringleaders of the **mutiny** were themselves killed by Inuits before they reached home.

▲ The Last Voyage of Henry Hudson, a painting by John Collier

◀ Henry Hudson entering New York bay on 11 September 1609, with a Native American family watching from the shore

The Lands Down Under

Dutch navigator Abel Janszoon Tasman (1603–1659) was the first European to discover Tasmania, New Zealand, Tonga, and the Fiji Islands. For most of his life, Tasman was based in Batavia (now Jakarta), where he kept a lookout for rebels and smugglers. In 1642, Tasman was commissioned to explore the southern stretches of the Indian Ocean and map its lands.

Tasmania and New Zealand

On 16 August 1642, Tasman embarked with two ships—the *Heemskerk* and the *Zeehaen*—to Mauritius. Sailing south and east, he discovered new land on 24 November, which he named Van Diemen's Land (now Tasmania). On 13 December, Tasman and his crew became the first Europeans to sight New Zealand's South Island. They entered the strait between North and South Islands, exploring Murderers Bay, North Island's coasts, the Cook Strait, Cape Maria Van Diemen, and the Three Kings islands. They spent Christmas just east of Stephens and D'Urville islands.

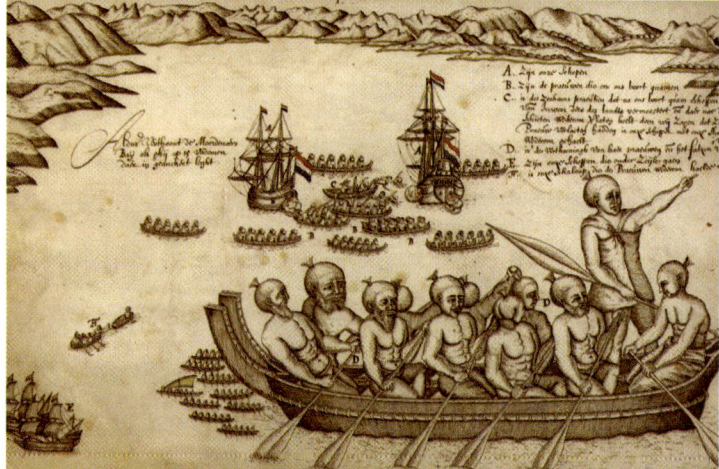

In Real Life

This was the first time the Maori people of New Zealand saw Europeans. Tasman and seven crewmen tried to land on a small boat, but the Maori attacked them, killing three and leaving a fourth to die of wounds. Tasman thus named this area Murderers Bay.

◀ A drawing by Isaack Gilsemans, Tasman's artist, illustrating the Dutch team surrounded by the Maori people at Murderers Bay (now Golden Bay), New Zealand

Tonga and Fiji

Sailing northeast, Tasman discovered Tonga on 21 January and the Fiji Islands on 6 February. The ships then turned west and sailed back to Batavia through the New Guinea waters. The whole trip took 10 months and Tasman went around Australia without ever seeing it!

Australia

In 1644, Tasman embarked on a new expedition to search for a southern continent. This time, he steered southeast below New Guinea, through the Torres Strait and into Australia's Gulf of Carpentaria. Coasting along, Tasman was able to map the northern coast of Australia.

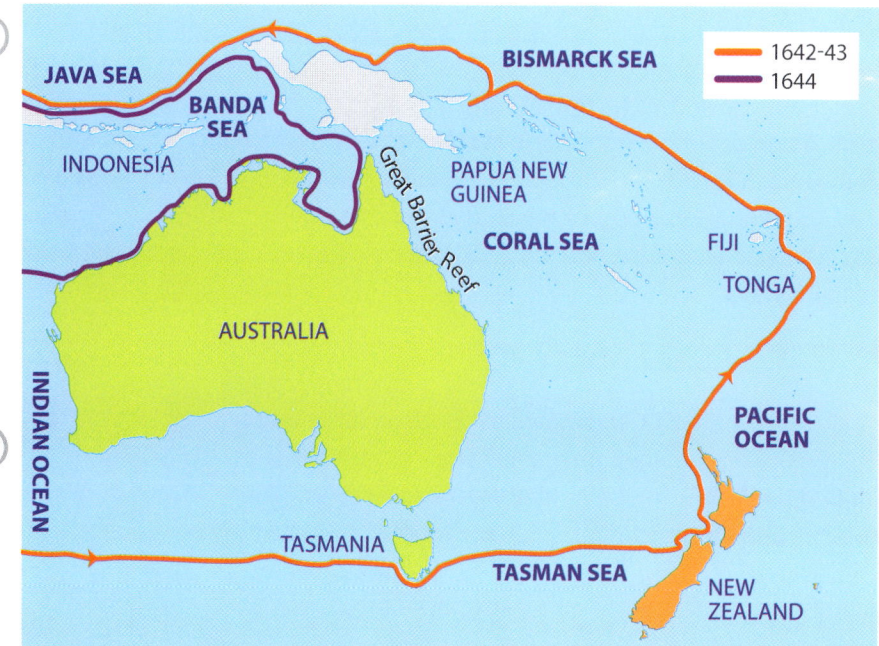

▲ The map shows the route of Abel Tasman's first and second exploratory voyage around New Zealand and Australia. The first voyage was taken between 1642–43 and the second voyage was taken in 1644

The Evolution Revolution

At the age of 22, Englishman Charles Darwin (1809–1882) set sail on HMS *Beagle.* On the way, he spent many months exploring the islands and coasts around South America. Here, Darwin noticed strong patterns between life on the islands and on the main continent. For instance, he saw daisies and sunflowers as large as trees on one of the islands!

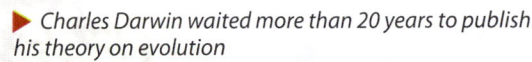 Charles Darwin waited more than 20 years to publish his theory on evolution

Darwin's Findings

Darwin realised that plants and animals on the islands must have changed to take advantage of the homes they were provided. Thus, on an island that had no trees, the sunflowers evolved to become its trees. Darwin called this the 'theory of natural selection'. He realised that it made plants and animals successful at conquering new environments. This supported the groundbreaking idea that life was not created by God; instead, it evolved over thousands and thousands of years from interactions with nature.

◀ A series of skulls show how human beings evolved from our ape-like ancestors

◀ The frigate bird lives near tropical oceans. Its wings evolved to take advantage of warm currents of air that rise upwards. The bird can thus soar without flapping its wings for hours and even days at a time

In Real Life

Genes are proteins in our bodies that decide whether we become a plant, a mouse, a human being, or something else. We inherit our genes from our ancestors. Did you know that 98 per cent of our genes are the same as a chimpanzee's? We share 92 per cent of our genes with mice. About half our genes are the same as a fly's. 18 per cent of our genes are the same as some weeds.

Voyage of the Beagle

On 27 December 1831, HMS *Beagle* set sail for South America. Her captain Robert Fitzroy was an aristocrat who feared being alone on the long voyage. So, he brought along Charles Darwin as a companion. Together, they faced five years of physical and mental hardships. They battled the seas, explored dense Brazilian jungles, and climbed inhospitable Andes mountains. By the end, Darwin had written a 770 page diary, with another 1,750 pages of notes. (He also had a collection of 5,436 skins, bones, and carcasses.) These were published as the famous book *The Voyage of the Beagle.*

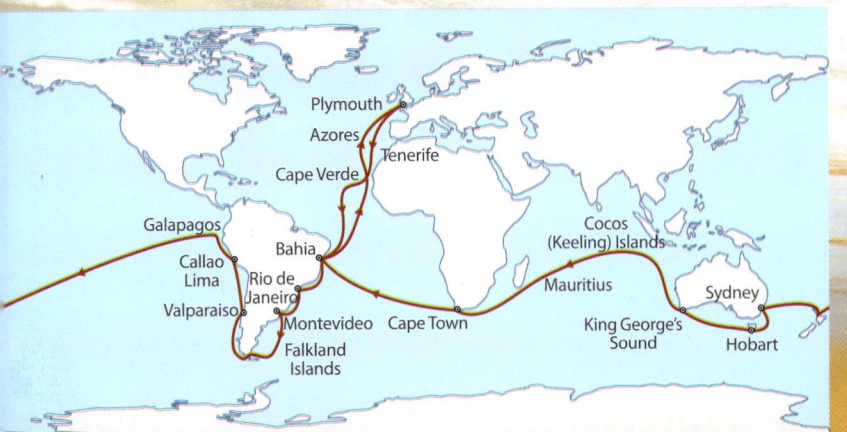

▶ A painting of HMS Beagle in South America, by crewman Conrad Martens

◀ The Beagle set out from Plymouth, England, and made its way around South America to the Galapagos islands. From there, it crossed the Pacific, Indian, and Atlantic oceans to reach England again

INVENTIONS & DISCOVERIES | EARTH DISCOVERIES

The Galapagos Archipelago

Darwin spent about five weeks on the islands of Galapagos, admiring and recording their extraordinary wildlife. Many of the creatures here are endemic, which means that they cannot be found anywhere else on Earth.

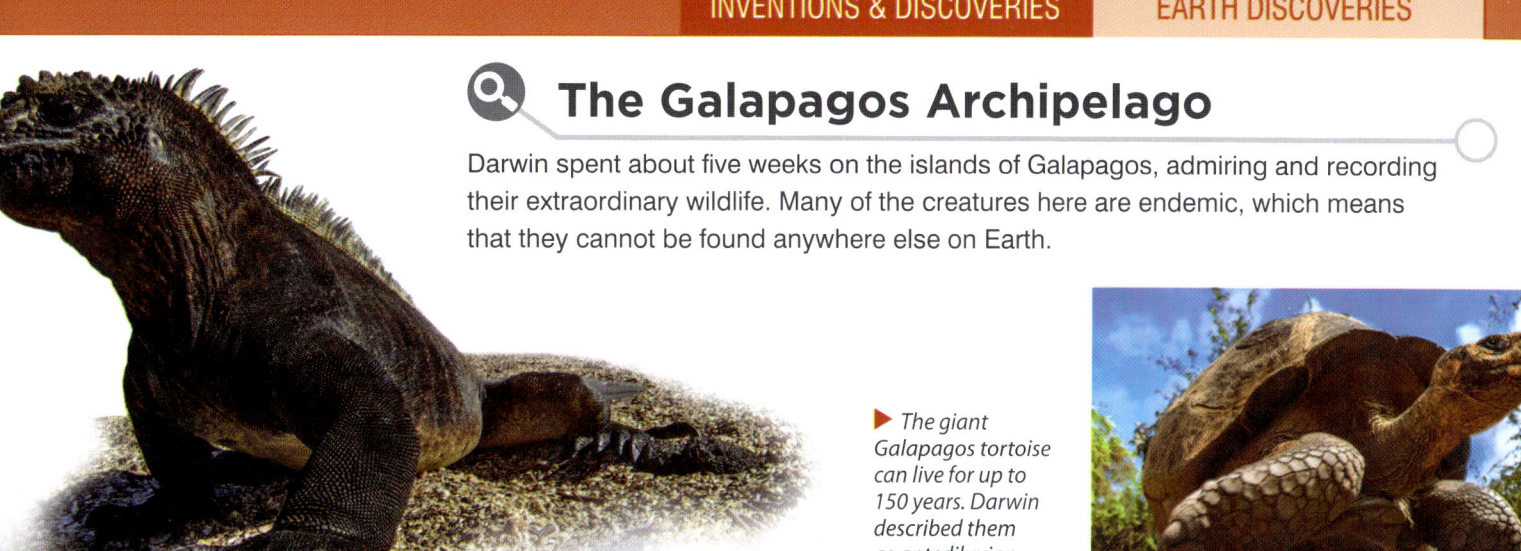

◀ Darwin came across a marine iguana for the first time. In amazement, he called them 'imps of darkness'

▶ The giant Galapagos tortoise can live for up to 150 years. Darwin described them as antediluvian, meaning they were so old, they probably lived before Noah and the great flood

Fossils

Darwin also discovered fossils of **extinct** animals in South America. Among them were the remains of giant sloths, mastodons, ancient armadillos, and animals that looked like rhinoceroses and horses. Darwin concluded that animals that could not adapt to changing environments would die out. Until he propounded his theory, people believed that the fossils found in South America were of mythical creatures destroyed by the gods in an ancient time.

▶ The giant sloth of South America was the size of an elephant

▲ A Galapagos sea lion

Discovering Africa

David Livingstone (1813–1873) was a Scottish missionary whose explorations of the African heartland gave Europeans their first look into the continent. Livingstone's first trip lasted 15 years. He spent this time travelling tirelessly across Africa, meeting its people, spreading his teachings, and condemning the abhorrent practice of slavery.

▲ Victoria Falls, a UNESCO World Heritage Site at Mosi-oa-Tunya National Park, Zambia

▲ A map of Dr Livingstone's westernmost explorations in Africa

The Hero of Victoria Falls

Between November 1853 and May 1854, Livingstone made an arduous journey to discover a path from Linyanti to the Atlantic coast. He then returned to Linyanti again and struck out east, exploring the Zambezi regions. On 16 November 1855, he came across a roaring, smoke-like waterfall on the Zambezi River. Claiming it for the British queen, he named it Victoria Falls. Livingstone returned to England and was received as a national hero. He returned to Africa in 1858 and stayed till 1864, making further discoveries.

Farthest West

Livingstone was back in Africa by January 1866, exploring the area around Lake Tanganyika. At this time, his followers deserted him. The man himself became the first European to reach Lake Mweru (1867) and Lake Bangweulu (1868). On 29 March 1871, he reached Nyangwe on the Lualaba River, the greatest source of the Congo River. This was farther west than any European had travelled within Africa.

At Rest in the South

Livingstone returned to Lake Tanganyika a sick man. Here, he was discovered by Henry M. Stanley, a reporter for the *New York Herald*. Stanley brought him much-needed medicine. Livingstone recovered, and journeyed south again. In May 1873, at Chitambo in northern Zambia, Africans found Livingstone dead by his bedside. His body was taken back to England and buried with ceremony in Westminster Abbey.

Undercover Adventures

An English spy named Sir Richard Francis Burton (1821–1890) was the first European to see Lake Tanganyika in Africa and a number of Islamic cities that were forbidden to Westerners. Over his lifetime, he wrote 43 travel books. He also translated 30 books from other languages. Most famous among them is an amazing 16 volume edition of *The Arabian Nights*.

▲ *The young scholar and spy Richard Burton*

 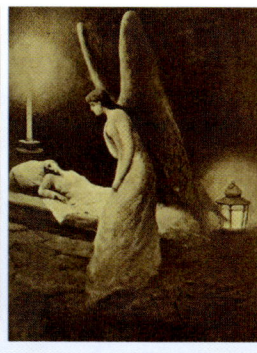 

▲ *Demons, angels, murderers, and mythical beasts from Burton's translation of The Arabian Nights*

▶ *Richard Burton disguised as a Muslim man*

🔍 Mecca and Medina

In 1853, Burton dressed as a Pathan—an Afghan Muslim—and travelled to Cairo, Egypt. He made his way to Arabia to visit the sacred Medina. Following bandit-infested roads, Burton then travelled on to Mecca. At the time, no foreigners were allowed inside these two holiest of Islamic cities.

Facing a death sentence if he were caught, Burton snuck into the shrine of Ka'bah. Burton published his journey as the *Pilgrimage to Al-Madinah and Mecca*. For the first time, people in the West saw the customs and manners of their Muslim contemporaries.

🔍 African Adventures

In 1854, Burton became the first European to enter the forbidden East African city of Harar, without being executed. In 1857–1858, he went hunting for the source of the Nile River but instead discovered Lake Victoria.

🔍 West Africa

In the 1860s, Burton was living on an island, near West Africa. During this time, he made frequent trips to the mainland and wrote five books about West African customs. Burton's writings made him very popular with scholars, but the government thought he was mad.

🔍 Banishment and Books

Calling him dangerous, the government banished Burton far from his beloved Africa and India. Burton spent his time writing more books. In 1870, he published a translation titled *Vikram and the Vampire, or Tales of Hindu Devilry*. He also wrote a volume on the Sindh, two volumes on the gold mines of Midian, and a number of other titles. Finally, in 1886, the government recognised the value of his life's work. In February 1886, he was knighted by Queen Victoria.

▼ *Burton's tomb at Mortlake, London*

▼ *The freshwater Lake Victoria is Africa's largest lake and the main reservoir for the Nile waters*

Around the World in 72 Days

Nellie Bly (1864–1922) was the most accomplished female journalist of her time. She lived a life full of adventure, and became famous by beating the fictional record for time taken to travel around the world.

The Fearless Journalist

Elizabeth Cochrane—better known as Nellie Bly—wrote articles that were phenomenal and profound. She first wrote on the condition of working girls and slum life. In 1886–1887, she spent months in Mexico, reporting on government corruption. Her sharply critical articles angered Mexican officials and caused her expulsion from the country. In 1887, she faked insanity to get into an asylum and report about how the mentally ill were being mistreated. Her work caught the attention of the public and brought about great social improvements. These important articles are now published as the books *Six Months in Mexico* and *Ten Days in a Madhouse*.

▶ Bly spent 6 months in Mexico writing about Mexican people before eventually upsetting the government

Racing Jules

In 1873, Jules Verne published his travel-adventure novel, *Around the World in Eighty Days*. In the story, fictional hero Phileas Fogg wins a bet by accomplishing the titular journey. In 1889, Nellie Bly was invited to beat this fictional record. On 14 November, Bly sailed out of New York. She boarded ships, trains, rickshaws, **sampans**, horses, and **burros** all along her fantastic race. She finally returned to New York on a special train and was greeted by brass bands and fireworks. Her record was 72 days, 6 hours, 11 minutes, and 14 seconds.

The Lost City of the Incas

Machu Picchu is an ancient place high in the Andes mountains of South America. The ruins of Machu Picchu were discovered by German adventurer Augusto Berns in 1867. But the world did not hear about it until American archaeologist Hiram Bingham (1875–1956) began his explorations.

The Search for Machu Picchu

▼ The ruins of Machu Picchu, hidden in the Peruvian Andes, high above the Urubamba River valley

In July 1911, Bingham led a hunt for Vilcabamba, the 'lost city of the Incas'. Vilcabamba was their name for a 16th century mountain stronghold. Its location was a secret known only to the Incas. They used it to fight against Spanish conquerors. About 400 years later, the only clue to the city was a rumour, which said it was somewhere near Cuzco, in Peru.

At Cuzco, locals told Bingham to search the Urubamba River valley for the legendary site, Choquequirao, meaning 'Cradle of Gold'. Bingham had to trek 2,350 m up into the formidable Andes. On 24 July, the Quechua-speaking Melchor Arteaga led him to spectacular Incan ruins that lay in a saddle between the peaks Machu Picchu (Old Peak) and Huayna Picchu (New Peak). In 1912 and 1915, Bingham led expert teams to Machu Picchu. They realised that the site was a vast palace complex belonging to the ruler Pachacuti Inca Yupanqui, who ruled from 1438–1471. The city was built using thousands of stone-cut steps, high walls, mysterious tunnels, and other inventive structures!

▶ Giant stone terraces made farming possible on the steep mountainside

Cool Conquests

Roald Amundsen (1872–1928) was an explorer from Norway. He was the first person to reach the South Pole. He was also the first person to navigate a ship through the elusive Northwest Passage. Amundsen is one of the greatest figures in the history of polar exploration.

◀ *The stake on the right of the sign board marks the South Pole, while the board marks the achievements of explorers Roald Amundsen and Robert Scott*

The Northwest Passage

The Passage was a shortcut from the Atlantic Ocean to the Pacific Ocean by sailing across the Arctic region. People believed that such a route lay above the coasts of modern Canada. Yet its exact location was a mystery.

Amundsen's Way

In 1903, Roald Amundsen took up the challenge. His goal was to sail through the Northwest Passage and around the northern Canadian coast. After a long, hard journey, Amundsen was able to reach Cape Colborne in August 1905. By the following month he had completed the greater part of the passage. At this point, he was stopped by winter and ice. The crew was forced to stay at Herschel Island in the Yukon. Once the ice melted, they resumed their journey. Late in August 1906, they completed the route at Nome, Alaska. Amundsen was given a hero's welcome for his successful discovery of the passage!

▲ *To conquer the Northwest Passage, Amundsen sailed out with six men on a sloop named Gjöa*

▼ *Amundsen and his crew aboard the Gjöa at the end of the trip at Nome, Alaska on 1 September 1906*

South Pole

In June 1910, Amundsen headed for the South Pole. Sailing the Fram Strait, he reached the Bay of Whale in Antarctica and set up a base camp. Experienced in the ways of ice and snow, Amundsen carefully prepared for the journey. He knew that accidents were common on polar lands. So, he made a trip halfway to the pole, to store emergency food supplies all along the way. He used sled dogs to transport his supplies.

▲ *On the way to the South Pole*

The Historic Trip

On 19 October 1911, Amundsen set out with four men, four sledges, and 52 dogs. The weather was on their side for the next couple of months. The group reached the South Pole on 14 December. The explorers stayed there until the 17th, making scientific observations. They safely returned to the Bay of Whales on 25 January 1912.

▲ *Roald Amundsen, Helmer Hanssen, Sverre Hassel, and Oscar Wisting at the South Pole on 17 December 1911*

Vacuum Tubes

Did you know that you could create electricity by heating certain materials? Thomas Edison (1847–1931) first observed this in 1875, when he was fiddling around with a light bulb. A few years later, British engineer John Ambrose Fleming (1849–1945) used his discovery to invent the first **vacuum tube**, called a diode.

After the diode, vacuum tubes became more complex. Until a few decades ago, they were used to power lots of communication devices. This included radios, televisions, and even computers.

▲ *Fleming's device began the age of electronics*

How Does it Work?

Electricity is generated when lots of tiny, invisible particles called **electrons** travel across a medium. A stream of moving electrons is called an electric current. The vacuum tube behaves like an electric switch. When you turn it on, electricity runs through it. The tube looks like a glass bulb. Inside it, is a plate called the **anode**, and a filament called the **cathode**. Air is removed from the bulb, creating a **vacuum**.

If you send electricity into the cathode, it will become glowing hot and give off electrons. These electrons travel through the vacuum to the anode, creating an electric current. If you stop heating the cathode, it will stop releasing electrons, and the current will be 'switched off'.

▼ *A vacuum tube with a glowing cathode filament*

Modern Uses of Vacuum Tubes

Vacuum-tube technology is rarely used in the 21st century, as it has become obsolete. Nevertheless, there are a handful of applications for this gadget. Vacuum tubes are used in high-quality stereo systems. These stereo systems are used by music professionals and sound technicians.

Vacuum tubes are also used in instruments such as electric guitars. They have vacuum-tube amplifiers. Similarly, fluorescent displays are often thin vacuum-tube displays used to convey simple information in audio and video equipment. X-ray machines, radars, and even microwave ovens sometimes are fitted with vacuum tubes.

▲ *A modern sound amplifier with vacuum tubes*

Incredible Individuals

J.J. Thomson (1856–1940) was the son of an English bookseller. He revolutionised the world of physics by discovering the electron. For this, he received a Nobel Prize in 1906 and was knighted by King Edward VII in 1908.

Semiconductors and Microchips

Vacuum tubes were known to be bulky and breakable. Thus, early electronic machines took up a lot of space and needed frequent repair. During 1947–1948, three Americans—John Bardeen, Walter Brattain, and William Shockley—invented the **transistor**, which replaced vacuum tubes in electronics. This is because the transistor was small and sturdy, required very little power, and released very little heat.

Semiconductors

A transistor is made primarily of silicon, a substance found in sand and glass. Silicon is a **semiconductor**. This means that the way it conducts electricity can be changed by adding other materials to it.

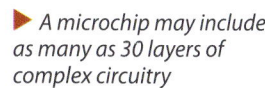

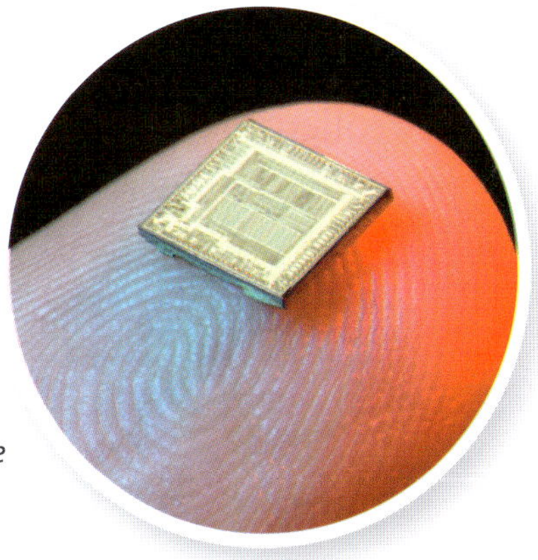

▶ A microchip may include as many as 30 layers of complex circuitry

Microchips

The first transistors were used to make lighter machines, like portable radios and hearing aids. During the 1960s and 70s, scientists began to draw tiny electric circuits on to silicon chips. This created Integrated Circuits (IC), also called **microchips**. These circuits acted like wires to conduct electricity.

These days, a single microchip—which is smaller than the tip of your finger—can hold thousands of transistors. They are used to make everything, from toasters and phones to super computers and robots.

▶ An Integrated Circuit board, with microcircuits connecting different parts of the board

👤 In Real Life

The first proper digital computer, Electronic Numerical Integrator and Computer (ENIAC), was built during World War II. It weighed 30,000 kg, used 18,000 vacuum tubes and gave off a lot of heat! This massive machine occupied an entire basement, where it was arranged in the shape of the letter U along three walls.

◀ Experts operating the gargantuan ENIAC, 1946

Batteries

A battery stores electrical energy in chemical form. In the year 1800, Italian physicist Alessandro Volta (1745–1827) invented the first modern battery. Volta arranged zinc and copper plates in a pile, like a stack of coins. In between the plates, he placed pieces of vinegar- or brine-soaked leather, or pasteboard. This was the first structure that allowed scientists to store and use electricity in a controlled manner. Volta's battery is called the voltaic cell. Today, there are many varieties of batteries.

▶ *A voltaic cell is sometimes called a galvanic cell*

 ## Commonly-used Batteries

Lithium-ion batteries are so light and small, they are called cells. They are rechargeable, long-lasting, environment-friendly, and used in phones and computers. You can even use solar power to recharge these cells.

Big rectangular lead-acid batteries are fitted into car engines. They are used to start the car and power its air-conditioner, radio, GPS, and other devices. AA and AAA batteries are most commonly used in remote controls, headphones, clocks, and portable players.

Most of our watches run on small alkaline batteries that are cost-effective and easily available. However, expensive watches use cells that contain lithium or silver oxide, which are much more reliable.

▲ *Lithium ion batteries have an average of 600 charge cycles*

 ## Disposing Used Batteries

Many batteries contain toxic chemicals that can leak out and affect your health and surroundings. So, deposit the used batteries at a recycling unit, where experts can safely get rid of harmful chemicals.

▲ *Used batteries should not be chucked away like regular dry garbage*

Calculators

The first calculators were mechanical, not electrical. They were simple wooden frames with rows of beads, representing 10s, 100s, and 1,000s. This invention was called an abacus and was used as far back as in 2,000 BCE in ancient Egypt.

▼ *The person who uses the abacus is called an abacist*

In the 17th century, a new type of calculator called the slide rule was invented. This contained different scales that could slide against each other to do multiplications, divisions, and other arithmetic calculations. In the 19th century we had mechanical calculaors.

Electrical Calculators

Today's digital calculators are based on a machine called the 'arithmometer', invented by French mathematician Blaise Pascal (1623–1662) in 1642. In the mid 1950s, electronic data processing gave rise to the first electronic calculators. By the late 20th century, they could perform arithmetic that most mathematicians could not solve using pen and paper. Nowadays, calculators are inbuilt in your phone and computer.

▶ *Modern calculators come with keys for unique arithmetic functions. Some are so sophisticated, they are powered by solar cells*

Telegraph

The telegraph was the first electric as well as the first wireless technology that allowed us to send long-distance messages quickly. In the early 1800s, electricity was still new. At this time, two Germans—Carl Gauss (1777–1855) and Wilhelm Weber (1804–1891)—built the first real electric telegraph. However, this machine could not send messages beyond 1 kilometre. During this period, other inventors came up with their own versions of the telegraph, but none of them really took off.

▲ *An illustration of an old telegraph office (1867)*

 ## Samuel Morse and the Code

In the 1830s, American inventor Samuel F. B. Morse (1791–1872) invented a system of dots and dashes to match the English alphabet. This system, called the Morse Code, made it easy to telegraph messages on a new model that he developed. In 1843, Morse was asked by the American government to build a 60-km-long telegraph system. Public use of this first telegraph line began on 24 May 1844, with Morse sending the message, 'What hath God wrought!' By 1851, the USA had over 50 telegraph companies.

▶ *The device used to tap out morse code signals*

 ## Radio Waves and the Wireless Telegraph

In 1888, a German physicist named Heinrich Hertz (1857–1894) discovered that it was possible to transmit electrical energy through the air. This energy travelled in invisible waves and eventually came to be called **radio waves**.

Over 1894–1896, Italian scientist Guglielmo Marconi (1874–1937) experimented with various ways of sending signals in Morse Code using radio waves. By 1906, he had refined his system so well that he was able to send messages across the Atlantic Ocean. He is thus the inventor of the wireless telegraph.

◀ *A telegraph operator sending messages by tapping them out in Morse code*

▼ *A stamp featuring Guglielmo Marconi, who won the Nobel Prize for Physics in 1909. His discoveries in wireless communication are the basis for our modern understanding of long-distance radio*

Radio

In the early 1900s, Canadian engineer Reginald Fessenden (1866–1932) was able to combine sound from a microphone with a type of electromagnetic wave to send messages over long distances. These electromagnetic waves are now called radio waves and are used by many devices other than the radio, including TV and mobile phones.

Fessenden made the first ever public radio broadcast in America on the eve of Christmas in 1904. He played 'O Holy Night' on his violin and could be heard by ships that were 160 km away. However, regular public broadcasting only began in 1920.

Incredible Individuals

In 1938, Orson Welles (1915–1985) rewrote *The War of the Worlds*—a book about Martians invading Earth—as a radio drama. Broadcasted as a Halloween special, the drama began with a series of fake news bulletins. The bulletins lasted an hour and seemed so real that many people believed they were truly being attacked by aliens. Entire cities became hysterical and were thrown into a turmoil!

▲ *Reginald Fessenden, the inventor of the radio, a photo from c. 1906*

The Early Days of Radio

All radio systems since then have worked using a transmitter that sends sound signals, and a receiver, which finds the signal and lets us hear radio programmes. Nowadays, radio broadcasting happens over two main types of channels: **AM** and **FM**.

AM channels can be heard over thousands of miles and are usually used to broadcast news, sports, and talk shows. FM channels offer better sound quality and are more popular. They travel shorter distances and are used by local police, taxis, and other groups to listen to information, music, and entertainment shows.

Surprisingly, when you listen to a live concert on the radio, the music reaches you faster than it does a person in the actual concert hall. This is because your radio transmits sound to you in the form of electric signals at the speed of light. In contrast, sound waves—the vibrations made by a voice or instrument—travel more slowly through the air to reach the person in the hall.

▲ *An electronic survey system of radio transmitters and monitors*

▼ *A radio from the 1950s*

In Real Life

If you have an AM radio, you can use the radio and a nine-volt battery with a coin to create radio waves! Switch on the radio and turn the dial till you hear static—steady crackling noises. While holding the battery near the radio's antenna, quickly tap the two terminals on the battery with a coin, so they are connected for an instant. Try this fun trick and you will be able to hear the radio waves.

▶ *A 9 volt battery*

Who Invented the Telephone?

Most people think that the telephone was invented by Alexander Graham Bell (1847–1922) in 1876. But nobody knows the amazing story behind the real inventor! In 1841, Italian inventor Antonio Meucci (1808–1889) had already designed a telephone. He applied to the government for recognition in 1871. But the officials stalled and ignored him.

The Full Story

Bell shared a lab with Meucci in 1870s. In 1876, Bell wrote to the government about the invention of telephone. It was a similar invention for which Meucci has earlier applied for but was ignored. This time, the officials responded, and he became rich and famous! A furious Meucci sued Bell for fraud. But he died before he could win the case.

American professor Elisha Gray (1835–1901) also developed a telephone. It is suggested that he filed for government recognition on the same day as Alexander Graham Bell!

▲ Elisha Gray also invented a musical telegraph

Battery-operated Phones

Early phones did not rely on the phone company for electricity. They had a built-in magneto, which used a coil and a magnet-generated electric current. To use these phones, you first "recharged" the battery by cranking up a lever on its right side. If you did not do this, the phone at the other end would not ring.

▲ Candlestick phones soon gave way to rotatory-dial and push-button telephones

▶ The first cordless phone was invented in 1962 for the World Fair in Seattle, USA

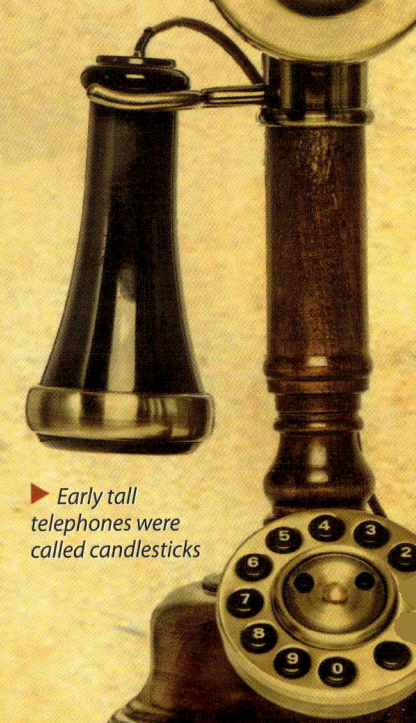

▶ Early tall telephones were called candlesticks

Isn't It Amazing!

The first words Bell ever spoke over the telephone were to his assistant. He said, 'Mr. Watson, come here. I want to see you.'

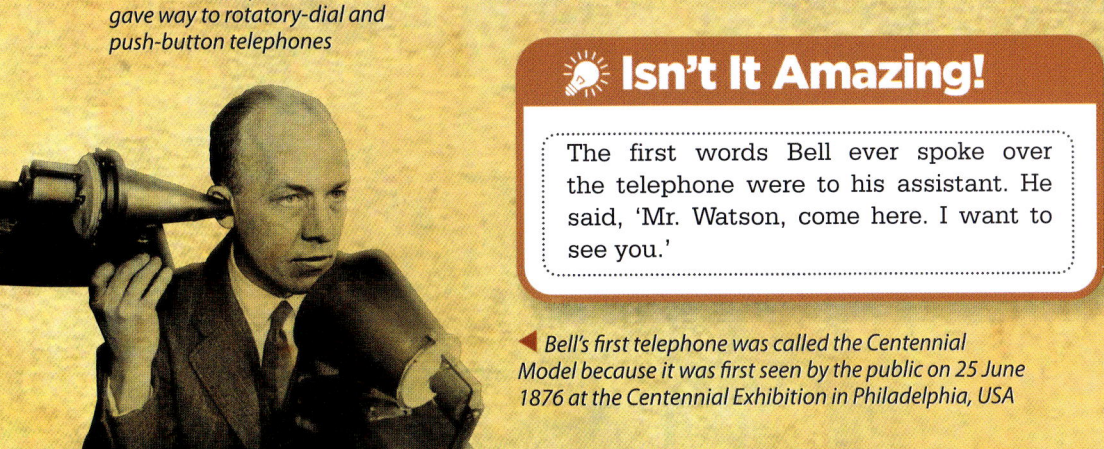

◀ Bell's first telephone was called the Centennial Model because it was first seen by the public on 25 June 1876 at the Centennial Exhibition in Philadelphia, USA

Television: Moving Pictures Sent on Radio Waves

All TVs need three things to function. These are the TV camera, which turns sound and picture into a signal; the TV transmitter, which sends the signal using radio waves; and the TV set at home or the receiver, which turns the signal back into image and sound.

Broadcasting and Cable

The earliest TV broadcasts were seen—mostly by scientists—in the late 1920s. But by the 1950s, there was steady public interest in TV shows. Cable TV was invented around this time and it streamed many more channels than regular radio transmission. These days, TVs use satellite dishes as transmitters and receivers to provide high-definition, high-quality programmes.

Some Brilliant Minds behind the TV

In the 1880s, people were thinking, if voices can be sent over the air, why not pictures? In 1884, German inventor Paul Nipkow (1860–1940) used spinning discs with small holes in them to break up images into smaller elements. He was then able to recombine these into a black-and-white image. In 1906, Boris Rosing (1869–1933) of Russia combined Nipkow's disc with the Cathode Ray Tube (CRT) to develop the first basic TV set. In 1931, the spinning disc was once and for all replaced by the electronic camera, invented by another Russian, Vladimir Zworykin (1888–1982).

◀ *John Logie Baird with his television receiver; he invented the first publicly demonstrated colour television system*

Flat Screen TVs and 3D Technology

With the invention of LCD, plasma screen, and OLED technologies, TVs became as flat as the walls they are mounted on. LCD and plasma TVs have millions of tiny picture elements called pixels, which give us sharp images. OLED TVs use electricity to generate light particles called **photons** to display even better images. Nowadays, engineers are trying to bring images out of the screen and into 'real' space.

In Real Life

The first TVs only had black-and-white content. Much later, engineers discovered that any colour can be made by mixing the three primary colours. So, inventors made cameras that could capture separate red, green, and blue signals; transmission systems that could beam colour signals; and TV sets that could turn them into multicoloured images.

▲ *3D and 4K televisions are becoming popular today*

Computers: A Fruit of the Loom

The idea of a computer first came from weaving. In 1801, French merchant Joseph Jaquard (1752–1834) developed the industrial loom. This machine could weave detailed images on to cloth. Images were stored as punched patterns on cards. Each row of holes was used for a row of threads in the pattern. About 2,000 punch cards were needed for one complete image.

◀ A used punch card

In Real Life

In order to aid the census process, Herman Hollerith built the Tabulating Machine Company. This was later renamed as International Business Machines or IBM. Today, IBM is one of the leaders in making all things computer-related.

The Personal Computer

Until the 1970s, most people had never come across a computer. At this time, there were two types of computers. One was the large, room-sized version that cost hundreds of thousands of dollars. The other was a mass-produced mini-computer in the similar price range and was used in laboratories and offices. The idea that everyone could have a computer at home—let alone a laptop—was considered a tall tale. What made this possible was the invention of the microprocessor. The processor is what allows the computer to make calculations instantly and respond to your commands. Lots of machines such as cars, dishwashers, TVs, etc., have them today. But the processor of your computer is a great deal more powerful.

The Future of Computing

In the Internet-linked 21st century, computers are getting smaller and microprocessors more powerful. In a few years, nano-computers could be small enough to fit inside your body to track your health, enhance your abilities, and help you control your surroundings. Experts are already creating environments that are fully computer-controlled. This means your home, car, clothing, and appliances will all respond to your signals. The exciting new field that is powering these possibilities is called quantum computing. This will use the principles of quantum theory—the study of atomic and subatomic particles—to create a new generation of super-fast computers. The full extent of its abilities is yet unimaginable.

◀ A computer operator with a punch-card sorter at the US Census Bureau (c.1940)

The Father of the Computer

British professor Charles Babbage (1791–1871) realised that the punched-card system could also be used to do arithmetic. He modified the loom to create the world's first computer. It was a mechanical invention called the 'Analytical Engine'.

Inventor Herman Hollerith saw Babbage's machine and was inspired to create the 'Hollerith Desk'. The desk used punched cards to gather information from the 1890 American census. Thus, the computer moved beyond calculation to information processing.

▲ Charles Babbage's brain is on display in the Science Museum in London

Incredible Individuals

Ada Lovelace (1815–1852) was a mathematician and the daughter of a famous British poet, Lord Byron. She met Charles Babbage in 1833. Both worked closely to further develop the computer. Among Ada's many contributions was a stepwise sequence for solving certain mathematical problems. For this amazing accomplishment, she is known as the 'world's first computer programmer'.

Ada was also the first to see the vast potential of the Analytical Engine, beyond simple number calculations. She has therefore been called the 'Prophet of the Computer Age'.

◀ At the age of 12, Lovelace conceptualized a flying machine

▼ The 1960s electronic computer URAL-2 was located in Tashkent, Uzbekistan, and relied on vacuum tubes

The Development of Computers

Computers have come a long way since Babbage and Lovelace first worked on them. Some countries even have super computers to help their governments and scholars with cutting-edge research. The development of computers can be divided into three main periods.

🔍 First Generation Computers: 1937–1946

Dr John Atanasoff and Clifford Berry built the first electronic digital computer in 1937. It was called ABC (Atanasoff-Berry Computer). In 1943, the military had an electronic computer built. They called it the Colossus.

Progress was further made until, in 1946, the first general-purpose computer, the ENIAC was built. Computers of this period did one task at a time and had no operating language or systems.

◀ *The mechanism used to make precise holes on computer punch cards at the US Bureau of the Census (c.1940)*

🔍 Second Generation: 1947–1962

Computers of this period used transistors instead of vacuum tubes. In 1951, UNIVAC 1 (Universal Automatic Computer) became the first computer to be introduced to the public. The first programming languages (about 100 of them) were written for this generation of computers. Storage also became possible through devices such as disks and tapes.

▲ UNIVAC 1 control station

🔍 Third Generation: 1963–Present

The invention of the microchip truly revolutionised computers. They became powerful, reliable and a lot smaller. Nowadays, they can run multiple complex programmes at the same time. In 1980, the MS-DOS (Microsoft Disc Operating System) was created.

A year later, IBM introduced the personal computer or PC. Now it was possible to undertake various tasks and even play basic computer games on smaller, more affordable systems. In the 90s, Bill Gates invented the Windows operating system. With this, the PC rapidly became a part of homes and offices across the world.

⊙ Incredible Individuals

The QWERTY keyboard was created by American inventor Christopher Latham Sholes. It was first seen on 1 July 1874.

◀ *A PC from the 1990s*

▲ *The first QWERTY keyboard on a typewriter*

Networking

Computer networking allows us to collect, organise, and share all the knowledge in the world with each other. There are two basic types of networks.

LAN

Local-area Networks (LANs) connect machines that are close by. This could be in your house, school, or in an office. The network can be created with wires or fibre-optics. More often, it is done by Ethernet cables or Wi-Fi.

💡 Isn't It Amazing!

In the 1950s, visionary Ted Nelson coined the term 'hyperlink' for the clickable link we see on the web.

▲ *Network of Ethernet cables at a data centre*

WAN

Wide-area Networks (WANs) connect small networks to larger ones, over entire continents. They use cables, optical fibres, and satellites to link up computers. The Internet is the largest WAN.

◄ *Satellite dishes ensure large-scale networking for banks, offices, schools, homes, etc.*

👤 In Real Life

Machines in a LAN follow rules to "talk" to each other. This is called protocol. For instance, if one device signals "I'm ready to send", it must wait until the other responds "I'm ready to receive." With many computers, protocols become complex; this helps avoid network errors.

Ethernet and Wi-Fi

The most popular system for linking computers is the Ethernet. It was created in 1973 by an American team led by Robert Metcalfe. It became available for public use in 1980.

Wireless technology already existed at this time. But Wi-Fi connectivity came in 1997–1999, after tech experts around the world formed the Wireless Ethernet Compatibility Alliance (WECA).

◀ *Wi-Fi uses a router and radio waves to connect computers to a LAN. The signals can only travel short distances—usually less than 100 m*

The World Wide Web and App Stores

The Ethernet became truly useful after the World Wide Web was created. This was done in 1989 by English programmer and physicist Tim Berners-Lee. The web's earliest form had a server, used **HTML** code, and was displayed on the first browser.

In 2009, the mobile phone web came into being. The first one was based on Apple's iTunes. App stores nowadays belong to specific companies. They are run directly on the Internet and are not a part of the World Wide Web.

▶ *Accessing the world through a smartphone has become the modern reality*

The Deep Web

Millions of people around the world use the web for games, news, communication, and more. Yet, people are finding it harder and harder to discover data online. This is because only a tiny portion of the World Wide Web is easily accessible. This is called the Surface Web. It is the part of the web that is accessed by search engines like Google. And it only consists of 0.03 per cent of the information that is truly available! The rest of it is buried in the Deep Web. No one really knows how vast the Deep Web is. Our current technology is simply not strong enough to access all of this material. Some part of the Deep Web, however, is intentionally hidden. This is called the Dark Web.

Incredible Individuals

In 2009, Chinese-born engineer Charles Kuen Kao (1933–2018) received the Nobel Prize in Physics for his discovery in 1966, of how light can be transmitted through fibre-optic cables. Fibre optics use hair-thin, transparent wires. This forms an alternative to Ethernet in creating LANs.

▲ *Charles Kuen Kao is known as the "Godfather of Broadband"*

The Dark Web

Layers and layers of protection are given to information in the Dark Web. It is often used by criminals as well as government spies to hide their activities. It can only be accessed through special codes or browsers. The special software offers privacy and hides the identity of the user. Thus, it offers security for people who deal with information and goods and services, whether legal or illegal. On the bright side, the Dark Web allows greater freedom to people who live in dictatorial and totalitarian nations. It is also routinely used to leak information about political and organisational wrongdoings, so that powerful but corrupt people are brought to justice.

A Balancing Act

The first transport invention that may be called a bicycle had two wheels but no pedals. It was the wooden **draisienne**, invented by a German named Baron Karl von Drais de Sauerbrun in (1785–1851). In 1817, he pushed and rode it for 14 kms, proving that it was possible to balance on two wheels while moving forward.

In 1818, some 300 modified draisiennes, called hobby-horses and **velocipedes**, were brought out by another inventor based in London called Denis Johnson. People found them expensive and difficult to use. Riders were even laughed at on the streets! Naturally, they went out of style quickly, but the idea of the cycle remained of interest to inventors. For the next 40 years, inventors created different kinds of three-wheeled and four-wheeled cycles.

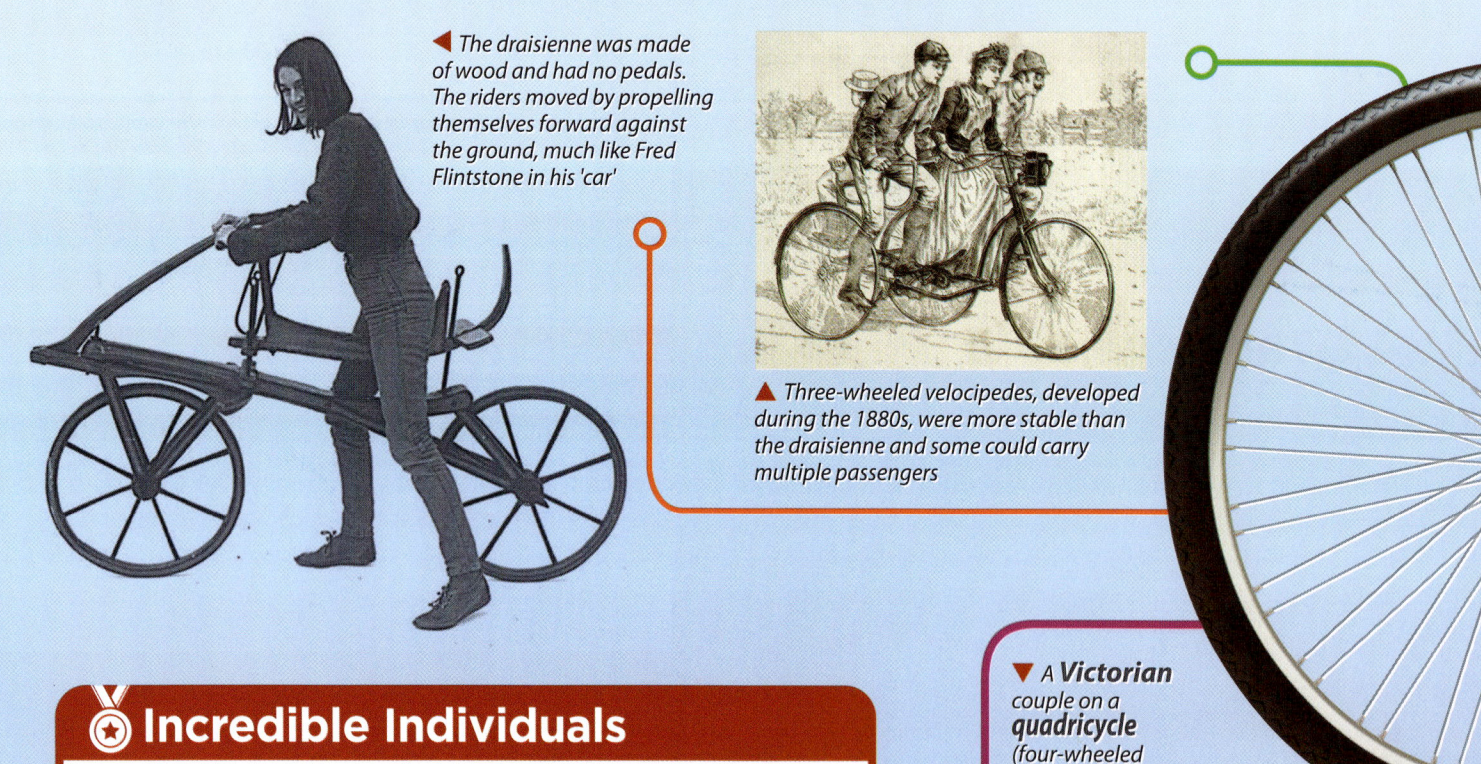

◀ The draisienne was made of wood and had no pedals. The riders moved by propelling themselves forward against the ground, much like Fred Flintstone in his 'car'

▲ Three-wheeled velocipedes, developed during the 1880s, were more stable than the draisienne and some could carry multiple passengers

▼ A *Victorian* couple on a *quadricycle* (four-wheeled cycle) designed for two people

⭐ Incredible Individuals

Early safety bicycles had solid rubber tyres. Though better than plain wooden tyres, these were still not very good shock absorbers. At the time, a Scottish vet by the name John Boyd Dunlop (1840–1921) was looking to make his son's tricycle less bumpy to ride. In 1887, he got the brilliant idea of pumping air into hollow rubber tubes. He is, thus, the inventor of the **pneumatic** tyre, which is used in all bicycles today.

▲ John Boyd Dunlop speeding along on pneumatic tyres

Pedalling to Fame

The first cycle with pedals was completed by a blacksmith named Kirkpatrick Macmillan (1812–1878) in Scotland in the 1840s. He felt that the cycle would be more usable if people could propel it forward without placing their feet on the ground.

By 1868, Europe had named velocipedes with pedals as bicycles. They were now being built out of cast iron instead of wood. Bicycles were made popular by the Olivier brothers, Rene and Aime, of France. In 1865, they pedalled a record 800 km from Paris to Marseille. Their enthusiasm caught on and cycling became a popular sport among the young and the rich.

In Real Life

The penny-farthing was a boneshaker with an oversized front wheel that was better at handling bad roads. One of its riders was the world champion cyclist William 'Plugger' Martin (1860–1942), who won a six-day race in New York in 1891.

▲ Early bicycles like the Oliviers' had wood-spoked wheels and iron rims. They were so jarring to ride, people called them boneshakers

▲ William Walker Martin, posing with the boneshaker cycle, was the long-distance champion cyclist of the 1890s

◄ The 1885 Rover Safety was designed by John Kemp Starley. It was the first bicycle to offer true advantages in stability, braking, and easy mounting

Ingenious Engines

Although we use electrical energy to power gadgets, we rarely use it to physically move objects. The prime movers in our world are engines. Most engines use either steam power or a process called internal combustion. Both types of engines are powerful technologies that came up during the 18th and 19th centuries.

Raising Steam

The first steam engine of practical use was patented by a British inventor named Thomas Savery (1650-1715) in 1698. The purpose was to 'raise water by fire'. It was used to raise water from underground mines. The machine worked by heating water until it turned into vapour. This vapour or steam moved to a higher container. As the steam condensed, it created a vacuum that drew up the water—similar to how you suck water through a straw. But there was little else that this steam engine could do. Also, it was a dangerous machine. The cylinder could burst in cases of excess steam! Imagine your pressure cooker blowing your kitchen to smithereens. Now imagine the havoc caused by an industrial-sized pressure chamber.

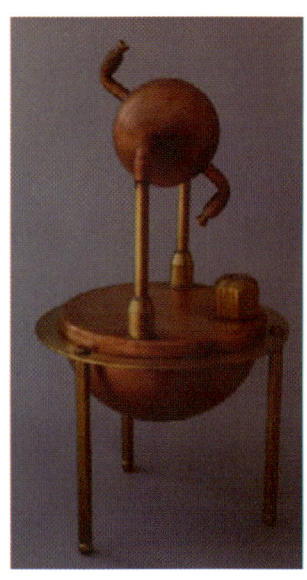

▲ Invented by Hero of Alexandria in the first century CE, the aeolipile is the first known steam-driven mechanism. It is named after Aeolus, the Greek god of air

The Industrial Age Wonder

1712, Thomas Newcomen (1664–1729) developed a better steam engine. James Watt (1736–1819) further improved it in 1765. Most importantly, Watt added a rotating shaft that produced wheel-like circular movements. At this point, the steam engine became immensely useful. Inventors used it to build the first locomotives—vehicles that were not pulled by animals—and kicked off the revolutionary Industrial Age!

◀ In 1802, Richard Trevithick (1771–1833) built the first steam locomotive. It ran on a horse-drawn tram route

▼ Robert Fulton (1765–1815) built the first commercially successful steamboat

What is Internal Combustion?

Combustion is simply another word for burning. Since the burning happens inside the engine, it is called internal combustion. An internal combustion engine can burn fuels such as gas, petrol, or diesel to move large objects like cars and planes. There are many types of Internal Combustion Engines (ICEs), to match the many types of vehicles we use.

The Four-stroke Engine

The first successful Internal Combustion Engine was built by Belgian inventor Etienne Lenoir (1822–1900) around 1860. It looked like a horizontal steam engine, but used an explosive mix of gases set afire by an electric spark. The heat and pressure from the burning fuel pushed pistons and wheels, and got the machine moving.

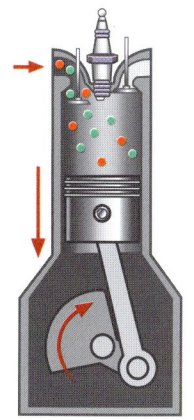 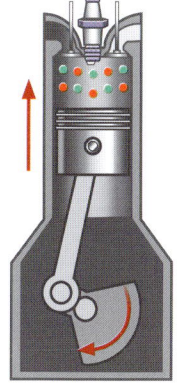 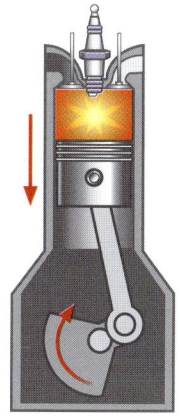 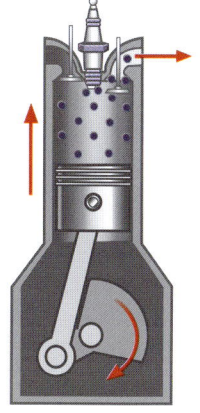

1. Intake   2. Compression   3. Fuel power   4. Fuel Exhaust

▲ Otto's ICE worked in four steps (or strokes)—intake of air and fuel, compression of the mix, firing of the mix, and release of the exhaust

▲ Daimler and Maybach's "grandfather clock engine"

The Diesel Engine

Rudolf Diesel (1858–1913) of Germany came across Otto's engine soon after it was invented. He set about making it more efficient and developed his 'combustion-powered engine'. In 1892, the government recognised it as the diesel engine.

Although this was truly a powerful engine, it was noisy, smelly—due to noxious exhaust fumes, and worked best at lower speeds. Today, we see them largely in heavy goods carriers such as trucks, ships, and road trains.

Smaller and Faster

In 1885, Germans Gottlieb Daimler (1834–1900) and Wilhelm Maybach (1846–1929) famously invented an engine that resembled a "grandfather clock", hence it was called the grandfather clock engine. It was the first small, high-speed ICE to run on petrol. It was the grandfather of all modern petrol engines. Daimler and Maybach fitted it on to a number of vehicles, including a cycle, a stagecoach, and a boat.

Engines and Pollution

Our engines release toxic gases into the air, such as carbon dioxide—the main cause of catastrophic climate change—or sulphur dioxide and nitrogen oxides, which cause acid rain, breathing problems, and ozone depletion, among other issues. Hence, it is important to use engines that use less harmful fuels like hydrogen, liquefied petroleum gas (LPG), and biodiesel.

The First Cars

In the early 20th century, nearly 80 per cent of all American cars ran on either steam or electricity. Petrol cars were noisy, shaky, and often broke down. Steam cars too had many complications. In contrast, electric cars were easy to start, silent, and needed little maintenance. Unfortunately, the ever-polluting petrol car squashed out its competition over time. It has dominated our roads ever since.

▲ The first automobile to speed over 100 kmph was the 1899 electric car La Jamais Contente, built by Camille Jenatzy (1868–1913)

▲ In the Motorwagen, the passengers and the engine sat above two wheels; the front wheel steered the car

▼ Benz invented the Victoria with four wheels. He wanted the car to be priced low enough for mass production, so more people could buy automobiles

🔍 Karl Benz and the Petrol Car

The car is a complex creature. Its many parts are the brainchildren of different people. However, Karl Friedrich Benz (1844–1929) of Germany is considered the inventor of the first 'true' automobile which was powered by gasoline. Called the Motorwagen, this three-wheeled car was built in 1885.

Benz also invented the **accelerator**, the battery-operated ignition, the **spark plug**, the **gear shift**, the **water radiator**, the **clutch**, the **carburettor**, and the axle-pivot steering system.
In 1896, he designed a high-performance engine that is still used in racing cars today!

💡 Isn't It Amazing!

Early cars were quite different from the ones we see today. The Motorwagen of early 1888 was pushed, not driven, up sloping roads and hills. Early car owners had to buy petrol at pharmacies where it was sold as a cleaning product. Naturally, they did not have it in large supply. Interestingly, the first Benz car was bought in the summer of 1888.

INVENTIONS & DISCOVERIES | INVENTIONS IN MOTION

◀ The photograph shows a reconstruction of da Vinci's self-propelled cart. Renaissance genius Leonardo da Vinci designed and described an automobile way back in 1509

In Real Life

Some countries historically banned women from driving. Locomotion has given humankind a great deal of freedom of movement, and some people wanted to withhold this freedom from women. In June 2018, Saudi Arabia became the last remaining country to lift the ban on female drivers.

◀ A poster from Saudi Arabia's #women2drive movement

Incredible Individuals

The story goes that Benz's wife, Bertha, once secretly took the Motorwagen to visit her mother, who lived 106 km away. Bertha started the drive on the morning of 5 August 1888 and brought along her sons Eugene and Richard.

On the way, she had to hunt for fuel at pharmacies and overcome numerous technical and mechanical problems. The trio finally arrived at night and sent off a telegram to Benz announcing their achievement! The event is now celebrated every year in Germany with an antique automobile rally.

▶ One of the official signposts along the 194 km long Bertha Benz Memorial Route, in memory of 'man's' first long-distance car journey

▲ Henry Ford (1863–1947) launched his famous Model T in 1908. This low-priced, easy-to-maintain car revolutionised the industry by turning cars into daily necessities; earlier, they were seen as luxury items

▼ France's motor industry began in 1890 with cars made by Armand Peugeot (1849–1915) and Emile Levassor (1843–1897). Peugeot cars were seen at this 1901 Paris Motor Show

A World on Track

A train is a long string of cars, or carriages that is pulled along by an engine. It transports either people or goods from place to place. There are many different kinds of trains, such as monorails, funiculars, turbo trains, bullet trains, double-deckers, and even 'toy' trains.

▶ The toy train of Darjeeling (India) runs on narrow rails along the Himalayas. This railway is now a UNESCO World Heritage Site

Passenger Trains

Trains that carry people over long distances are called passenger trains. They are powered by diesel engines. Faster, modern passenger trains are powered by electricity. Long-distance trains are designed to be comfortable. Their seats often double up as beds. They also have plenty of luggage space. Some passenger trains even have dining cars.

▲ A double-decker hi-speed train in France

City Trains

A commuter or city train carries large numbers of people over short distances. They are most often used to travel between work and home. Commuter trains have a lot of standing space, which allows them to carry more people during each trip. Seating and luggage space are minimal. Most commuter trains run on electricity.

▲ The commuter trains of Mumbai, India, carry hundreds of thousands of passengers each day

Metros

Another way of travelling in large cities is the metro system. This consists of electrically powered trains that run on tracks which are either underground or flyovers. Metro trains can accelerate much faster than long-distance trains.

▲ London metro tube

Monorails

The monorail is a special type of metro. It consists of a single track instead of two parallel rail tracks. The train straddles the track, that is, covers it from side to side. Sometimes, the track runs above the train! In such cases, the train is suspended from the track.

▲ Tokyo Monorail

Freight Trains

Freight trains are also called goods trains. These are used to transport overland cargo. Traditionally, workers would load the cargo into box wagons. Nowadays, cranes lift large containers of goods into and out of the wagons. Sometimes, trucks carrying goods drive on to the freight trains. At their destination, the trucks disembark and continue onwards by road.

▼ A freight train carrying cargo containers

To Keep the Wheels Turning

Another exciting form of transport is the motorcycle. It provides the flexibility of a bicycle along with the convenience of a car! In November 1885, Daimler installed a smaller version of the grandfather clock engine on a wooden bicycle, creating the first two-wheeled petrol-powered motorcycle. It was named the Reitwagen (the riding car). Daimler's partner Maybach rode it for 3 km by the River Neckar, reaching speeds of 12 kmph.

◀ *In 1884, Edward Butler built the first commercial motorcycle. It had three wheels and ran on petrol*

Evolving Motorcycles

In the early 1900s, inventors everywhere were attaching engines to cycles and creating their own versions of the motorcycle. A lot of them were sold on the streets and were called touring machines.

In an effort to discover top-notch bikes, the first motorcycle races were set up at the Isle of Man. Of these, the 1907-established Tourist Trophy (TT) race became the most famous and most extreme form of bike racing in the world.

▲ *The BAT twin-cylinder motorcycle of 1910 set a new track record of 80 kmph at the TT race*

Springing to Action

Nowadays, motorcycles come in a variety of designs depending on what you need them for. People enjoy riding motorcycles for long journeys, navigating city roads, adventure biking, and racing, to name just a few.

▲ *By the end of WWI, Harley Davidson was the largest motorcycle manufacturer, selling in 67 countries*

Incredible Individuals

Born on 17 November 1906, Soichiro Honda (1906–1991) was the pioneering force behind Honda motorcycles, one of the largest motorcycle manufacturers today. Starting out as a teenage mechanic, he began inventing automobile parts during WWII. Over his lifetime, he gained recognition for over 100 inventions!

In 1945, he founded what eventually became the Honda Motor Company, which built light motorcycles that ran on small but efficient engines. By the 1980s, Honda was the third-largest Japanese automaker.

Honda himself had strong ethics. He built close relationships with his workers. He stood firm against the government when it tried to limit Japan's auto industry. And even in his 60s, he was still personally testing new models of motorcycles.

▲ *Soichiro Honda had no formal education*

▼ *Nowadays, the Japanese manufacturers Honda, Yamaha, Kawasaki, and Suzuki dominate the world of motorcycles*

Ships Ahoy!

Human beings have been using rowing boats since prehistoric times. The first sailboats were seen on the River Nile and belonged to the ancient Egyptians. By the Iron Age, ships were large enough to carry several tonnes of cargo between prosperous trading port cities.

Until the Industrial Age, all river and seafaring vessels, large and small, were powered either by oars or by wind sails. The speed of a sea craft is measured in knots. A speed of 1 knot means the boat is travelling at 1.8 kmph.

In Real Life

Did you know, Queen Elizabeth I of England had an official person who uncorked 'ocean bottles'? His duty was to open messages from bottles that washed ashore. This was a serious and important job! In fact, it was a capital crime for anyone else to do this, as the Queen believed that these seafaring secrets may have come from spies abroad.

The trireme was the deadliest warship of the 5th century BCE. It needed 170 oarsmen arranged in three rows, one above the other, to propel the ship.

In the 16th century, the Chinese were inspired by Portuguese treasure ships to build their own galleys, called Wugongchuan (centipede ships).

All at Sea

After 1200, sailing ships truly came into their own. The stern rudder was invented to guide the ship more firmly. Deep-draft hulls were successfully engineered to hold more cargo and speed across oceans.

By the 14th century, shipbuilding got so specialised that warships became separate from merchant vessels. From the 15th century onwards, ships also had multiple masts and complex arrangements of sails.

Christopher Columbus's 15th century ship, named *Santa Maria*, was the flagship on his first voyage to the Americas.

Queen Anne's Revenge was the ship of the most famous pirate, Blackbeard.

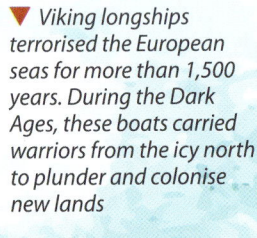

▼ Viking longships terrorised the European seas for more than 1,500 years. During the Dark Ages, these boats carried warriors from the icy north to plunder and colonise new lands

▶ Mayflower—the ship that carried the pilgrims to America

Making Waves

Steam-propelled boats were first seen during the late 1700s. Some of them worked and some did not. By the early 19th century, American inventor Robert Fulton (1765–1815) had developed steamboats that were strong enough for commercial use. He also built the US Navy's first steam warship, the *Demologos*. These vessels moved using steam-powered paddles arranged in the form of a wheel, at the boat's side or stern. The paddle was later replaced by the screw propeller, which was more resistant to storm damage and easier to steer with. Eventually, screw propellers were combined with steam-turbine engines, as seen in modern steamships. By WWI, coal and oil were also being used as fuel.

The famous *Titanic* was powered by multistage steam turbines, an 1894 invention of Sir Charles Algernon Parsons (1854–1931), who first used them in the yacht *Turbina*.

The 19th century paddle steamer, *Queen Victoria*.

The 1843 built *SS Great Britain* was the first ship to have a full iron hull. Iron-clad warships were extensively used in the American Civil War (1861–1865).

Military Matters

During WWII—and even after it—a great number of ships were constructed with ever-advancing technology. Such vessels served naval forces both as warships and cargo vessels. Many technologies made their way into luxury cruisers and merchant ships. While steam engines continued to run passenger ships, diesel and oil engines became popular for freighters. Earlier inventions such as radars also went through refinements.

▲ In 1910, the USS Birmingham became the first ship to launch an aeroplane. Eight years later, HMS Argus became the first true aircraft carrier that could transport, launch, and land aeroplanes

Radar

Radar is a type of active electromagnetic sensor. It is used for finding, identifying, and tracking objects that are far away. The objects are usually air or sea crafts and weapons. The radar works by sending out electromagnetic waves through the air and listening for any echoes that come back. The waves sent out are usually microwaves, which are very similar to what heats your food at home.

Oil tankers are the behemoths of the ocean. This supertanker can carry 2 million barrels of crude oil.

Flights of Fantasy

Human beings have wanted to fly like birds since time immemorial. Our myths and legends are full of heroes who found ways to fly, such as Icarus of Greece who flew too close to the Sun on wings of wax and feathers, or King Kaj Kaoos of Persia who harnessed eagles to his throne and flew over his kingdom. Even so real a figure as Alexander the Great is mythologised as flying in a basket pulled by gryphons!

🔍 A Timeline of Flight

The first person to design realistic flight was Leonardo da Vinci. In the late 15th century, he illustrated his theories of flight with the ornithopter. Since then, flying has come a long way. However, it was only in 1903 that the Wright brothers made the first flight, setting in motion man's eternal tryst to fly.

💡 Isn't It Amazing!

The modern conception of the aeroplane dates as far back as 1799. The concept was another of Sir George Cayley's achievements.

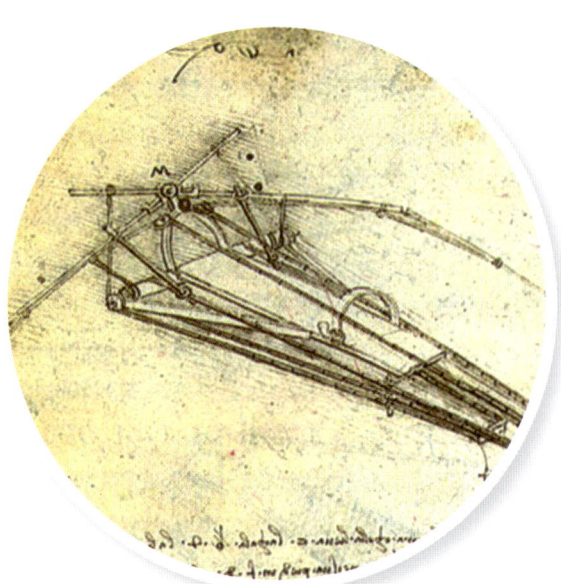

▶ The ornithopter was never actually built, but da Vinci's concept can be seen in modern-day helicopters

Manfred von Richthofen (1892–1918), or 'the Red Baron' was possibly Germany's top flying ace during WWI. He shot down some 80 enemy aircrafts, many of them from a German Fokker, which was a triplane. The Baron himself was killed while flying this plane on 21 April 1918.

⭐ Incredible Individuals

Amelia Earhart is one of the most inspiring aviators of all time. Even as a child, she was independent and adventurous. Earhart fell in love with flying in the 1920s. In 1928, she became the first woman to fly across the Atlantic Ocean.

Throughout her life, Earhart's exploits captured the public's imagination. On 1 June 1937, she set off to fly around the world. Until 2 July she was recorded making regular fuel stops. But she was never seen again, after that day. A massive rescue party was launched to find her. It did not turn up with any clues. On 5 January 1939, Earhart was declared dead. An eternal celebrity, Amelia Earhart is the subject of many books, movies and plays.

▶ Amelia Earhart, one year before her fateful journey

Soaring High

The Wright brothers' Flyer is a biplane. This is a flying machine with two sets of wings, one above the other. Throughout WWI, this was the most popular model for planes. From the 1930s onwards, advancements such as stronger engines and better building materials led to improvements in the monoplane. These became the regular aeroplanes we see today. The conquest of the skies gave some countries a huge advantage over others. Over the 20th and 21st centuries, it led to fierce technological competition, which has given us some truly advanced planes.

Supersonic Passengers

The Douglas DC-8 was the first commercial plane to break the sound barrier. However, the most memorable has been the Concorde. It reached top speeds of 2,179 kmph (**Mach** 2.04), which allowed it to cross the Atlantic in 2 hours 52 minutes and 59 seconds. It started flying in the 1970s but turned out to be so noisy and expensive, it was shut down in 2003.

▼ The sleek Concorde

Around the World in Nine Days

In 1986, the Voyager became the first plane to fly non-stop around the world. Piloted by Dick Rutan and Jeana Yeager, the super-light aircraft was actually made using layers of carbon-fibre tape glued together and epoxy-saturated paper.

▲ Almost all parts of the Voyager's frame, including the wings, were filled with fuel which were four times heavier than the plane itself

When Cars Fly

The incredible Terrafugia Transition is a flying car! This small plane can fold up its wings in less than 30 seconds and turn into a car. It can then continue on the road and drive up to a regular petrol station if it needs to refuel. It is not yet on sale, as engineers continue to improve its technology.

Environment-friendly Planes

Modern planes are among the biggest gas guzzlers harming our planet. In 2003, Swiss pilot and engineer Adre Borschberg began the project Solar Impulse. Its aim was to develop a plane that ran on clean, renewable solar energy. This led to the invention of the Solar Impulse II in 2014. Running entirely on batteries powered by sunlight, it circumnavigated the globe in 2016. The non-stop flight was 118 hours long—that is almost five days!

In Real Life

After 1969, international air travel became affordable with the invention and introduction of the Boeing 747. This was the first jet plane to have a wide body, seat 400 passengers, and still fly safely and speedily across large distances.

▲ Any plane carrying the President of the USA is called Air Force One. Since 1991, this name has belonged to a pair of specially outfitted Boeing 747 jets

The Rocket Launch

The invention of the rocket engine kicked off the exploration of the vast, mysterious universe. This remarkable engine is not the creation of any one person; rather, it came about over centuries through the hard work of many scientists. Notably, in the 17th century, Sir Isaac Newton gave us the three laws of motion, which form the basis for modern rocketry. Another key figure is Robert H. Goddard, whose lifelong research in rocketry led to many innovations. Among other things, he was the first person to use liquid fuel successfully to fly a rocket.

▶ Newton's third law says that to every action there is an equal and opposite reaction. Rocket engines act by forcing hot gases downwards. This creates an equal force in the opposite direction, which causes the rocket to shoot upwards

The Making of Missiles

Thought to be a Chinese idea, rockets themselves were first used as weapons several hundred years back. In 1232, flaming rockets destroyed a Mongol army besieging the Chinese city of Kaifeng. These missiles were most likely made of explosive gunpowder—another Chinese invention. In Europe, rockets were first used by Mongol raiders against an army of Christian knights at the 1241 Battle of Legnica, in Poland.

Missile Revival

Despite its initial success, the rocket missile was more or less forgotten by the 17th century. It was revived again in 18th century India by Hyder Ali, the ruler of Mysore. His rockets were made of metal cylinders, which could harness the power of the rocket and travel well over a kilometre. His son, Tipu Sultan used them successfully against the British in the famous battles at Shrirangapattana. This technology caught European interest and led to many rocket-propelled missiles being developed during the two World Wars. Over the 20th century, a number of other inventions were combined with rocket technology to give us the extremely sophisticated missiles of modern times.

An Accurate Missile

After Congreve's metal rockets, the next 19th century innovation in rocket technology came with British engineer William Hale's invention, the rotary rocket. This used jet vents to create spin, which made the rockets more stable and accurate—much like a bullet from a modern gun.

▲ Tipu Sultan, the Tiger of Mysore, had 5,000 rocket troops in his army. Their gunpowder came from Calcutta, which had one of the largest gunpowder factories of its time

Incredible Individuals

As a 16-year-old, Robert Goddard read HG Wells's thrilling science-fiction novel *The War of the Worlds*. It inspired Goddard so much, he actually dreamed of building a machine that could fly to space. On 19 October 1899, he climbed a tree behind his house and "imagined how wonderful it would be to make some device which had even the possibility of ascending to Mars…" In his diary, he wrote, "Existence at last seemed very purposive." Today, Robert Goddard is considered the father of modern rocketry.

Reaching for the Stars

Space is a scary, unpredictable place for us earthlings. Things we take for granted, such as sunlight, heat, gravity, atmosphere, sound, and water are out there, but in warped and extreme forms.

Space science is still new and we are still discovering the rules of this alien environment. Institutes like NASA have large teams of scientists who work together to explore our universe. Some of their most basic research involves moving about in space. After all, if we cannot move, how will we ever begin our journey?

▲ *Yuri Gagarin, the first man to walk in space*

🔍 Man-made Satellites

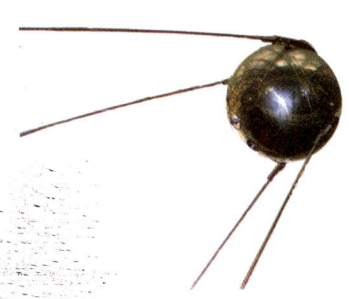

Launched on 4 October 1957, Sputnik-1 was the first spaceship to successfully orbit the Earth. It moved on an elliptical path, completing its orbit every 96 minutes. In early 1958, it fell back towards Earth and burned up in the atmosphere. A month after Sputnik-1's launch, Sputnik-2 shot into space carrying the dog Laika, the first living creature to orbit the Earth.

◀ *Sputnik-1 was a little smaller than a basketball but weighed as much as an adult man*

🔍 Zero Gravity, Zero Atmosphere

On Earth, we are able to move by interacting with forces like gravity and air pressure. Space, however, is a near-vacuum. You can float weightlessly in it. Large crafts move using the rocket engine to thrust forward. But there is only so much rocket fuel you can carry into space.

The rocket engine is simply not fast enough to cover the enormous distances of our solar system—let alone our galaxy or the universe!

🔍 Space Stations

Another way to overcome the problem of moving through space is to build space stations that can refuel spaceships. Since 1971, some 11 space stations have successfully orbited our planet, most famously the International Space Station (ISS). Since 1981, scientists have also launched reusable crafts called space shuttles, some of which were used to build the ISS.

◀ *Six years after it was launched, New Horizons flew to the edge of our solar system in July 2015, becoming the first spacecraft to explore Pluto and its five moons up close*

▲ *People have lived on the International Space Station since November 2000. It is as big as a house with five bedrooms, and even has two bathrooms, a gym and work spaces*

A Peek Inside the Body

When doctors first began to look for natural causes of illnesses, they did not have the proper tools to help them. Devices like the thermometer and stethoscope had not been invented. So, doctors had to use their eyes and ears to observe patients and diagnose diseases.

Modern Medical Equipment

These days, medical experts have hi-tech imaging equipment that shows what is happening inside a patient's body. Such technologies include X-ray, ultrasound, and MRI. Other machines like the **EEG** and **ECG** chart our brain waves and heartbeats, so doctors can tell if they are functioning normally.

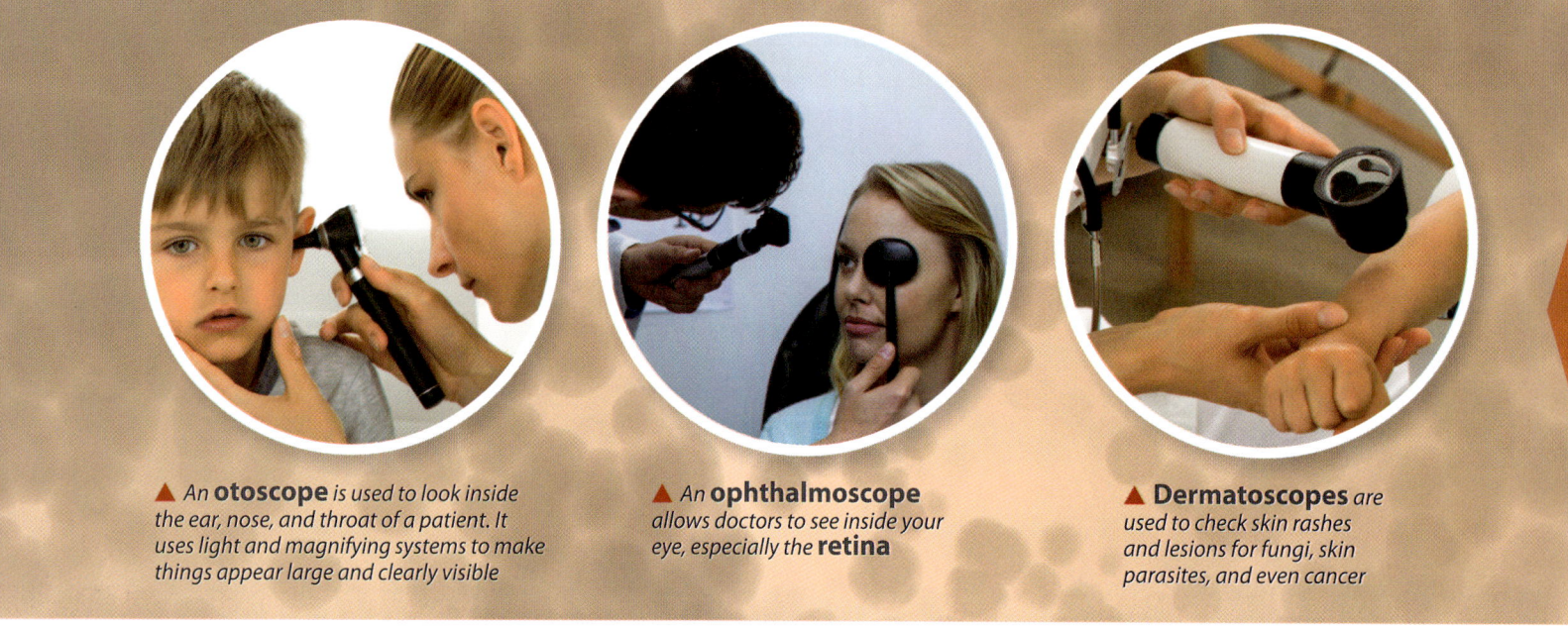

▲ An **otoscope** is used to look inside the ear, nose, and throat of a patient. It uses light and magnifying systems to make things appear large and clearly visible

▲ An **ophthalmoscope** allows doctors to see inside your eye, especially the **retina**

▲ **Dermatoscopes** are used to check skin rashes and lesions for fungi, skin parasites, and even cancer

Checking Your Temperature

When you feel ill, the first thing to do is to check if you have a fever. The tool with which you measure your body temperature is called a thermometer. The Italian mathematician Galileo Galilei invented the earliest known thermometer in 1592. The first accurate mercury thermometer was created in 1714 by German physicist Daniel Gabriel Fahrenheit. The Fahrenheit scale of temperature measurement, in which ice melts at 32° F and the temperature of a healthy human body is 96° F, was named after him. In 1742, Swedish astronomer Anders Celsius gave us the other popular scale, the centigrade or Celsius.

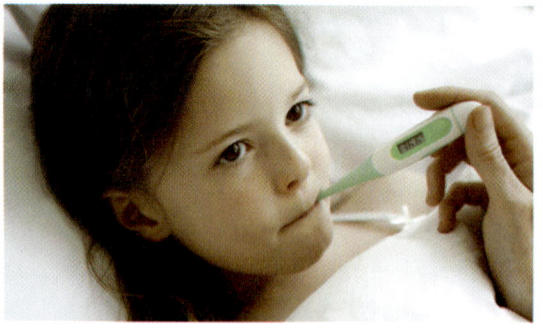

▲ A patient using a modern digital thermometer

◄ When heated, the air inside the glass tube of Galileo's thermometer expands, changing the level of the liquid. The glass bulbs carry temperature markers corresponding to the liquid

💡 Isn't It Amazing!

Celsius originally used 0° C as the boiling point of water and 100° C as the melting point of snow. It was later turned around and became more popular with 0° C as the melting point of ice and 100° C the boiling point of water.

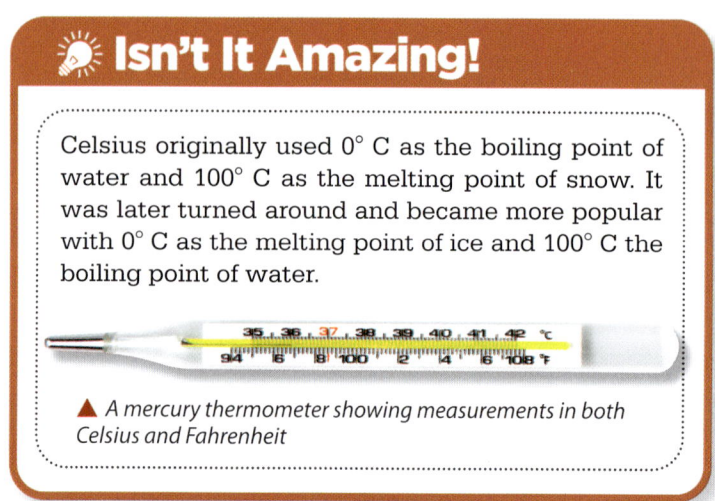

▲ A mercury thermometer showing measurements in both Celsius and Fahrenheit

INVENTIONS & DISCOVERIES | MEDICAL INVENTIONS

Listening to the Body

The first stethoscope was invented in 1816 by French physician Rene Theophile Hyacinthe Laennec. The stethoscope allows doctors to clearly listen to sounds within a patient's body. Most often, doctors listen to the sounds made by the heart and lungs using the stethoscope.

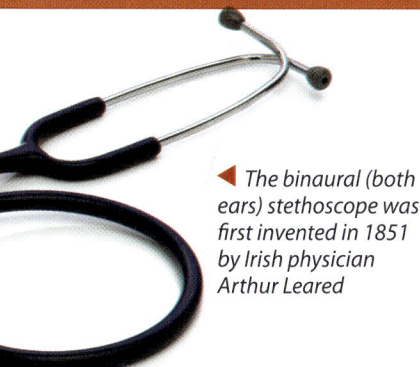

◀ The binaural (both ears) stethoscope was first invented in 1851 by Irish physician Arthur Leared

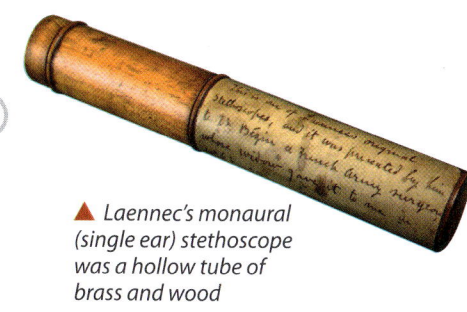

▲ Laennec's monaural (single ear) stethoscope was a hollow tube of brass and wood

Digital Thermometers

Nowadays, mercury thermometers are being replaced by digital models. Digital thermometers work by using a thermistor—a material whose resistance to electricity changes with changing temperatures. This resistance is measured by a computer chip inside the thermometer. The measurement is converted into a temperature reading, which is then shown to us on a display screen.

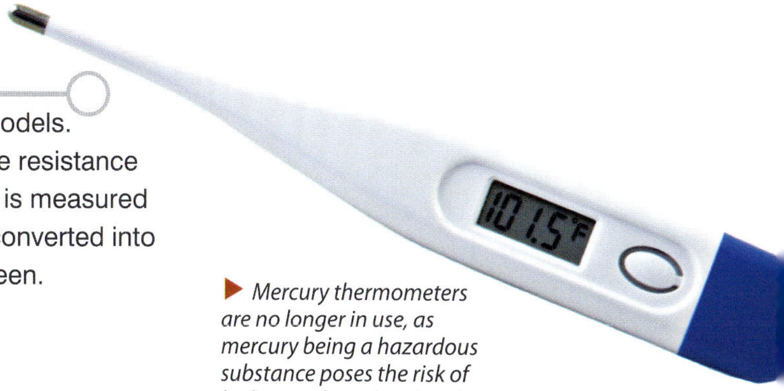

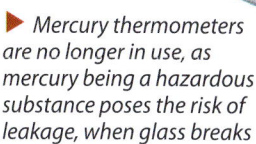

▶ Mercury thermometers are no longer in use, as mercury being a hazardous substance poses the risk of leakage, when glass breaks

Measuring Blood Pressure

A healthy heart is necessary for pumping blood throughout the body. When blood is pushed into blood vessels, it naturally presses against the walls of the vessels. This pressure is measured using a machine called a **sphygmomanometer**. Blood pressure can be affected by a huge number of illnesses. It is, therefore, one of the first things that doctors check to understand the state of your health. The first useful sphygmomanometer was invented by Austrian physician Karl Samuel Ritter von Basch in 1881.

An inflatable pad on the sphygmomanometer is wrapped around your upper arm and air is pumped through it, until it squeezes your arm. The doctor then measures your blood pressure using a stethoscope and the measuring counter attached to the sphygmomanometer.

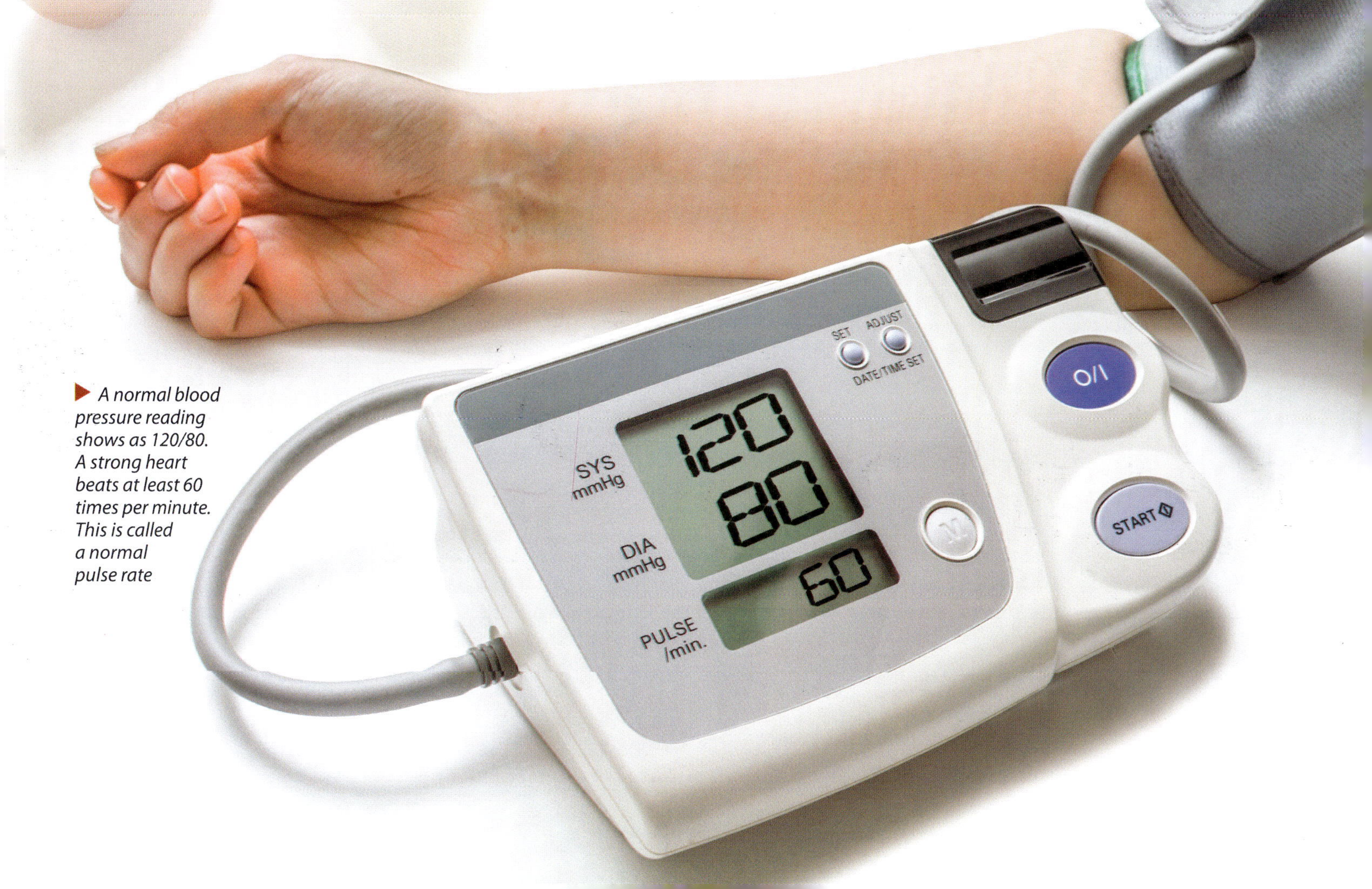

▶ A normal blood pressure reading shows as 120/80. A strong heart beats at least 60 times per minute. This is called a normal pulse rate

Photography for Physicians

Colours are made of electromagnetic rays called light. Apart from light, there are numerous other electromagnetic waves that are invisible to our eyes. Light cannot get in and out of our body, but certain sounds and electromagnetic waves can. Using these, inventors have built incredible machines to 'photograph' what is inside the body. Such imaging devices are used by doctors to diagnose your illness without cutting you open.

The Invisible X Factor

In 1895, German physicist Wilhelm Röntgen first discovered the presence of invisible **electromagnetic rays**. He called these mysterious waves X-rays. Unlike light, X-rays can pass through our bodies, but only through some parts. Bones and dense tissue are too thick for X-rays to penetrate.

If you put a piece of photographic film in the background, the X-rays that pass through the patient will hit the film and turn it black. The parts of the body that stop X-rays from going through will be outlined in white. Thus, X-ray photographs are used to look for damaged hard tissues, such as bone fractures.

▲ *This image shows a series of MRI scans of the brain from different angles*

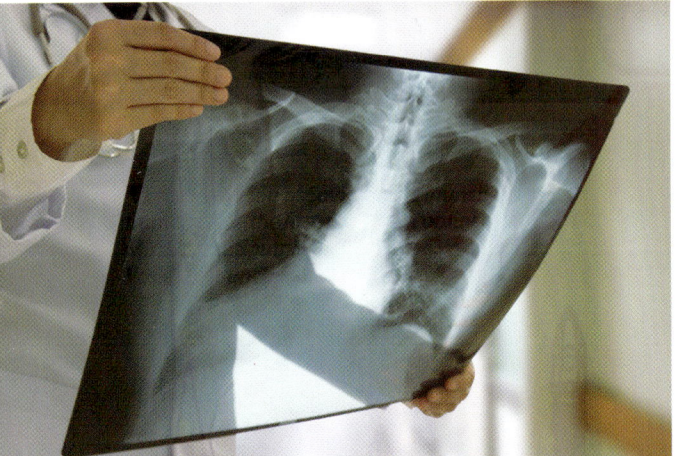

◀ *An X-ray film of the chest cavity; bones of the rib cage, spine and shoulders appear in white*

▶ *The first Nobel Prize for Physics was given to Röntgen in 1901, for his extraordinary discovery of invisible rays all around us. It ushered in a new era for physics and revolutionised medicine*

CT Scan

A Computed Tomography (CT) scan is a special type of X-ray machine. It was developed in the 1970s by Godfrey Newbold Hounsfield and Allan MacLeod Cormack, who shared a Nobel Prize for it in 1979. CT scans are popular in medicine for their detailed, high-resolution images. More importantly, they are able to photograph cross-sections of organs, so doctors can see what your organs look like from the inside.

Incredible Individuals

During WWII, a brilliant scientist named Marie Curie equipped vans with X-ray machines, so doctors could look for bullets inside wounded soldiers. The vans were fondly called 'petites Curies' (little Curies).

INVENTIONS & DISCOVERIES MEDICAL INVENTIONS 63

🔍 The Amazing MRI

Another Nobel-winning invention of the 1970s was Magnetic Resonance Imaging (MRI). This method gives high-contrast, 3D images of organs without using X-rays. Instead, it uses powerful magnetic fields about 1,000 times stronger than your fridge magnet.

The results are incredibly detailed images of soft tissues inside your body. Sir Peter Mansfield and Paul Lauterbur were the prize-winning minds behind MRI science. However, it was physician Raymond Damadian who invented the first full-body MRI scanner.

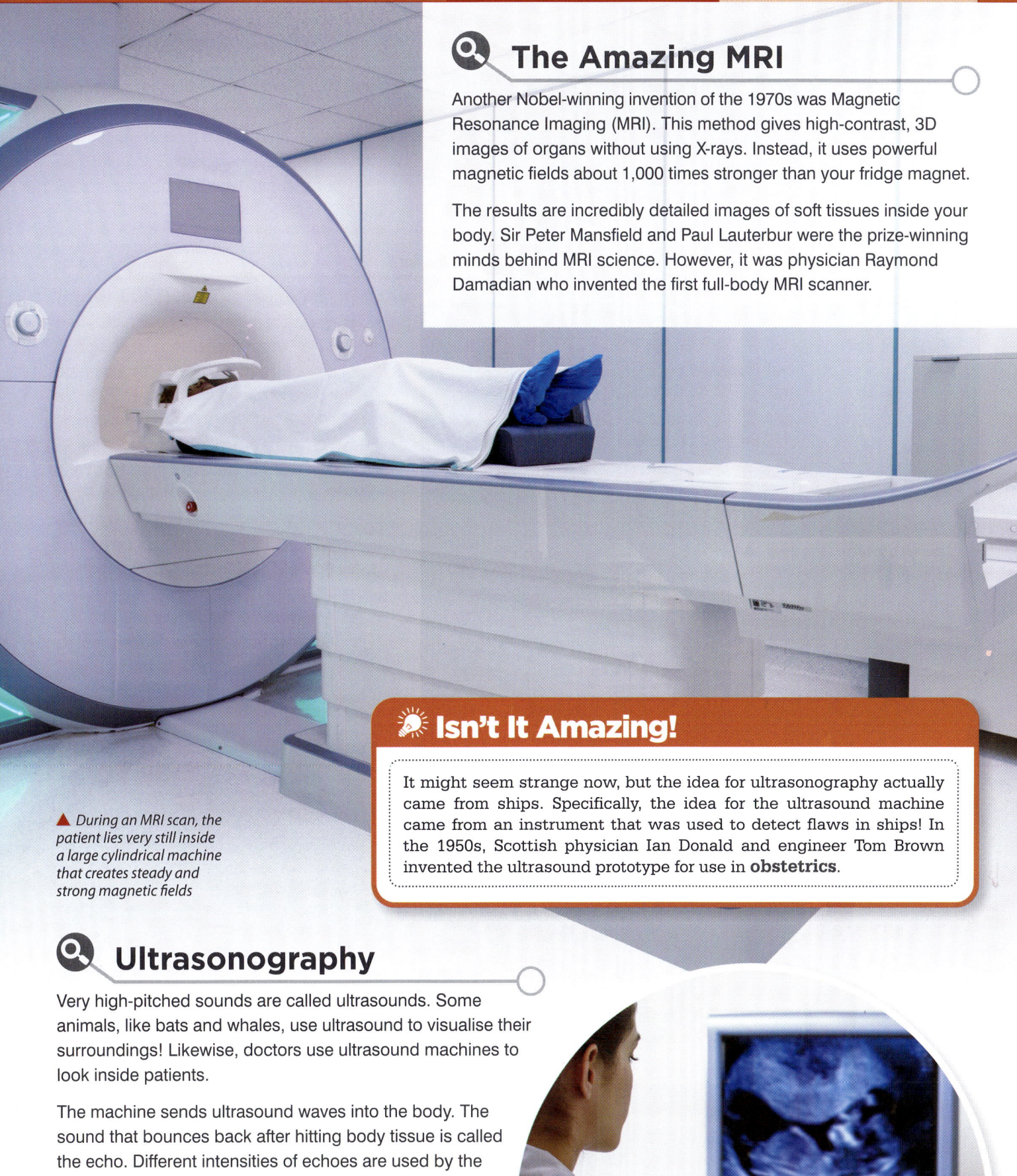

▲ During an MRI scan, the patient lies very still inside a large cylindrical machine that creates steady and strong magnetic fields

💡 Isn't It Amazing!

It might seem strange now, but the idea for ultrasonography actually came from ships. Specifically, the idea for the ultrasound machine came from an instrument that was used to detect flaws in ships! In the 1950s, Scottish physician Ian Donald and engineer Tom Brown invented the ultrasound prototype for use in **obstetrics**.

🔍 Ultrasonography

Very high-pitched sounds are called ultrasounds. Some animals, like bats and whales, use ultrasound to visualise their surroundings! Likewise, doctors use ultrasound machines to look inside patients.

The machine sends ultrasound waves into the body. The sound that bounces back after hitting body tissue is called the echo. Different intensities of echoes are used by the machine to understand the relative position of tissues. This information is used to create an image of the tissues inside the body.

▶ Unlike X-rays, there are no health risks associated with ultrasound. It is therefore used to check the health of a baby inside a mother's womb. CT scans and MRIs are also prohibited for pregnant women

Preventing Infections

Most diseases that spread from person to person are caused by bacteria and viruses. If the infection is not too serious, our bodies are able to create chemicals called antibodies that fight off the disease. But wouldn't it be great if we had antibodies even before the infection? Then, the disease would not affect us at all.

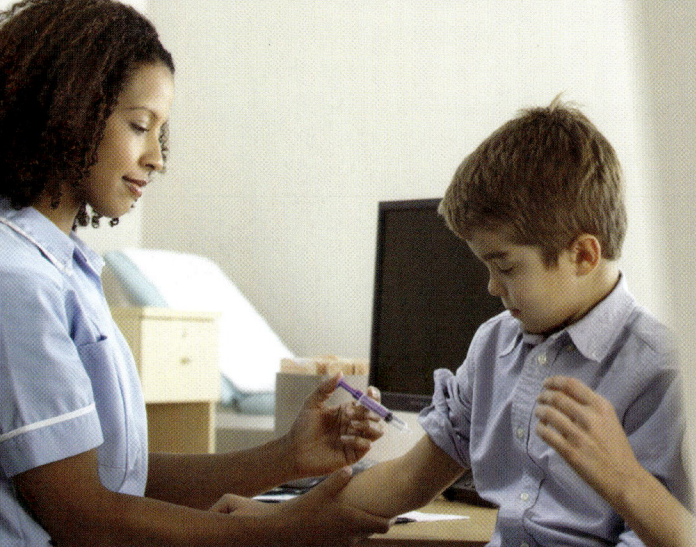

🔍 The Miracle of Vaccination

Vaccines are made up of weak or dead bacteria and viruses. They trick our body into thinking that it is being infected. The body then starts producing protective antibodies, even though we are not really ill.

Before vaccines, people used **variolation** (or inoculation) to prevent infections. This was done by applying old scabs or pus from infected boils on to a healthy person. The body responded by producing antibodies.

1000–1700 CE
Records from this time describe how people in China and India inoculated against the smallpox virus.

1796
Edward Jenner inoculates eight-year-old James Phipps with cowpox, a mild virus that spreads from cows to people. This breakthrough technique protects Phipps from the deadly smallpox virus. Jenner thus introduces vaccines to the world.

▼ *An illustration of Dr Edward Jenner injecting young James Phipps with the cowpox virus*

1805
Napoleon Bonaparte's sister Maria Anna Elisa Bonaparte becomes the first ruler to try to make vaccination mandatory. However, her initiative fails due to a lack of feasible methods to make the vaccination process compulsory.

▲ *Maria Anna Elisa Bonaparte (1777–1820)*

1884
Louis Pasteur creates a vaccine that protects dogs from the fatal rabies virus. The following year, he saves a badly bitten nine-year-old boy named Joseph Meister, with a course of 13 rabies injections.

▲ *Louis Pasteur*

1885
Pasteur's student Jaime Ferran develops the first anti-cholera vaccine. During a cholera epidemic in Spain, he undertakes the first mass vaccination of some 50,000 people.

INVENTIONS & DISCOVERIES | MEDICAL INVENTIONS

Incredible Individuals

In 1661, China's Emperor Kangxi came to power when his father died of smallpox. Emperor Kangxi himself had survived the disease as a child. Therefore, he had his sons and daughters inoculated against the disease. The successful procedures made him a firm supporter of the practice.

▶ The Qing Dynasty's fourth ruler, Emperor Kangxi

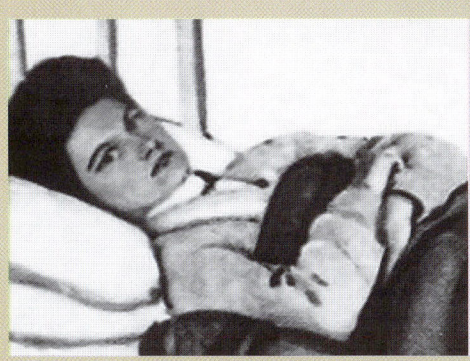
▲ An American maid named Mary Mallon became infamous as 'Typhoid Mary' in the 19th century. She knew she was ill, but continued to work at various households due to ignorance. By the time she was diagnosed, at least 51 people had been infected

1890s
British bacteriologist Sir Almroth Edward Wright invents an effective vaccine against typhoid. In 1899, the British army tests it on 3,000 soldiers in India during the Second Boer War.

1921
After 13 years of research, French scientists Albert Calmette and Camille Guerin develop the tuberculosis vaccine, calling it BCG (Bacillus Calmette-Guerin).

1936
Max Theiler creates the Yellow Fever vaccine, for which he later receives the Nobel Prize, becoming the only person to win the prize for the invention of a virus vaccine.

1938
Jonas Salk and Thomas Francis invent the first vaccine against influenza. It is used to protect US armed forces during WWII.

1939
American duo Pearl Kendrick and Grace Eldering develop the first effective vaccine for the deadly whooping cough.

1955
Jonas Salk's polio injection is approved. It is replaced in the 60s by an oral vaccine created by Albert Sabin.

1963
Dr John Enders and his team develop a safe measles vaccine.

2005
Measles, mumps, rubella and varicella are now combated using a single MMRV vaccine.

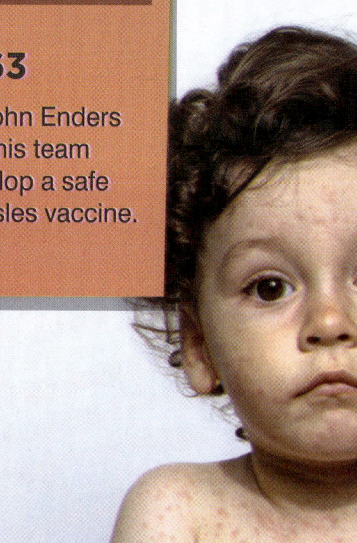
▶ A boy infected with measles

▲ The horse-drawn ambulance used during the last Yellow Fever epidemic in New Orleans, USA

An Infectious Theory

Antibiotics are chemicals produced by living creatures, which can affect the growth of other microorganisms. The chemicals are used to kill disease-causing microorganisms like bacteria. Before their invention, a great many people died from badly infected wounds. Even after bacteria were discovered in the 17th century, many doctors did not believe in their ability to cause infections.

Finally, in the 19th century, people were convinced that infections were caused by invisibly small organisms. The three heroes responsible for this achievement were Louis Pasteur, English surgeon Joseph Lister, and German physician Robert Koch.

▼ *Salmonella is a group of rod-shaped bacteria that cause many types of diseases, notably typhoid and food poisoning*

Isn't It Amazing!

Although we think of microbes as harmful creatures, our bodies survive by hosting a wide variety of microbes. For instance, without a healthy population of bacteria in our gut, we wouldn't be able to digest our food properly. Many scientists now believe that being obsessively hygienic destroys good microbes and leads to issues like asthma, skin conditions, and allergies.

 The greenish mould (a fungus) penicillium produces the invaluable antibiotic penicillin

 The Human Immunodeficiency Virus (HIV) is one of the deadliest viral diseases, as it takes away the body's ability to protect itself

From Stale to Sterile: Penicillin

Antibiotics gained prominence during the 1940s, thanks to penicillin taken from the fungus penicillium. This powerful antibiotic was popularised by Alexander Fleming, Howard Florey, and Ernst Chain. All three shared a Nobel Prize for it in 1945. However, penicillin was neither the first antibiotic to be discovered, nor was Fleming the first person to discover penicillin.

Alexander Fleming

After he returned from a long holiday, Fleming set about clearing out some petri dishes in his lab. The dishes contained colonies of a deadly bacteria called *staphylococcus*. Somehow, a fungal mould had entered the bacterial culture. Fleming noticed that the mould was producing a 'juice' that was killing the bacteria. He got his assistants to isolate this liquid and studied its properties. It turned out to be the antibiotic penicillin.

INVENTIONS & DISCOVERIES | MEDICAL INVENTIONS

A History of Antibiotics

Though they did not know about bacteria, people in ancient Egypt, China, Greece, and Rome knew how to use antibiotics. They used mouldy bread (which releases antibiotic chemicals) to treat infected wounds.

In the 19th century, Rudolf Emmerich and Oscar Low isolated pyocyanase from a green bacterium found in injured people's bandages. When this antibiotic was used in hospitals, different patients displayed different reactions and some even felt no difference.

In 1909, German physician Paul Ehrlich discovered the chemical arsphenamine, a successful cure for adults affected by the syphilis bacteria. Arsphenamine became the predecessor of the modern antibiotic.

▲ *Paul Ehrlich in his lab*

Incredible Individuals

Most schools teach us that penicillin was discovered in 1928 by Alexander Fleming. But this may not be true. In 1870, Sir John Scott Burdon-Sanderson noted that certain types of mould stopped bacteria from growing. Soon after, Joseph Lister experimented on penicillium and proved its anti-bacterial effect on human tissue. In 1875, John Tyndall also presented his experiments with penicillium. Most importantly, in 1897, Ernest Duchesne saw Arab stable boys applying mould from horse saddles on to their own saddle sores as a cure. He found that this mould was indeed penicillium and used it to successfully cure typhoid fever in guinea pigs.

The Works of Louis Pasteur

Little was known about microorganisms in the early 19th century. It was French chemist and microbiologist Louis Pasteur (1822–1895) who proved that germs were living beings. He discovered that milk turned sour because of microbes like bacteria. Further, heating milk killed the bacteria and made it safer to drink. This process is called pasteurisation. It is now a standard practice for many foods and drinks. Pasteur's idea also led to the boiling of instruments before surgery, to rid them of infectious bacteria. Most importantly, his work led to the development of vaccines against infectious diseases.

▲ *Louis Pasteur had 5 children, sadly he lost 3 of them to typhoid*

Indispensable Medicine

The 20th century saw groundbreaking advances in the invention of medicines. As a result, the average human life is much improved and the human lifespan is steadily increasing. We live longer, healthier lives thanks to the medicinal marvels of the 20th century.

Allergies

When foreign substances enter our body, our immune system responds in a variety of ways to remove them. A strong immune system thus protects us from parasites and microbes. But sometimes, harmless bits of fluff may enter our bodies and cause the system to react. This unnecessary response is called an allergy.

Common things that cause allergies include pollen from flowers, dust, pet hair, insect bites, and even some foods like peanuts and shellfish. The term allergy was coined in 1905 by Austrian physician Clemens von Pirquet.

Incredible Individuals

Clemens von Pirquet was an Austrian physician. He invented a test for tuberculosis. In this test, a drop of a bacterial protein called tuberculin is scratched on to the surface of the skin. If the area becomes red and raised, it confirms that the person is infected with tuberculosis.

Pirquet also discovered serum sickness, a mild allergic reaction to an injection of serum. This eventually led him to coin and define the term 'allergy'.

▲ People can take tests to find out what they might be allergic to

Tackling Allergies

Allergies have existed since ancient times, affecting rich and poor alike. Famously, the Roman emperor Claudius was terribly allergic to his own horse! Allergies can be as mild as a bout of sneezing and deadly enough to cause shock and death.

Unfortunately, we are yet to find a permanent cure for allergies. However, it is easy enough to control them by using medicines called anti-allergens. These range from injections to ointments, tablets, and inhalers. Mild anti-allergens like Benadryl (used for hay fever, hives, and motion sickness) are easily available at pharmacies.

Pain Relief

Any drug that takes away your pain without putting you instantly to sleep is called an **analgesic**. The best-known analgesic is aspirin. It is used to reduce fever and inflammation, and to remove aches in your muscles, joints, or head.

Aspirin is made from salicylic acid, a chemical that can be acquired from lots of herbs, fruits, grains, and even the bark of the willow tree. Clay tablets left by people from 4,000 years ago show that willow bark was used for pain relief. It has been a popular part of herbal medicine ever since. But it was only in the 19th century that salicylic acid was manufactured separately as a medicine.

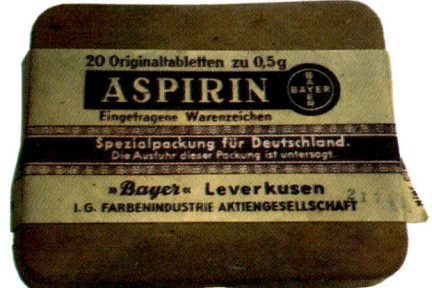

◀ Modern aspirin was made by the chemical researcher Arthur Eichengrun. The first tablet appeared in 1900 and rapidly became popular in this form

What is a Transplant?

In medicine, a transplant (or a graft) means taking tissue from its original location and using it to heal some other part of the body. It can be done with an entire organ or with some part of it. When a tissue is grafted from one part of your body to another part of your own body, it is called an autograft. Organ transplants are also made from one human being to another.

The History of Autograft

As far back as the sixth century, surgeons in the Indian subcontinent were practising tissue grafts. The Sushruta Samhita, an ancient Indian text, outlines the process of skin grafts. Specifically, they could rebuild shattered noses using skin flaps from the patient's arm. The flap would remain attached to the arm until the nose area grew new blood vessels. After about two to three weeks, the arm would be freed from the nose.

This method spread to Western medicine in the 16th century through the efforts of Italian surgeon Gaspare Tagliacozzi.

Transplant Successes

The body's immune system treats most transplants as foreign bodies and attacks them. All transplants—even autografts and transplants between identical twins—are prone to such rejection. To prevent this situation from arising, transplant recipients are given drugs called immunosuppressants, which help the body successfully cope with the transplant.

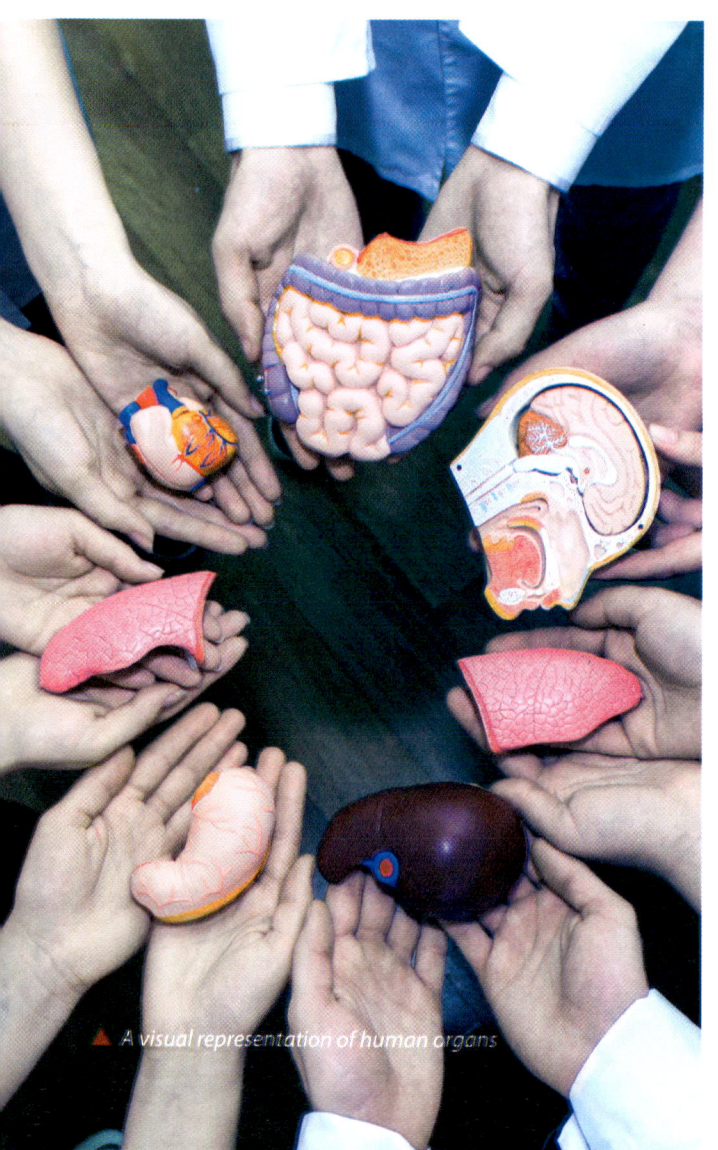
▲ A visual representation of human organs

Facts about Transplants

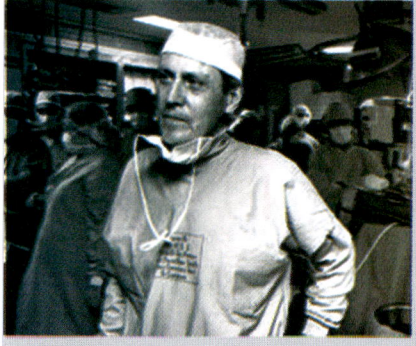

▲ In 1969, Thomas Starzl performed a successful liver transplant. In the same year, Christiaan Barnard completed the first successful heart transplant

In 1998, a full hand was successfully transplanted for the first time. The surgery was done in France.

A partial face transplant was also first successfully performed in France. Five years later, in 2010, a full-face transplant was achieved in Spain.

Incredible Individuals

Alexis Carrell developed groundbreaking ways to sew blood vessels together, for which he received the Nobel Prize in Medicine in 1912. His work laid the foundation for organ transplant surgery. In 1990, Joseph Murray received the Nobel Prize for his revolutionary work in advancing organ transplants using radiotherapy and immunosuppressants. He shared it with Donnall Thomas, who invented methods of providing bone marrow cells for transplant.

▲ Alexis Carrell

Sussing out Surgery

Often, acute injuries and illnesses cannot be treated by simply taking medicines. In such cases, doctors may open the affected part of the body and physically set things right.

Specially trained doctors called surgeons operate in specially equipped rooms called Operation Rooms (OR). They work under sanitised conditions to repair any damage or remove infected parts from inside the body.

In Real Life

During a heart attack, a person's heart stops beating. To revive it, doctors send an electric shock through the heart using a device called the defibrillator.

6500–3000
A form of surgery called trepanation (drilling a hole in the skull) is done by ancient humans in France. The purpose of this procedure is not yet known.

335–280
Alexandrian physician Herophilus **dissects** human cadavers in public. He is known as the 'father of **anatomy**'.

1452–1519
The multitalented Leonardo da Vinci dissects and draws human bodies with stupendous accuracy.

1728–1793
British surgeon John Hunter carries out groundbreaking studies in human biology. He is called the 'father of modern surgery'.

1735
The first known **appendectomy** takes place.

1792
Napoleon Bonaparte's military surgeon Dominique-Jean Larrey creates an ambulance service for soldiers on the battlefield.

1818
In Britain, James Blundell performs the first successful transfusion of human blood. He transfers blood from a husband to his wife, soon after childbirth.

▲ A skull showing evidence of the practice of trepanation

◀ Many modern surgeries are performed by robot arms, which are controlled by a surgeon using a computer. This helps doctors perform very precise and delicate operations.

▲ Larrey's Flying Ambulances would take wounded soldiers to field hospitals, located a few kilometres away from the battle. Before this invention, injured men were simply left on the field until the battle ended

▶ Type AB Plasma can be transfused to people of all other blood types, but it is short in supply

INVENTIONS & DISCOVERIES | MEDICAL INVENTIONS

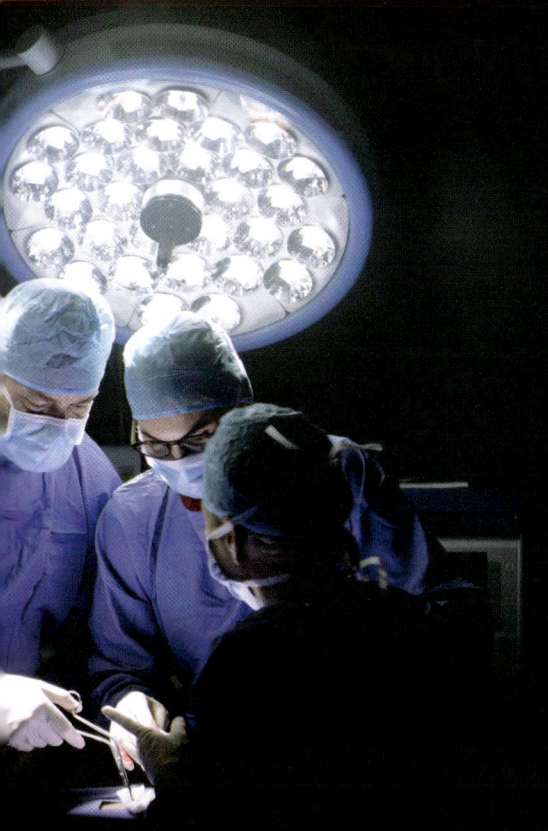

Isn't It Amazing!

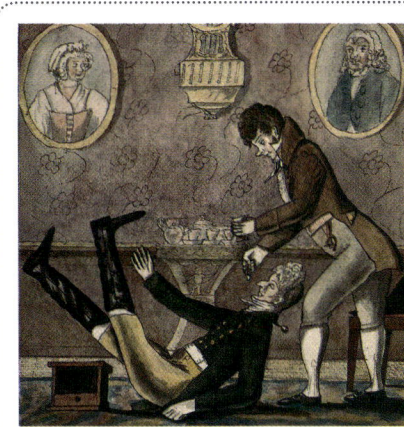

Many ancient cultures, like India, China, and Egypt were familiar with surgery. However, in medieval Europe, surgery was done by barbers rather than doctors! In 1540, the United Company of Barber Surgeons of London was set up to finally bring some standards and training to the profession.

◀ *A painting depicting dentistry by a fashionable dentist in 17th century*

1843
Ether is used as an **anaesthetic** for the first time. Four years later, James Simpson uses chloroform as an anaesthetic.

1865
British surgeon Joseph Lister discovers the use of antiseptics in surgery.

1893
The first successful open-heart surgery is performed in the USA, for a wound extremely close to the heart. Three years later, the first successful heart surgery is completed in Germany to repair a stab wound.

1905
The cornea of the eye is transplanted for the first time.

1940
A metal hip replaces bone for the first time.

1937
Blood banks come into being. They aid quicker blood transfusions.

1930
In Germany, a man undergoes an operation to become a woman named Lili Elbe.

1954
A whole organ (a kidney) is transplanted from one body into another. The patient lives on for eight more years.

2008
A laser is used in minimalist keyhole surgery to treat brain cancer.

2013
A successful nerve transfer allows a patient to move their formerly paralysed hand.

Incredible Individuals

Born in 1797, Dr James Barry was actually a woman who lived her whole life as a man, because women were not allowed to become surgeons. Dr James Barry became a British military surgeon and, upon her death, was buried as a man.

▶ *Barry's real name was Margaret Ann Bulkley*

Genetics

Have you ever wondered why the biologically related members of a family look like each other? The answer lies in the nucleus of the cell. This dark nucleus is made up of microscopic matter called genes. The study of genes is called genetics. Genes give our cells their basic form and function.

Children inherit genes from their parents. Thus, they look like a mix of their parents, and can also resemble their siblings, grandparents, aunts, uncles, cousins, etc. Genes decide the colour of a flower, give the lion its mane, and differentiate a fish from a bird.

 DNA

Genes are made up of a chemical called deoxyribonucleic acid or DNA. Lots of DNA and protein come together to form thread-like structures called chromosomes. Different creatures have different number of chromosomes. A garden pea has 14 chromosomes and an elephant has 56. DNA itself has a peculiar shape called a double-helix. This was discovered by scientists Francis Crick and James Watson in the 1950s.

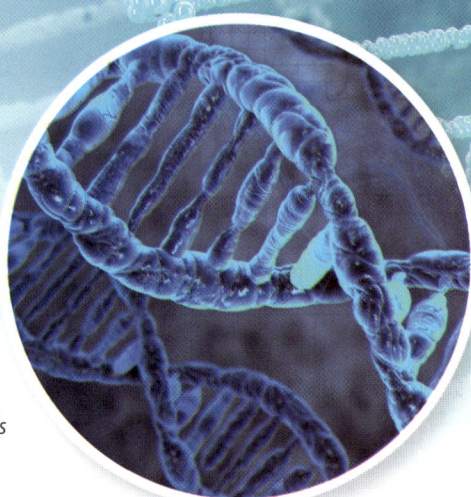

▶ The double-helix DNA is formed by two entwined strands

Human Genome Project (HGP)

A genome is the genetic make-up of an organism. Over 1990–2003, the Human Genome Project (HGP) identified and published all the thousands of genes that make up a human being. Going forward, this will help doctors and scientists understand how to improve human life, especially how to reverse ageing and cure inherited diseases.

Incredible Individuals

In 1962, Crick, Watson, and Maurice Wilkins won a Nobel Prize for discovering the structure of the DNA. However, they could not have done it without Rosalind Franklin's work. It was Franklin who obtained the images of DNA. She did so using X-ray techniques, which tragically led to her death by cancer. When the prize was awarded, Franklin—most unfairly—was left out!

   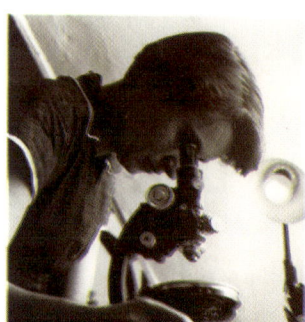

▲ Dr Francis Crick   ▲ Dr James Watson   ▲ Dr Maurice Wilkins   ▲ Dr Rosalind Franklin

Royal Rarities

Royalty has always considered itself special. In an effort to keep their blood 'pure', members of royal families often married their relatives. Eventually, they became so interrelated, new marriages were taking place between cousins. This is called inbreeding. It sometimes results in people being born with rare and tragic defects.

Haemophilia

The most infamous 'royal disease' was haemophilia. It occurs when blood clots do not form to stop a wound from bleeding. The illness affected many male descendants of Queen Victoria of England. She married her first cousin, Prince Albert. Their son Leopold fell and hurt himself. He died from blood loss. Through her daughters, haemophilia spread to other royal families of Europe. The two sons of the German Kaiser Wilhelm II, as well as the son of the Russian Tsar Nicholas II, were all haemophiliacs.

▲ After 16 generations of inbreeding, the royal Habsburg family of Europe started showing physical deformities. The Habsburg Jaw, seen here in Charles II of Spain, is the name for a jutting lower jaw—usually under a thick lower lip

Porphyria

Another disease of the blood, porphyria comes in different forms. James V of Scotland most likely passed it to his daughter Mary, Queen of Scots. She suffered from ulcers, mental illnesses, physical disablement and rheumatism since her teens. Her son James I of England had urine as 'purple as Alicante wine'—another sign of porphyria. Their descendent George III, nicknamed 'Mad' King George, would wander through the castle, blind, deaf and dirty. Unable to recognise anyone, he was sadly neglected by his caretakers. In 1810, his son forced his removal from the throne.

▲ A painting of George III of Great Britain commissioned during his younger, happier days

In Real Life

King Henry VIII of England suffered from the very common disease, malaria. The first cure for malaria was found in South America. A feverish man, desperate with thirst, drank from a pool of water and was cured. He noticed that the water was bitter. It had been 'poisoned' by the surrounding cinchona trees. Over the 18th and 19th centuries, scientists found and purified the chemical from the tree. It is called quinine and is used to cure malaria to this day.

Cosmology:
From Ancient Times to the 19th Century

We have slowly but steadily managed to glean many secrets of the universe over the centuries. The course of cosmology has weathered the pressures of religion and superstition, the suppression of female scientists, the prejudices of class and race, and many other odds. Let us take a look at some of the most brilliant champions of this triumphant science.

Anaximander (610–546 BCE)

The first known person to develop a systematic view of the world was the Greek philosopher Anaximander. He was also the person who recognised that Earth moved freely through space. This idea may seem obvious to us now, but most civilisations of that time believed that the planet was upheld by pillars, heroes or beasts. So, he was quite a path-breaker at that time.

▲ An ancient Roman mosaic depicting Anaximander holding a sundial

◀ A 1628 oil painting of the cheerful Democritus, by Dutch artist Hendrick Terbrugghen

Democritus (460–370 BCE)

Democritus was also known as the 'laughing philosopher'. He believed that the universe was made of tiny particles called atoms. According to him, the universe contained infinite, diverse worlds that followed a set of physical laws rather than the whims of gods. He also worked out that the Milky Way's appearance was caused by the light of stars.

Aristarchus of Samos (310–230 BCE)

In ancient times, people thought Earth was at the centre of the universe. Mathematician Aristarchus first proposed that the Sun was at the centre of the universe. He proposed this model 18 centuries before Nicolaus Copernicus discovered the same.

▶ A statue of Aristarchus at the Aristotle University of Thessaloniki, Greece

▲ Although not the first one to propose the theory, Nicolaus Copernicus (1473–1543) was the man who popularised heliocentrism, which theorises that the planets revolve around the Sun

INVENTIONS & DISCOVERIES | SPACE DISCOVERIES | 75

★ Incredible Individuals

Born a nobleman, Tycho Brahe (1546–1601) was kidnapped and brought up by his uncle. Brahe later refused to take his place at the royal court. Defying his family, he became a scientist. Brahe's work was revolutionary and brought new light to the understanding of planetary motion and gravity.

▶ A brilliant group of women known as 'Harvard's Computers' made significant contributions to astronomy. Among them were Henrietta Swan Leavitt (1868–1921), Annie Jump Cannon (1863–1941), Williamina Fleming (1857–1911), and Antonia Maury (1866–1952)

▼ The Kepler crater on the Moon is named in honour of Johannes Kepler

Hipparchus (190–120 BCE)

Hipparchus was one of the greatest Greek cosmologists. He was the first to accurately measure the distance between Earth and the Moon. His work revealed the existence of over 850 stars. He also discovered the 'wobbling' of Earth that causes the equinoxes. This is called **precession** and it was the third movement of Earth that was discovered after rotation and revolution.

◀ Almagest, written by Claudius Ptolemy (100–170 CE) was the ultimate guide to thousands of stars and constellations and to the movement of planets for 1500 years

Johannes Kepler (1571–1630)

Blessed with a keen intellect, Kepler propounded the laws of planetary motion. He also discovered that tides occur due to the gravitational pull of Moon. His work on planetary motion led Newton to discover the laws of gravity.

Isaac Newton (1643–1727)

Newton's laws of gravity and motion completely changed our understanding of physics and nature. Newton also invented the first reflecting telescope and showed how sunlight could be split into all the colours of the rainbow.

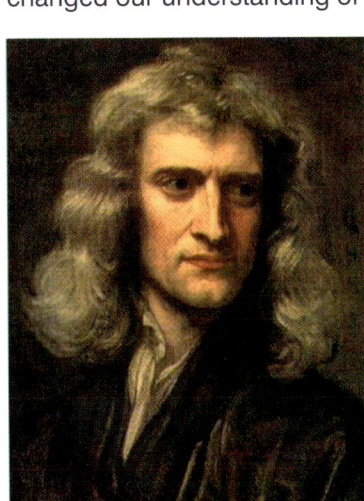

◀ Isaac Newton was a key figure of Europe's scientific revolution

John Herschel (1792–1871)

Nephew of the brilliant astronomer Caroline Herschel, John did the first global survey of stars. He built the first telescopic lab in the southern hemisphere and catalogued about 500 nebulae and over 3,000 double stars. He named seven of Saturn's moons and four of Uranus's moons.

▶ John Herschel took the first-ever photograph on a glass plate. He even coined the word 'photography'

The Space Race

The World War II ended in 1945. The US and Soviet Union had been allies during this war. But without a common enemy, the capitalist US and the communist Soviet Union soon turned against each other. Instead of clashing openly, they fought to establish their supremacy in various other fields of interest, such as race for outer space. This period is known as the Cold War.

The Space War

One of the few good things to come out of the Cold War was a spate of space-related technologies. In 1955, the US declared that it would launch a satellite into the outer space. The USSR decided to launch its own satellite first. Thus, began a fierce competition known as the space race.

▲ Taken at the height of the space race, this photograph shows Soviet leader Nikita Khrushchev with Valentina Tereshkova, the first woman in space and (in the far left) Yuri Gagarin, the first man in space. Between them is Pavel Popovich, another pioneering cosmonaut

4 October 1957
The USSR becomes the first nation to successfully launch an artificial satellite. It is called Sputnik, a Russian word meaning fellow wanderer.

3 November 1957
A live animal, the dog Laika, orbits Earth for the first time on the USSR's satellite Sputnik-2.

1960
NASA launches the first successful weather satellite, Tiros-1. Its ability to detect cloud cover and predict hurricanes encouraged the development of the Nimbus programme of weather satellites.

29 July 1958
America establishes the National Aeronautics and Space Administration (NASA) after the success of Sputnik.

▲ NASA Headquarters in Washington D.C.

1 February 1958
The US successfully launches a satellite called Explorer. It discovers the Van Allen radiation belt, which causes the polar lights called Aurora Borealis (in the Northern Hemisphere) and Aurora Australis (in the Southern Hemisphere).

◀ In 1958, TIME Magazine portrayed Soviet leader Nikita Khrushchev as the Man of the Year with the satellite Sputnik in his hands

◀ A statue of Laika in her space harness in Moscow, Russia

▶ The Aurora Borealis photographed over Norway

INVENTIONS & DISCOVERIES | SPACE DISCOVERIES

12 April 1961
The Soviets manage another first by launching the cosmonaut Yuri Gagarin into space.

◀ Yuri Gagarin, the first man in space and the first to orbit Earth

💡 Isn't It Amazing!
Did you know that fiction predicted the launch of satellites? They appeared in the 1869 short story, *The Brick Moon* by Edward Hale and in the 1879 novel, *The Begum's Fortune* by Jules Verne.

25 May 1961
US President John F Kennedy publicly commits the US to achieving the first human landing on the Moon.

◀ US President John F Kennedy addressing Congress in 1961, announcing his ambitious goal of "landing a man on the Moon and returning him safely to Earth"

16 June 1963
The Soviet Union launches Vostok-6 with Valentina Tereshkova, the first female cosmonaut to travel to outer space.

◀ The first woman in space, Valentina Tereshkova, presenting a badge to the first man on the Moon, Neil Armstrong

20 February 1962
NASA's 'human computers', an all-woman team of mathematicians, undertake mind-boggling calculations that give the US an edge in the space race. Katherine G Johnson's impressive mathematics skills help put American astronaut John Glenn into orbit around Earth.

◀ Katherine G Johnson, whose calculations in orbital mechanics led to many successful missions, including the first Moon landing

▲ This USSR stamp from 1965 commemorates Leonov's historic walk in space

28 November 1964
The Mariner-4 explorer is launched. It becomes the first spacecraft to fly by Mars and send photographs and data about the planet.

18 March 1965
The Soviet cosmonaut Alexei Leonov becomes the first man to 'walk' in space. He leaves the spacecraft wearing an early spacesuit and walks in the vacuum of space for just over 12 minutes.

20 July 1969
After a series of missions under the Apollo programme, the US spacecraft Apollo-11 lands on the Moon. Crew members Neil Armstrong and Buzz Aldrin spend 21 hours and 36 minutes on the Moon before successfully returning to the spacecraft. This brilliant achievement marks the end of the Cold War space race.

◀ Buzz Aldrin on the Moon; reflected in his visor is Neil Armstrong taking the photograph

Kicking off Space Exploration

Scientists have been working on fulfilling the human dream of space travel for centuries. During 1642–1727, Isaac Newton published his laws of motion and described gravity. This gave us a scientific basis for understanding rockets and orbits. Russian scientist Konstantin Tsiolkovsky (1857–1935) showed how rockets could be used to launch spacecrafts. He also calculated the minimum speed required to stay into the orbit around Earth. Finally, in 1942, the German aerospace engineer Werner von Braun and his team built V2, the first rocket to reach the boundaries of space, about 100 kms above Earth.

Rocket Development

A rocket is any weapon or vehicle propelled by a rocket engine. The medieval Chinese inventors of rockets used gunpowder for propulsion. Liquid-fuel rockets were developed by Robert H Goddard (1882–1945), the father of modern rocketry.

Modern ion rockets use solar-powered electricity to produce a stream of **ions**, which propel the rocket forward. The latest **plasma** rockets use radio waves to heat chemicals at such a high temperature that they turn to plasma (which is what the Sun is made of)! A powerful rocket like this could travel to Mars and back within a few weeks. But scientists have yet to figure out how to stop the rocket from melting in the heat it generates.

▼ US officials, including Werner von Braun, with a model Explorer-1, the first satellite launched by the USA into outer space.

In Real Life

Many space exploration devices are launched on multi-stage rockets. These are made of two to five rockets, each of which carries its own engine and fuel.

▼ The evolution of Soviet space launch vehicles from the R-7 (the first-ever Intercontinental Ballistic Missile), the Sputnik launcher, the Vostok, the Voskhod launcher, and the Soyuz launcher

▶ India's PSLV, a four-stage launch vehicle with both solid-fuel and liquid-fuel rockets

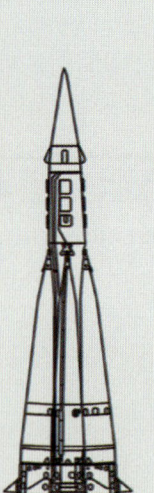
R-7 (8K71) Test vehicle 1957

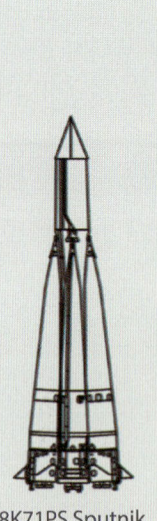
8K71PS Sputnik (PS) Launcher 1957

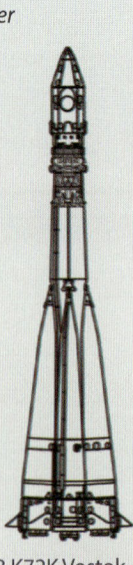
8 K72K Vostok (3KA) Launcher 1960

11A57 Voskhod (3KV) Launcher 1963

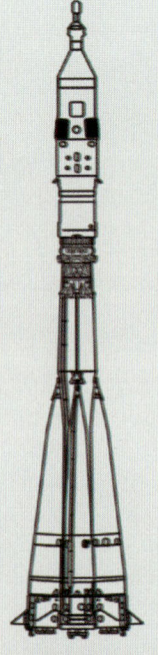
11A57 Soyuz (7K-OK) Launcher 1966

Sputnik

Launched on an R-7 liquid-fuel rocket, the Soviet Union's Sputnik was the first artificial satellite to orbit Earth. It weighed 83.6 kilograms and travelled in an elliptical path above Earth for three months. At 29,000 kmph, it took 96.2 minutes to complete each orbit. After 1440 circuits, it burned up in Earth's atmosphere on 4 January 1958.

▲ The Sputnik spacecraft

A Cosmic Zoo

The first beings to go up in a rocket were most likely accidental passengers like bacteria or other microbes. In 1947, scientists sent up some fruit flies in a V2 rocket. They were given some corn to snack on during the trip. On 14 June 1949, Albert II became the first monkey to fly up in a rocket. He travelled 134 kilometres to the very beginning of space. Since then, 32 monkeys and a chimpanzee have journeyed to space. Several mice were launched during the 1950s. The dog Laika was the first animal to orbit Earth. Sputnik-5 was the first spacecraft to return with its passengers alive on 19 August 1960. These included 2 dogs, a rabbit, 42 mice, 2 rats, and fruit flies!

▲ After some confused attempts, Arabella became the first spider to spin a web in space. Launched in 1972, Arabella and Anita were the first spiders in outer space

◄ The US launch of the V2 rocket carrying Albert II

The First Spaceman

Flying the rocket Vostok-1, Yuri Gagarin (1934–1968) became the first man in outer space. From there, he was launched into orbit on the Vostok 3KA spacecraft, in which he successfully completed one orbit of the Earth. He famously whistled the tune of 'The Motherland hears, the Motherland knows, Where her son flies in the sky', a 1951 song by Dmitri Shostakovich. Awed by the sight before him, he reported to ground control, "The Earth is blue... How wonderful. It is amazing."

◄ The Vostok-1 was notable for being the world's first space flight with a human on-board

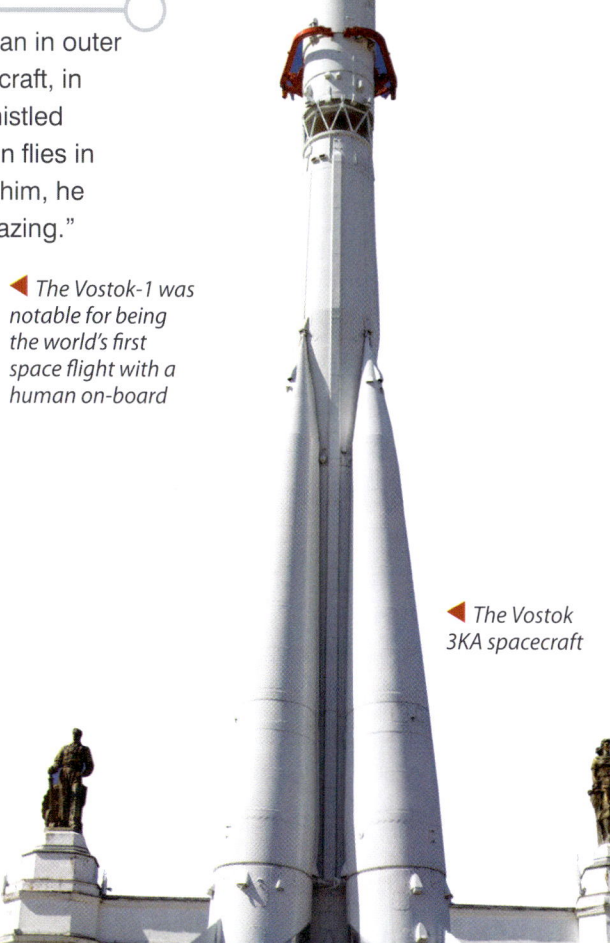

◄ The Vostok 3KA spacecraft

To the Moon and Back

In 1961, President John F Kennedy announced that the US would put men on the Moon before 1970. NASA achieved this goal when, on 20 July 1969, the manned Apollo-11 spacecraft made a successful landing. Nearly 530 million people watched the event on live broadcast. Since then, there have been several missions to the Moon launched by the US, Russia, Japan, China, India, and Europe.

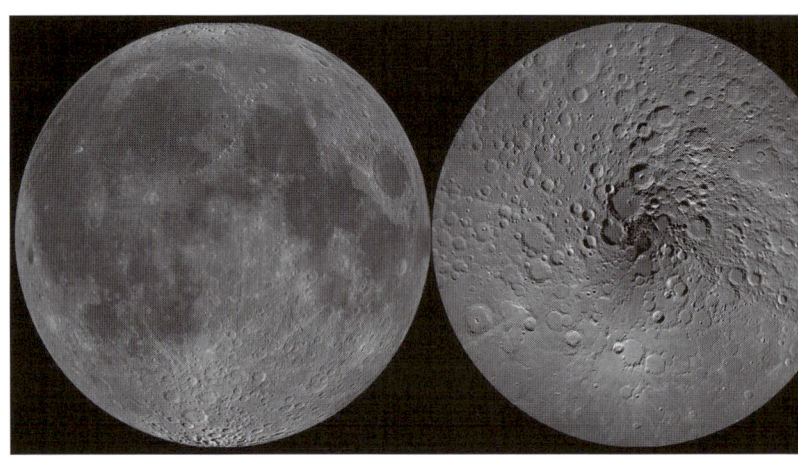

▶ From left to right, this shows the Moon's near side, far side, north pole, and south pole

Isn't It Amazing!

Just between the mid-60s and the mid-70s, there were some 65 Moon landings! However, only 6 Moon landings have carried human beings on board and only 12 people have ever walked on the Moon's cratered surface.

◀ On 30 May 1966, the US robot spaceship Surveyor-1 reached the Moon. Its photographs gave NASA some vital information on how they might successfully land a crew of astronauts on the satellite

The Dark Side of the Moon

The first human beings to orbit the Moon were the crew of Apollo-8. It comprised Frank Borman, James Lovell, and William Anders. The event occurred on 24 December 1968. While orbiting the Moon, they also became the first people ever, to see the dark side of the Earth's Moon.

▶ William Anders's photo of Earth rising over the Moon's horizon, taken from Apollo-8, is one of the most iconic photographs in human history

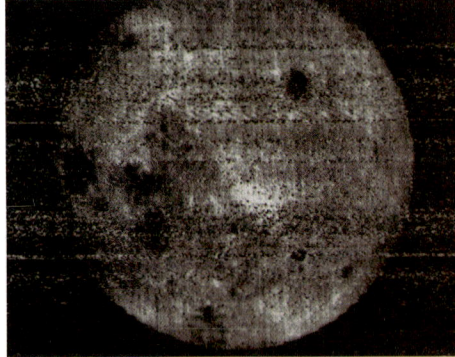

◀ Our first view of the far side of the Moon came from a photograph taken by Soviet probe Luna-3 on 7 October 1959

Man on the Moon

Apollo-11 launched on 16 July 1969. It carried Neil Armstrong, Michael Collins and Edwin 'Buzz' Aldrin. On 20 July Armstrong and Aldrin donned their spacesuits and climbed into a lunar landing module called Eagle, while Collins remained in orbit in the Columbia module.

The Eagle landed on a volcanic plain called Mare Tranquillity. Armstrong and Aldrin spent 21 hours and 36 minutes resting, exploring, and deploying experiments. Later, they re-joined Collins. On 24 July, Apollo-11 splashed down in the Pacific Ocean and the three astronauts were safely brought back home.

INVENTIONS & DISCOVERIES | SPACE DISCOVERIES

◀ The Apollo-11 lunar crew (from left to right): Neil Armstrong, Michael Collins, and Buzz Aldrin

▶ The Eagle with its spidery landing pods and sensors, photographed in orbit by Columbia

▶ Apollo-11 lifting off on the three-stage, liquid-fuelled Saturn V rocket on 16 July 1969 from Kennedy Space Centre

The Miraculous Apollo-13

Apollo-13 was meant to be the third manned mission to land on the Moon. But within two days of its journey, the oxygen tank in the service module failed, which ignited the damaged wire insulation. This caused an explosion which led to the relentless flow of oxygen in the outer space. The astronauts thought that they were doomed. Fortunately, NASA's scientists came up with prompt solutions using the limited equipment on board. They guided the astronauts to make the repairs and brought them home safely. The heroic story is celebrated in books, films, theatre, and even comics!

Lunar Road Trips

From 1971 onwards, American astronauts used a Moon car to explore the vast surface of Earth's satellite. This electric-powered vehicle, with a top speed of less than 13 kmph, was called the Lunar Rover. The Moon buggy made its first trip on 31 July 1971 with Apollo-15 astronauts David Scott and James Irwin.

Modern Explorations

Since the 1990s, Japan's Institute of Space and Aeronautical Sciences, the European Space Agency, the Chinese Lunar Exploration Agency, and the Indian Space Research Organisation have all successfully sent missions to the Moon. The first private enterprise to do so was the Manfred Memorial Moon Mission (4M), launched on 23 October 2014. On 3 January 2019, China's Chang'e 4 (named after the Moon goddess) became the first mission to achieve a soft landing directly on the far side of the Moon!

In Real Life

Neil Armstrong's words "One small step for man, one giant leap for mankind" were not the first words said on the Moon. In reality, the first words were a practical post-landing checklist! Armstrong's first communication from the Moon was simply, "Houston, Tranquillity Base here. The Eagle has landed."

▲ The Lunar Reconnaissance Orbiter orbiting the Moon and mapping its polar regions

Artificial Satellites

The idea of putting a man-made object into orbit around Earth was proposed as early as 1928. Slovenian rocket engineer Herman Potocnik (1892–1929) described how we could communicate with such a satellite using radio signals. He also described a space station and its usefulness in Earth-related experiments. Since then, human beings have developed many kinds of satellites. There are close to 2,000 satellites around our planet. Inventors have also created sophisticated networking systems to communicate with them.

▶ An Advanced Extremely High Frequency (AEHF) communications satellite

Deep Space Network

The awe-inspiring Deep Space Network (DSN) is an array of giant radio antennae located in three far-flung places—California, USA; near Madrid, Spain; and near Canberra, Australia. This careful placement allows DSN to remain in continuous contact with spacecrafts, even as our planet keeps rotating. The DSN guides spacecrafts and probes that are travelling far in space. It also receives information and photographs from these unmanned explorers.

Building a Satellite

These days, a satellite is designed to be strong and as light as possible. It is made of a platform (called bus) which contains the main systems. This includes batteries, computers, and engine thrusters. The antennae, solar cells, and instruments for research and communication are attached to the bus. The solar cells are usually designed on the foldable wings that are many metres long. Satellites are also covered with blankets of aluminium foil that can protect it from extreme heat and cold.

Finding the Way

The Global Positioning System (GPS) in your car, which tells you how to get from one place to another, functions because of navigation satellites. These are the same satellites that guide ships, aircrafts, and many other important systems.

Monitoring the Weather

About 36,000 kilometres above us are geostationary satellites that track weather patterns and changes. **Geostationary** means that the satellite keeps up with Earth's spin, so it is always looking down on us from the same spot.

Planet Observation

Earth observation satellites detect changes in our planet's green cover, ocean surfaces, and radiation. They also map Earth. Along with communications satellites, they are used by military and spy agencies to collect information that is of national importance.

▼ The giant parabolic antennae of the DSN are located in a bowl-shaped area created by hills to increase the antennae's sensitivity to specific radio signals

▶ The first television image of Earth taken from TIROS-1, the first successful weather satellite

Telescopes: A Distant Look

Space scientists these days have incredibly powerful telescopes locked on to far-off galaxies and planets. They even have telescopes in space. These astronomical satellites study the cosmos without suffering from any atmospheric disturbances. The idea of space telescopes came from physicist Lyman Spitzer in 1946. The first successful one, the OAO-2, was launched by the US in 1968.

▼ The Hubble Space Telescope

Space Telescopes

NASA's 'Great Observatories' refers to four powerful space telescopes. The Compton Gamma Ray Observatory observes **gamma rays** in space, the Chandra Observatory observes **X-rays**, the Spitzer Space Telescope observes **infrared rays**, and the Hubble Space Telescope observes visible light.

◄ Images from Chandra, Hubble, and Spitzer combined show the Crab Nebula spewing energy at the rate of 100,000 Suns

Gemini Observatory

Famous for its twin 8.1 m diameter telescopes, the Gemini Observatory is located in the mountains of Hawaii and Chile. From here, Gemini's telescopes are able to keep the entire sky under scrutiny.

European Southern Observatory (ESO)

Created in 1962, ESO observes the skies from three sites in the Atacama Desert, Chile—La Silla, Paranal, and Chajnantor. With its 3.6 m New Technology Telescope, ESO invented the method of using computers to control telescopes' mirrors. ESO also runs the Very Large Telescope (VLT), which discovered the first **exoplanet**. The VLT is currently observing stars that are close to the supermassive black hole at the centre of our galaxy.

WM Keck Observatory

The two-telescope WM Keck Observatory lies 4,145 m high, near the peak of old volcano Mauna Kea, in Hawaii. With their 10 m primary mirrors, these telescopes are among the largest astronomical telescopes in the world. They are responsible for achievements such as discovering the existence of galaxies at the edge of the universe and studying supernovas to find out how fast the universe is expanding.

Isn't It Amazing!

The ESO 3.6 m telescope uses an instrument called HARPS, which has discovered 130 extrasolar planets till date!

▲ Located 2,400 m high in the mountains of the Atacama Desert, La Silla has several sophisticated optical telescopes pointed towards the sky

► Located at the Roque de los Muchachos Observatory in the Canaries, Spain, the 10.4 m Gran Telescopio Canarias is the largest single-aperture optical telescope in the world

SCIENCE

THE MARCH OF SCIENCE

Welcome to the fascinating world of chemistry, where the ordinary becomes extraordinary. Have you ever thought of yourself as a chemical composition? It's true! Your very being is made up of proteins, carbohydrates, lipids, nucleic acids, and water. In fact, everything around us, including the food we eat and the matter in the Universe, is made up of chemicals. From the smallest atoms to complex molecules and ions, everything can be traced back to about 100 elements that were born during the Big Bang.

Long ago, humans dabbled in alchemy, seeking the elusive secret of turning everyday objects into gold. While they didn't succeed in that endeavor, alchemy paved the way for the modern science of chemistry. Along the journey, they discovered the nature of chemical reactions, the uses of petroleum, and even the chemical basis of life itself.

Advancements in science and technology have revolutionized our lives over the years. Remember typewriters? While they once dominated the world of writing, computers have rendered them obsolete. But the spirit of the typewriter lives on in our digital keyboards. Innovations in physics, chemistry, and biology have led to the creation of amazing devices and technologies. Engineers harness scientific knowledge to build superior transportation systems, explore genetic engineering and cloning to combat diseases, utilize robots and artificial intelligence to revolutionize industries, and enhance various sectors of our society.

Progress, however, comes at a cost. Automation eliminates traditional jobs while giving rise to unforeseen ones like web designers and drone pilots. Economists call this creative destruction, where old jobs are replaced by new ones. But even amidst change, humanity has always endured and adapted.

Let us embark on a journey through science and technology, exploring incredible breakthroughs that shape our lives. From the transformative discovery of electricity to the fundamental building blocks of matter and energy, we will unravel the mysteries of force, movement, and the intricate workings of our Universe. Get ready to soar through the realms of machines, rockets, planes, and the celestial dance of the planets around our magnificent Sun.

▼ Modern chemistry owes its origins to ancient alchemists' quest for gold

Space Stations: Stellar Base Camps

▲ A 1971 stamp commemorating Salyut-1 and its three brave astronauts

Certain artificial satellites stay in low Earth orbit and people can live inside them. These are called space stations. The earliest such station was Salyut-1, launched by the Soviet Union on 19 April 1971. It was built as one complete piece and sent up to space; the crew followed afterwards. Space stations have come a long way since then.

The Salyut Programme

Over 1971–1986, the Soviet Union explored the possibility of living in space. They called the mission Salyut. Over these 15 years, they successfully sent up four space stations for scientific research and two for military purposes. All six had human crew members. Of course, there were failures too.

Skylab

Skylab, NASA's first space station, was inhabited for some 24 weeks over 1973–1974. It bore a solar observatory (Apollo Telescope Mount), two docking ports, EVA capabilities, and a main working area called Orbital Workshop. Skylab teams made breakthrough progress in solar science and Earth observation.

The International Space Station (ISS)

The ISS is the biggest man-made object that has ever flown in space. It orbits Earth 16 times a day. Five space agencies came together to create the ISS—NASA, Roscosmos, JAXA, ESA, and CSA (Canada). ISS has since been occupied continuously for over 19 years! The space station has been visited by cosmonauts and even tourists from 18 nations.

▲ The International Space Station with its vast array of solar panels

Mir

The first space station to be put together in space was the Soviet Union's Mir. The core unit and modules (with specific functions) were launched separately and assembled in orbit over 1986–1996. This became the standard way of building space stations. Mir was continuously inhabited for 3,644 days.

Isn't It Amazing!

During its launch, Skylab hit a micro-meteoroid. The impact deprived the craft of electricity and thermal protection! Fortunately, the crew was able to repair Skylab. It was the first time such a large repair was conducted in space.

▶ Astronauts building part of a space station as it orbits Earth

SCIENCE · CHEMISTRY & ELEMENTS

Living in Space

As you can imagine, living in outer space is vastly different from living on Earth. The atmosphere, gravity, warmth, water, regular day-and-night cycles, and even the freedom to move about are simply not possible in space. Large teams of people have been working to recreate the well-being of life on Earth for astronauts in space vehicles and stations.

◀ Astronauts on the ISS rise from their sleeping quarters on Christmas morning in 2010

In Real Life

On the ISS, astronauts can watch DVDs and talk to their families once a week.

Mental Fitness

Cosmonauts on the early space stations like Salyut and Mir were the first to show signs of mental stress from extended stays in outer space. Their experience led the Russians to set up studies in aerospace psychology. In the mid-1990s, Russian space psychologists shared their insights with NASA. Today's aerospace psychologists ensure that the people going up to space possess strong, sturdy minds. They also support the astronauts throughout training, the mission and in adjusting to life after the mission.

▲ Mealtime aboard the ISS

Zero Gravity

In space, a body has no weight. Astronauts simply float from one place to another. Without any work to do, their back and legs quickly lose muscle density. Even the heart, which is a muscle, shrinks in size. Without the need for a strong skeleton, bones lose calcium, which forms stones in the kidneys. Blood and body fluids settle in the upper body (instead of flowing downwards) making the astronauts feel congested.

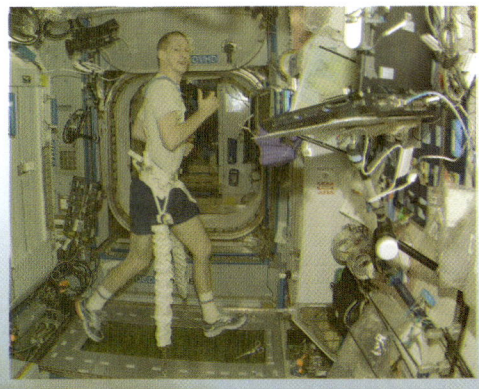

▶ Astronaut Marsha Ivins in zero-gravity outer space

Spacesuits

When astronauts leave a spacecraft, they do so wearing a protective spacesuit. It is made of interchangeable parts that can be adjusted to fit various sizes. It is puncture-proof and equipped with cameras, drinking-water and even a diaper-like pouch to contain urine. The first one to be worn in outer space was the Soviet SK-1 suit, worn by Yuri Gagarin.

What Makes Up Matter

In the past, people thought that the Universe was made of five elements: earth, water, fire, air, and ether. Today, we know that none of these are elements. Air is a mixture of gases, and earth is a complicated mixture of solids, liquids, and gases. Water and ether are compounds, while fire is simply the light emitted when a compound is **oxidised** at high temperature. Let's read on to find out what these words mean.

🔍 Element

An element is anything that cannot be broken down into simpler things by ordinary **chemical reactions**. So far, we know of 118 elements, of which about 20 are artificial elements made in nuclear laboratories. The rest all occur naturally. The most common elements on our planet are nitrogen—which encompasses most of our atmosphere—oxygen, silicon, aluminium, and iron in the Earth's crust. The core of our planet is made of a molten mix of iron and nickel, and deep inside is a ball of solid iron.

Chemists use one or two letters which represent elements when writing down chemical reactions. These letters are known as chemical symbols that are based on the elements' names.

For most elements, the first letter of their English name, such as C (carbon) or O (oxygen) is their symbol. Some elements have two letters, like Cl for chlorine. Elements known to science before the year 1800 have different names in different languages. Therefore, scientists use symbols based on their Latin names, such as K for potassium which is *kalium* in Latin, or Na for sodium which is *natrium* in Latin. Most metals and elements discovered recently have names ending in -ium—such as sodium or rutherfordium, while non-metals have names ending in -on, -gen, etc.—such as argon or nitrogen.

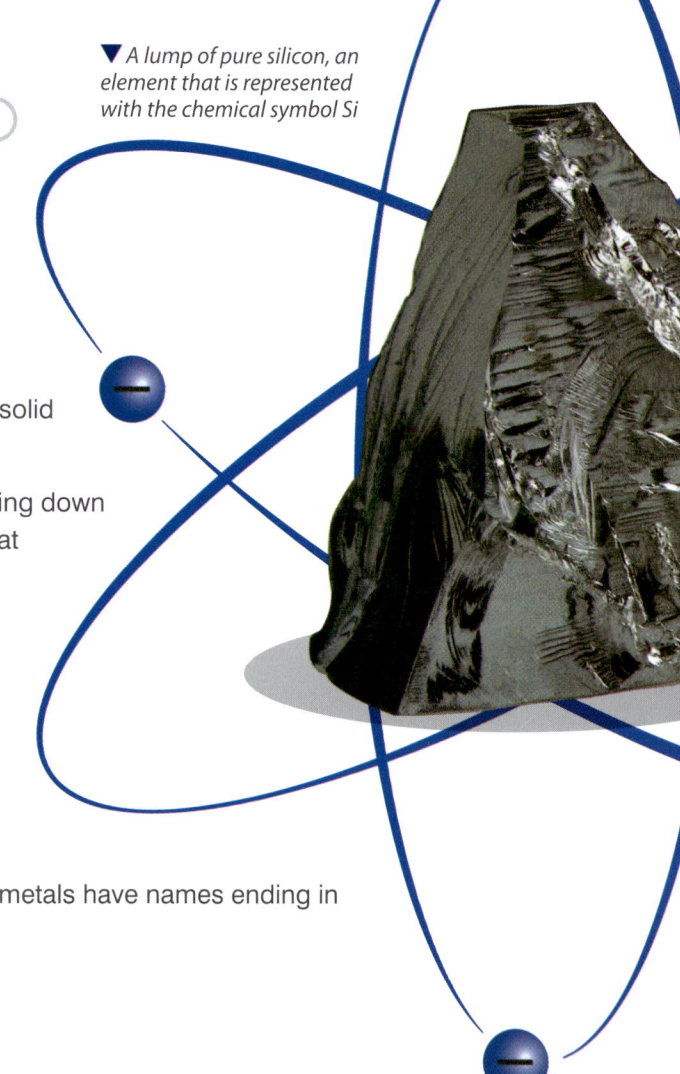

▼ A lump of pure silicon, an element that is represented with the chemical symbol Si

▼ There are just 118 elements, but millions of different chemical compounds

Compound

A compound is a substance made of two or more elements that can be broken down into its constituent elements by ordinary chemical reactions. Some compounds, such as deoxyribonucleic acid (DNA), can be very complicated and made of billions of atoms of different elements. A compound is written using the symbols of the elements in it, and numbers which depict the ratio these elements are found in. (The numbers are written in subscript after the symbol of each element in a compound).

For example, common salt is made of sodium (Na) and chloride (Cl) in equal proportions, so it is written as NaCl. Water is made of two parts hydrogen (H) and one part oxygen (O), so it is written as H_2O.

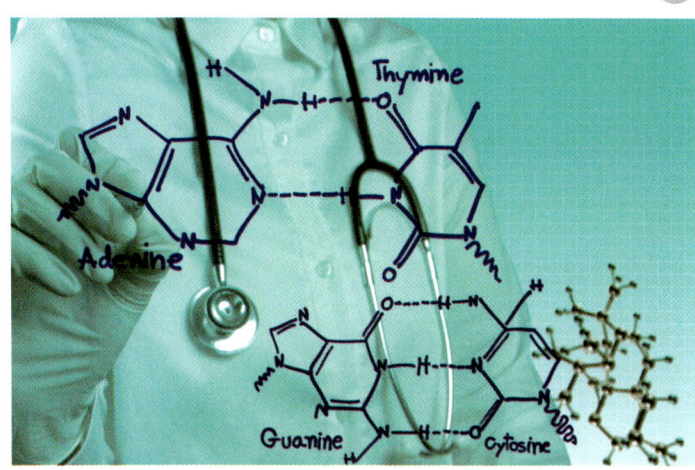

▲ DNA is a complicated chemical compound made of carbon (C), hydrogen (H), oxygen (O), nitrogen (N), and phosphorus (P)

Atom

Every element has a number of traits by which it can be distinguished. These are called its chemical properties, which include things such as mass, reactivity, density, and hardness. All of these in turn depend on the atoms that make it up. An atom is the smallest thing in the Universe that exists by itself at ordinary temperatures. In turn, an atom is made of three things called subatomic particles:

1. Electrons, which weigh almost zero, have a tiny negative electric charge and revolve around the **nucleus** (like the Earth revolves around the Sun).
2. Protons, which have a tiny positive electric charge.
3. Neutrons, with no charge. Protons and neutrons live in the centre of the atom, forming its nucleus.

An atom of an element always has the same number of protons and electrons, while atoms of different elements have different numbers of protons (and electrons). So helium has two protons and two electrons, while helium and lithium have two and three protons and electrons respectively.

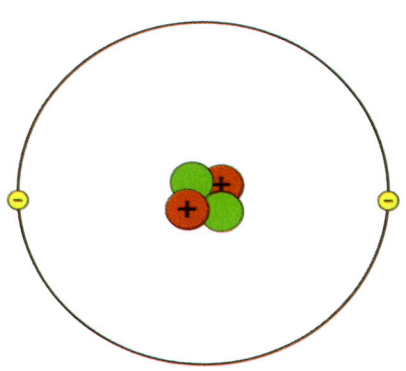

▲ Model of a helium atom, which has two protons, neutrons, and electrons

Molecule

A molecule is made of two or more atoms that have come together in a chemical reaction. A molecule may be made of atoms of the same element or different elements. Some elements—such as nitrogen, oxygen, or chlorine—can exist in nature only as molecules.

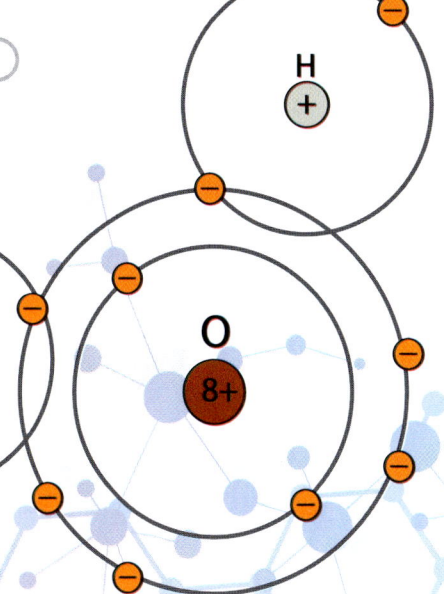

▶ A water molecule is made of hydrogen and oxygen atoms that have come together in a chemical reaction

The Periodic Table

All atoms are made of electrons, protons, and neutrons. The number of protons in an atom—called its atomic number—decide which element it belongs to. For example, if there is only one proton in an atom, then it is an atom of hydrogen; if it has six protons, then it is an atom of carbon, and so on. The number of protons and neutrons together make up an element's atomic mass. Atoms of the same element may have one or more additional neutrons, which increase its atomic mass, but not its atomic number. Such atoms are called isotopes of the element.

Elements can be lined up based on their increasing atomic number. Scientists originally discovered that the chemical properties of elements were similar in periods of eight, so lithium, sodium, and potassium are similar to each other as highly reactive metals, while helium, neon, and argon are similar to each other as unreactive gases. This is now known as the periodic law, and the table is called the periodic table.

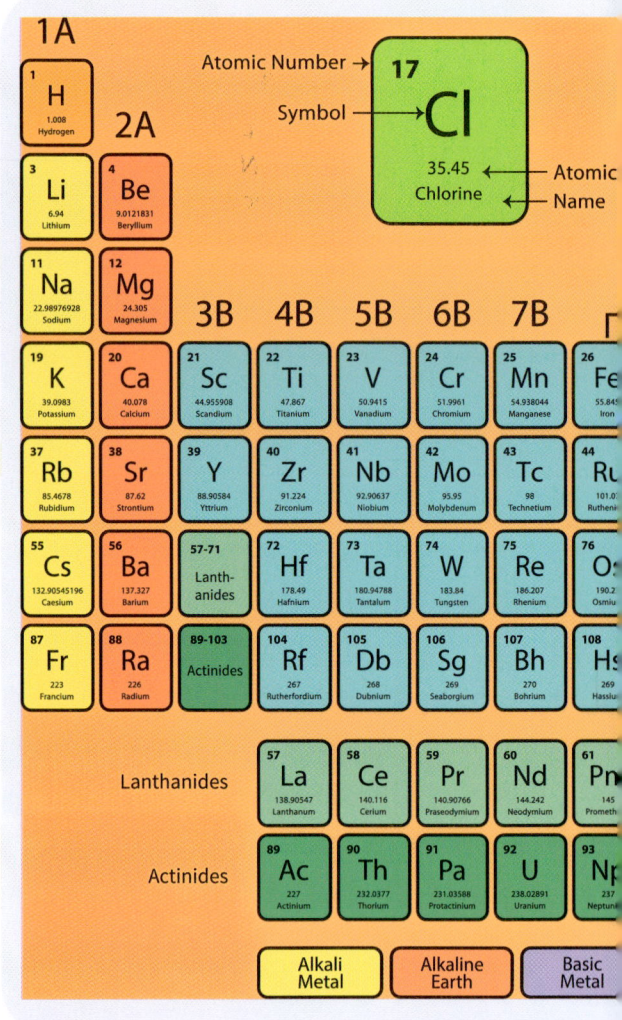

Hydrogen
Hydrogen (H) is the simplest element made of one proton and electron and no neutron. This element is abundantly available in the Universe and is known as the mother of all elements.

Alkali Metals
These are some of the most reactive elements in nature. They do not exist in their pure state, but are always found as compounds known as salts.

Alkaline Earth Metals
After alkali metals, these are the most reactive elements. Magnesium (Mg) is needed for photosynthesis, and calcium (Ca) is needed for our bone formation.

Transition Metals
These make up the biggest section of the periodic table. They have chemical properties between alkali metals and non-metals, so they behave like metals sometimes and like non-metals at other times. They form some of the most industrially useful chemicals, such as copper, iron, and manganese.

Incredible Individuals

The Russian scientist Dmitri Mendeleev (1834–1907) created the periodic table in 1869, after studying the properties of all the elements known in his time. He even predicted the chemical properties of elements that were unknown at the time, such as gallium. When gallium was discovered in 1875, it had the same properties Mendeleev had predicted for it!

▲ *In 1969, Russia printed a stamp honouring Dmitri Mendeleev*

Post-transition Metals

These metals are closer to semiconductors and are relatively inert. Aluminium (Al) and lead (Pb) have many uses while the rest are used as semiconductor dopes. Transition metals are on their left in the periodic table, while metalloids are represented on their right.

Metalloids

These are also known as semiconductors. They are used in modern electronics.

Non-metals

This is a diverse bunch of elements. Apart from selenium (Se), they are the elements most needed for life, such as carbon (C), nitrogen (N), oxygen (O), sulphur (S), and phosphorus (P). They are usually plastic (i.e. they will not regain their shape if bent) and cannot conduct electricity, as opposed to metals and metalloids that are elastic and can conduct electricity.

Halogens

These are the most reactive non-metallic elements. We use them for many purposes such as making lamp fillings, cleaning agents, and plastics; and they often partner with alkali metals in forming salts.

Noble Gases

These elements exist as gas in their natural state. Since they do not react with anything, they are called inert gases; and as they are not very abundant, they are also called rare gases.

Lanthanides

These elements are also called rare earths. They have many uses in modern electronic devices such as semiconductors and switches.

Actinides

Most of these are radioactive elements. Uranium (U) is the most important and is used in nuclear reactors to make electricity, while others like plutonium (Pu) are used in nuclear weapons.

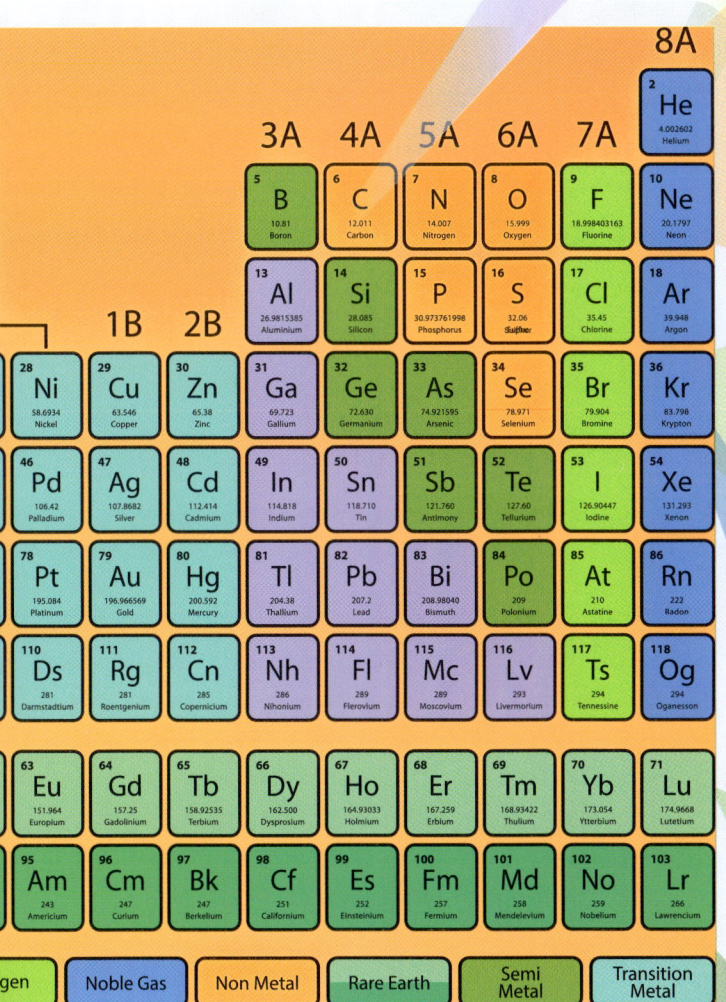

▲ The periodic table showing all the 118 elements

▼ Atomic structure for Hydrogen, Oxygen, Carbon, and Nitrogen

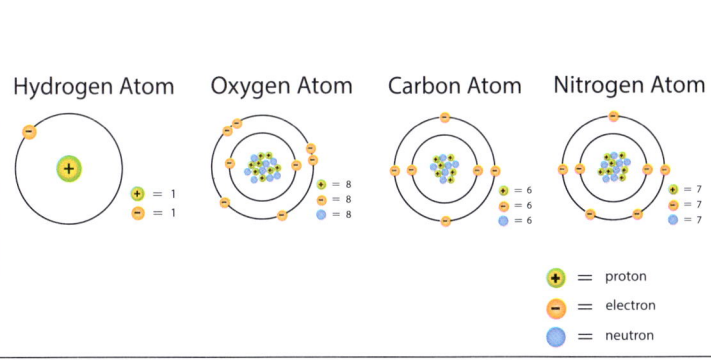

In Real Life

An element that is yet to be discovered is named after its atomic number using Latin numbers and '-ium'. So, element no. 119 is called un-un-enn-ium. Once an element's discovery is verified by other scientists, the people who first discovered it are free to give it any name they like.

States of Matter

Chemists define matter as anything that can be touched or felt. At any given temperature and pressure, matter will exist in a phase (also called a state of matter), in which its atoms or molecules have a certain amount of freedom to move and can be separated from another phase by physical means. The natural phase of all materials is their physical condition at 20°–25°C ('room temperature'), and atmospheric pressure at sea level. For example, water is liquid in its natural state, but it turns to gas (steam) when heated above 100°C, and solid (ice) when cooled below 0°C.

If you heat or cool a material, at some temperature, it will change from one phase to another. Scientists call this a phase transition. In daily life, there are two main transition temperatures. The melting point is when a solid becomes liquid, and when the opposite happens (liquid becomes solid), it is called the freezing point. Further, the boiling point is when a liquid becomes gas, and the condensation point is when gas becomes liquid.

Gas

This is a state of matter when all the atoms or molecules of a pure substance have complete freedom to move; imagine a classroom when the teacher is absent. This is called **fluidity**. Nitrogen (N), oxygen (O), hydrogen (H), the **halogens** (F, Cl, Br, I, At, Ts), and the **noble** gases (He, Ar, Xe, Kr, Rn, Og) are elemental gases, while carbon dioxide (CO_2), ammonia (NH_3), sulphur dioxide (SO_2), and methane (CH_4) are compound gases.

▶ *Steam is the gas form of water. It is used to power engines and turbines*

Liquid

This is a state of matter when the atoms or molecules have lost some freedom to move; similar to a parade of soldiers moving under the officer's orders. Liquids move at a speed known as their **viscosity**—the more of it they have, the less fluid they are. Mercury (Hg) and iodine (I) are the only elemental liquids at room temperature. On the other hand, thousands of compounds are liquids at room temperature. Water (H_2O) is the best-known liquid. Many liquids are used as **solvents**, in which other solids or liquids (such as sugar or salt) can be dissolved for carrying out chemical reactions.

You may often hear or read that glass is a very viscous liquid, but that is not true. Glass is an amorphous solid, that is, it has no internal structure.

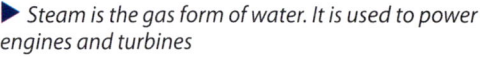

▲ *Water dissolves so many things that it is called the universal solvent*

Solid

When there's no freedom to move at all, the atoms or molecules become a solid. Solids come in two forms: crystal, in which the atoms are arranged in rows and columns (called lattices) like soldiers in a parade; or amorphous, in which there is no organisation. One glass-like substance commonly called crystal is quartz, a mineral whose molecules are arranged in a regular lattice. Most elements and solid compounds are crystalline, such as sugar, salt, metals, and rocks. Many others, often made from living things, are amorphous, such as wood, chalk, cloth, and paper. Earth is a mixture of both kinds.

▲ *Ice is the crystalline form of solid water, while snow is its amorphous form*

Isn't It Amazing!

The coldest temperature possible is –273.15°C, at which all the atoms and molecules of a substance completely freeze over. This is called absolute zero. In 1995, scientists found that near this temperature, atoms are no longer separate but merge to form a Bose-Einstein Condensate.

Metals

Chemically, a metal is an element that can form a cation by giving up an electron, and a non-metal is an element that forms an anion by accepting an electron. A common property of metals is that they should be malleable (easily hammered into sheets), or ductile (drawn into wires). They exist as crystalline solids in nature (except mercury, Hg), often do not react easily, and can readily conduct heat and electricity. They also have great tensile strength, that is, they can be stretched without breaking.

▲ *Ingots or blocks of various metals*

Silver, gold, copper, and iron are among the oldest metals known to humanity, along with bronze, an alloy of copper and tin. The history of humanity is divided into the Stone Age, the Bronze Age and the Iron Age. The Stone Age ended around 3300 BCE when humans discovered that they could make better tools out of metals instead of stone. As the hardest metallic substance available was bronze, the period is called the Bronze Age. Around 1200 BCE, humans discovered how to purify iron from its ore, thus starting the Iron Age. Iron is tougher and more flexible than bronze, and can be used for making many more things. We still live in the Iron Age.

Let's look at the periodic table on pages 6–7. Why do different kinds of metals take up so much space on it, and if they have common properties, why do they seem to be of different kinds?

🔍 Reactive Metals

Chemically, metals should be able to give up their electrons easily. Alkali metals, such as sodium and potassium, and alkaline earth metals, such as calcium and barium, do this the best. They almost never exist in pure form and will react with the oxygen in the air if purified.

▶ *Pieces of potassium. Potassium is so reactive with air that it has to be covered in unreactive mineral oil*

🔍 Transition Metals

These are what we commonly mean when we say metal. When they react with alkali metals, they can behave like non-metals. They are found in nature in a compound form called **ore** and can be converted to pure metal through a chemical process called refining. After refining, they stay in a pure state but react with the oxygen in the air very slowly by a process called corrosion. Some, such as gold and platinum, do not react at all and are known as noble metals.

💡 Isn't It Amazing!

For long, the toughest swords were said to come from the city of Damascus (present day capital of Syria), with beautiful patterns on the surface. They were made of wootz steel found in southern India. While the technique was lost for a period, some individuals have recreated techniques that are of the calibre of original Damascus steel.

🔍 Alloys

An alloy is a mixture of metals that is stronger than either of them separately and is used for many purposes. Brass (copper and zinc), bronze (copper and tin), and stainless steel (iron and carbon) are the most common alloys.

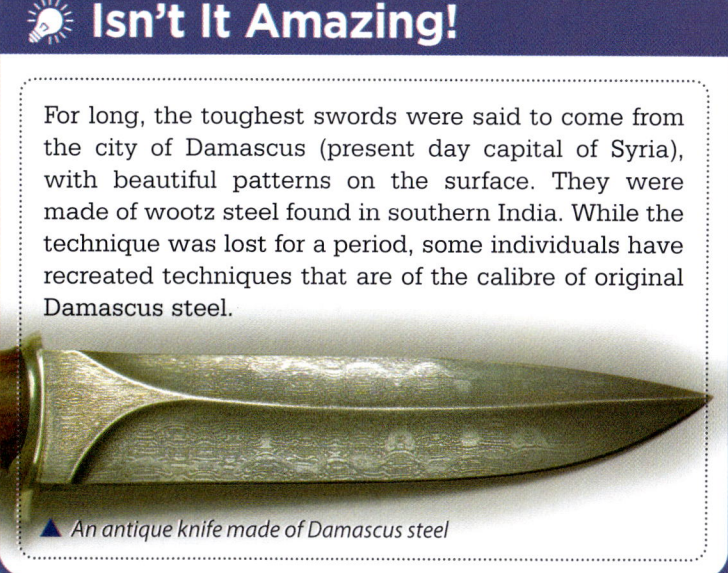

▲ *An antique knife made of Damascus steel*

Purification Methods

When all the atoms or molecules in a material are of the same kind, it is called pure. In real life, nothing is ever 100% pure. There are always other things called impurities that are mixed in. When there are lots of impurities, it is impossible to predict what will happen when the material is used for chemical reactions. Therefore, chemists use purification methods to make a material.

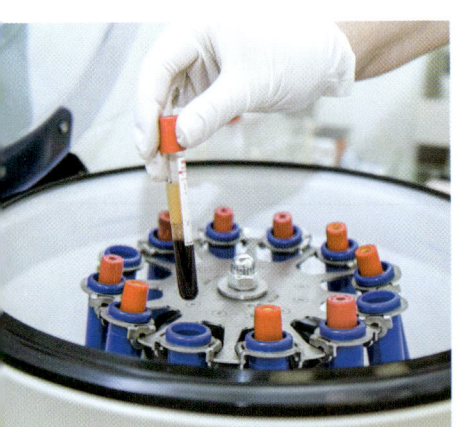

▲ *Centrifugation is used to separate plasma from blood cells before the plasma can be given to a patient who needs it*

Sedimentation

This process uses gravity to separate solids from liquids. If you leave muddy water undisturbed in a glass, the mud will settle down and leave a clear layer of water above.

A machine called a **centrifuge** helps sedimentation happen faster by spinning mixtures in special tubes at very high speeds. The solid collected at the bottom is called sediment. Centrifugation is used in laboratories and chemical plants.

Filtration

A filter is a material that has holes of a certain size. Anything smaller than those holes will pass through, while bigger things will not. Filtration is used to separate floating particles from liquids and gases. When two solids are separated, it is called sieving.

Adsorption is a method by which impurities stick to a filter (usually finely powdered carbon) while water passes through.

Distillation

This is a method that makes use of the boiling point of a liquid. An impure liquid, like tap water, is boiled in a special distillation still. The water boils off, leaving solid impurities behind. At the other end of the still, the steam is condensed back to water.

One of the best-known methods for distillation is fractional distillation. Using this process, a mixture of two liquids, whose boiling points are far apart, is separated.

Crystallisation

Try this: add salt to water in increasing amounts and watch it dissolve. After some time, the salt will stop dissolving with water. This is called saturation. If you heat this solution, the undissolved salt will dissolve, and you can keep adding more salt as the water heats further. Stop adding salt when you reach the boiling point. Now let the solution cool. It has now reached **supersaturation**. If you add a grain of salt to the solution now, you will see highly structured crystals of salt forming in the solution. This is called crystallisation and is used to purify soluble solids from supersaturated solutions.

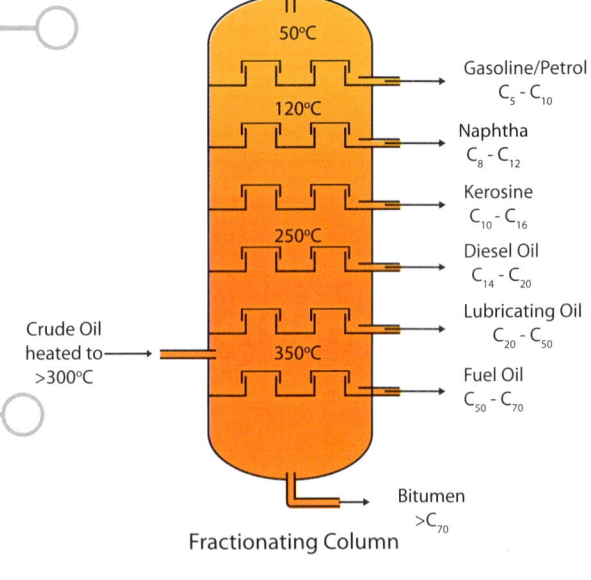

▲ *Fractional distillation is used to separate crude oil (petroleum) into useful chemicals. This is also called refining*

Sublimation

Some solids directly turn to gas when heated without going through the liquid phase. This is called sublimation. Sublimation can be used to separate two solids, if one of them becomes gas on being heated. Sublimation in vacuum is used to purify the materials used in electronics.

Incredible Individuals

Cleopatra the Alchemist (not to be confused with the queen of the same name) is believed to have lived in Egypt around the 2nd or 3rd century CE. She invented the alembic, a glass vessel used for distillation even today.

SCIENCE | CHEMISTRY & ELEMENTS

Acids, Bases, and pH

In most books and films, an acid is shown as a coloured liquid fuming in a laboratory, or something that causes an upset stomach. However, scientists define acids and bases in a very different way. Acids and bases form much of the groundwork of modern chemistry and have hundreds of uses. They are often used to convert raw materials into the plastics, paints, medicines, preservatives, dyes, and many other chemicals we use in daily life. The balance of acids and bases in our body is an important part of staying healthy.

Acid

Scientists define an acid as something that easily gives up a hydrogen ion (H^+) or ends up with extra electrons at the end of a reaction. Another definition of an acid is that it is any chemical in which one or more hydrogen atoms can be replaced by a positively charged ion (cation). The three most common acids used for chemical reactions are hydrochloric acid (HCl, which is also found in your stomach), sulphuric acid (H_2SO_4), and nitric acid (HNO_3).

Fatty acids, which are made of carbon molecules, do not dissolve in water. All others dissolve in water and break up into anions and hydrogen ions:

$$HCl + H_2O \rightarrow H^+ + Cl^- + H_2O$$

Salt

A salt is formed when an acid reacts with a base by the neutralisation reaction:

$$NaOH + HCl + H_2O \rightarrow Na^+ + Cl^- + 2H_2O$$

Many acids and bases react very strongly with each other, releasing a lot of heat. Such reactions are called exothermic reactions.

Base

A base is the opposite of an acid. It is something that easily takes up a hydrogen ion (H^+) or ends up with fewer electrons at the end of a reaction. The three most common bases used for chemical reactions are sodium hydroxide (NaOH, also called caustic soda), potassium hydroxide (KOH, also called caustic potash), and ammonium hydroxide (NH_4OH). Bases that react really fast are called alkalis.

$$NaOH + H_2O \rightarrow Na^+ + OH^- + H_2O$$

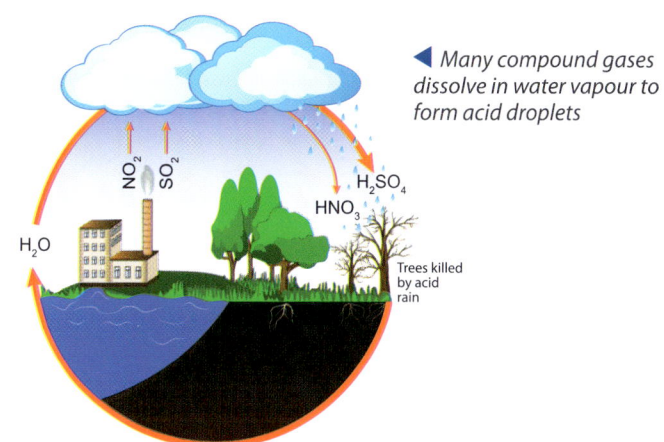

◀ Many compound gases dissolve in water vapour to form acid droplets

In Real Life

Some chemicals change colours if the pH of their solution changes. They are therefore used as pH indicators. Your school lab may have pH papers, which are special paper strips soaked in chemical and dried. When dipped into an acidic or basic solution, the paper changes colour.

◀ A pH paper changing colour to show that there is alkali left over in a bar of soap, which may burn your skin

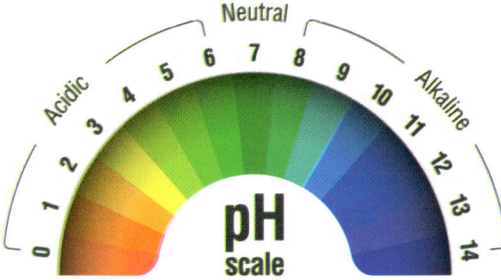

▲ The higher the pH, the fewer the hydrogen ions present

pH

pH stands for potential of Hydrogen. It is a way of determining how acidic or basic a solution is, by measuring the number of hydrogen ions present in it. The pH scale is inverse logarithmic, that is, an increase of 1 on the scale means that there are 10 times fewer hydrogen ions. Closely related to it is the pOH scale, which measures the number of hydroxyl (OH^-) ions. At a pH of 7, there are equal number of hydrogen ions and **hydroxyl ions**, so the solution is said to be neutral. Below 7, the solution is acidic and above 7, it is basic or alkaline.

Electricity: The Basics

Before we learn how our devices work, let's understand what electricity is. For that we need to understand a few terms of physics.

All electricity can be divided into two: static and current. **Static electricity** is what happens when your woollen clothes rub against rubber, or when lightning strikes the ground. This is because of opposite electric charges on them, as we will see ahead. **Current electricity** is what we commonly call electricity; it's 'current' because it is always on the move (dynamic). Both depend on a fundamental property of all things on Earth—an **electric charge**. Electric charges exist because of electrons, the tiny things that move around the nuclei of atoms.

Charge

Different materials have different charges on them. These charges arise because there are electrons on the surface of every atom, which move around the nucleus. Very often, these charges are balanced by an equal number of protons in the atoms, which stop the electrons from straying. This is because electrons have a negative charge and protons have a positive charge, and they attract each other. Such materials are called **dielectric**. Other materials, however, have an imbalance of electrons and protons. If there are fewer electrons, the material possesses a positive charge. If it has more electrons, the material has a negative charge.

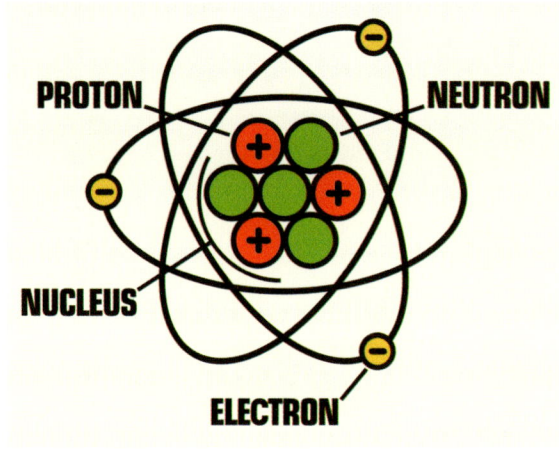

▲ Materials become charged when they have too many or too few electrons

Ions

The atoms of some elements can easily lose an electron or two to another atom. Such elements are called metals. When a metal atom loses an electron, it becomes a positively charged ion or cation. Other elements have atoms that are hungry for electrons. When they get an extra electron, they become negatively charged ions or anions. At very high temperatures, cations and anions can form a gas-like material called plasma. All stars are made of this material.

👤 In Real Life

Most clouds are made of plasma, in this case being comprised of charged water ions. When these ions come close to the Earth (or to a cloud with ions of opposite charge), they meet an opposite charge and are strongly attracted towards it. The clouds emit a spark, and the excess charge suddenly travels to the Earth, causing lightning.

◀ Lightning is an example of a static electric discharge

Electrons

When an electron moves, it produces a tiny **current**. In many metals, electrons can hop between atoms very easily. Some materials are rich in anions, while others are rich in cations. If you bring them together, there will be a chemical reaction. But if you keep them separate and connect them by a wire on one side and an electrode (a metal rod dipped in the substance) on the other side, the current will flow through the wire. This is because electrons will move from the anion-rich side (now called anode) to the cation-rich side (now called cathode). The difference in the charge between the anode and cathode is called the electric potential, which is also often called voltage.

▲ *Electric transmission happens when electrons move from an anode (from the power station) to a cathode (back to the power station), through the whole electric grid*

Isn't It Amazing!

AC/DC, the name of a famous rock band, does indeed stand for alternating current and direct current. As reported: "The band members Malcolm and Angus Young got the idea for the name from their sister, who saw the initials 'AC/DC' on a sewing machine."

Current

Current that flows only in one direction is called direct current or DC. But it can also be made to switch directions, which is called alternating current or AC. The latter happens because of **electromagnetism**. If you rotate a magnet, it creates a tiny electric field. If you put a metal coil around a rotating magnet, the electrons in it will start moving (this is called induction). However, for half a turn, current moves one way, and for the other half it changes direction. The more powerful the magnet, the stronger the current it generates.

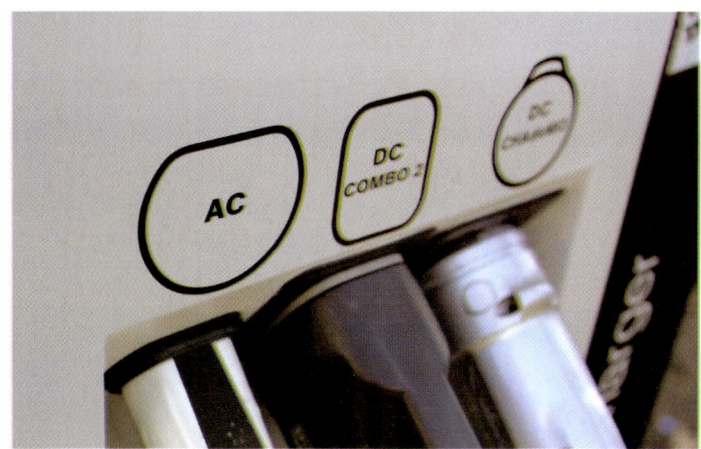

▲ *Most devices (such as coffee makers) work either on AC or DC*

Current and Resistance

Why does electricity pass through metals, but not other materials? For this, we have to understand the idea of conduction and resistance. **Conduction** happens when there are enough loose electrons that will move when a potential is applied, that is, there is an anode and a cathode between which there is a difference of charge. What if there aren't any electrons to spare, or too many protons hungry for these electrons? Then there will be resistance to the flow of current. These two principles are how most electronic devices work.

▲ *Air is a bad conductor, but if two opposite charges are close enough, it allows a 'spark' to travel between them*

Good and Bad Conductors

Most materials will allow some electricity (i.e. some electrons) to pass through them, and resist the rest. A material that lets most of the electrons pass through it is called a good conductor. Most metals are good conductors, and that's why they are used as electric cables. A material that lets all the current pass through it with no resistance at all is called a superconductor. Most good conductors become superconductors only below -253°C, so none of them can be used to make cables that transmit electricity.

On the other hand, bad conductors let little electricity pass through them, which means they resist most electrons. Some materials, like wood and plastics, allow almost no electricity to pass at all. These are called insulators and are used to wrap electric cables so that electricity does not leak out of them.

Yet other materials are neither too bad nor too good and thus they are **semiconductors**. These are important in turning up or turning down the flow of current. Hence, they are the ones that make modern electronics possible.

▲ *Insulators protect conductors from leaking electricity and electrocuting people*

🧑‍🔬 In Real Life

In theory, your body should be a bad conductor of electricity as 70% of it is made of water (since pure water is a bad conductor of electricity). But it will still let current pass through you, since the body has a lot of salt, which makes it a good conductor. This is why you can get an electric shock. You shouldn't touch an electric device when wet or sweaty as the salt in your skin can conduct electricity.

▶ *Electricians always work with safety equipment, including insulated gloves, hats, shoes, and glasses*

Resistors

So, what happens to electrons as they move along a conductor? Some of them get trapped by positive charges and are lost, reducing the current. This is called resistance (symbol R), and it was worked out by a person called Georg Ohm (1789–1854). The amount of resistance of a conductor can be calculated by measuring the current (symbol I) it lets through and the difference in voltage (symbol V) at either end of the conductor. This is called Ohm's Law, and the unit of resistance is called Ohm (symbol Ω) in his honour.

$$R = V/I$$

Yet other electrons are turned into different forms of electricity. The most common example you see is electric light. Some materials will emit light if current passes through them. This is because as electrons pass through them, they 'excite' the atom and transfer some energy to them. When the electron has passed, the atom becomes 'de-excited' and gives up that energy as a photon, the unit of light. Millions of electrons create millions of photons, and they light up a room. The reverse is also true, and that's how you get solar power. Other resistors turn electricity into heat or sound.

◀ *Electric devices work by converting electrical energy into other forms*

Optic Cables

These cables are used in connecting you to the internet, but they carry light inside them, not electricity. These work on a principle called total internal reflection. They are made of a material (called optical fibre) that reflects photons so that they bounce along the walls all the way from end to end with zero resistance. Hundreds of optical fibres are bundled together to form optical fibre cables (OFCs). These cables are laid all over the world, connecting computers across the globe.

▶ *Optic cables help move millions of bytes of data at the speed of light, all around the world, by turning them into photons*

Making Electricity

We cannot actually make any electricity, because it is a form of energy. As you know, energy can neither be made nor destroyed, but only changed from one form to another. So when we 'generate' electricity, we are only turning some other form of energy into it. In great power plants, this could be thermal, nuclear or mechanical energy; in a battery (cell) or home generator, it is chemical energy which is released by a reaction. Batteries can be rechargeable, such as car batteries; or non-rechargeable, such as in TV remotes, which have to be discarded once exhausted.

▶ *Batteries run every portable electronic device, from cars to smart watches*

How a Cell Works

Remember that you need an anode and cathode to create an electric potential for electricity to flow. A cell is a device where chemical reactions happen and create the necessary electric potential. Actually, there must be two reactions:

1. The **anode reaction**, which generates electrons that will travel through the electric cables.
2. The **cathode reaction**, which creates a lack of electrons, so that the electric potential is created.

But electricity will not pass unless there is something to connect the anode and cathode internally, so that the cycle is complete. This is called an electrolyte. The electrons come back into the cell, where they meet the cations and neutralise them, i.e. the charge disappears. These electric cycles are called circuits. Many reactions can turn chemical energy into electrical energy this way, but for them to work as a battery, they must be controllable by us.

◀ *Batteries come in many sizes and shapes, but all are made of rows of electric cells*

In Real Life

A cell is a single unit that produces electricity. However, many cells can be coupled together in rows to increase the total amount of electricity generated. In the 19th century, when inventors worked on these, they were reminded of artillery guns lined up together in a battle. The word for that is 'battery', and that's why a group of cells working together is called a battery.

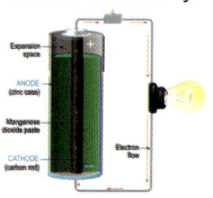

▶ *Four lead-acid cells are joined together to make one battery*

SCIENCE | ELECTRICITY & ELECTRONICS | 101

Non-Rechargeable Batteries

Most cells cannot be recharged. This is because once the chemical reaction has taken place, it cannot be reversed. Their main advantage is that they are cheap to make and can be made in large numbers, so they are used to power our flashlights, electric toys, music players, and hundreds of other devices. The most common ones use zinc (Zn) as the source of electrons (anode), and manganese dioxide (MnO_2) as the cathode, with a paste of ammonium chloride (NH_4Cl) as the electrolyte. A graphite (carbon) rod is used to take up the electrons, so the cell is also called a zinc-carbon cell.

Dry Cell Battery

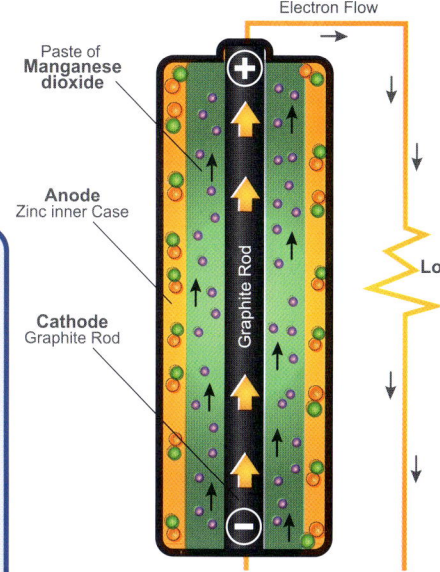

▲ Zinc-carbon cells are among the most commonly used and have a gel-like electrolyte in them

At the anode, zinc releases electrons into the circuit:
$$Zn \rightarrow Zn^{++} + 2e^-$$

At the cathode, the electrons arrive and make manganese dioxide react with ammonium chloride to make manganese trioxide, water and ammonia:
$$2MnO_2 + 2NH_4Cl + 2e^- \rightarrow Mn_2O_3 + 2NH_3 + H_2O + 2Cl^-$$

The chloride ions travel through the electrolyte to react with the zinc ions to make zinc chloride:
$$Zn^{++} + 2Cl^- \rightarrow ZnCl_2$$

Once all the MnO_2 is exhausted, the cell will stop working.

Rechargeable Batteries

Some chemical reactions can be made to run the other way if you apply an electric current to them. This is the principle used in car batteries and other rechargeable ones. The most common is the lead-acid battery, made of alternating plates of lead (symbol Pb) as anode and lead dioxide (symbol PbO_2) as cathode, both dipped in sulphuric acid (symbol H_2SO_4).

▲ Wireless charging of a smartphone battery

Anode reaction: $Pb + H_2SO_4 \rightarrow PbSO_4 + 2H^+ + 2e^-$

The hydrogen ions (H^+) travel to the cathode attracted by the electrons.

Cathode reaction: $PbO_2 + H_2SO_4 + 2H^+ + 2e^- \rightarrow PbSO_4 + 2H_2O$

When the car engine is running, it generates electricity that 'charges' the battery, and the lead and lead dioxide plates regenerate.

Electric Circuits

We've learned how power is generated from other sources of energy. But electricity only moves as a current if it can complete a circuit from the power source and back to it. On the way it will meet various kinds of resistors and other devices that will convert electrical energy to other forms of energy, which we use for our purposes—such as lighting and cooling a room, or powering TVs and computers. Some of the electricity will be used to power a motor (see pages 16–17). But not all devices use the same amount of electricity, nor do they need to be switched on all the time.

▼ Transformers at a power station

Transformers

In most countries, electricity travels through metal cables high in the air or underground at electric potentials of up to 765,000 volts, or 765 kilovolts (V and kV respectively). However, when it has to be connected to your home, it needs to be reduced to as little as 440V. For that, it needs a transformer.

Transformers act on electricity like the volume controls on a TV remote, by a method you already know—electromagnetic induction. But now there's a twist. If an induction coil is placed next to another (without touching) and alternating current is passed through it, there will be a new current in the other coil! The current in that coil depends on the number of turns there are in that coil. So, if you have a coil with more turns than the first one, it will have more current. In this manner, you will have made a step-up transformer. If there are fewer turns in the coil than the first one, then you have a step-down transformer. Power companies pass the electricity they generate through several step-up transformers before it is loaded onto the electricity grid. The power from the grid passes through many of these before reaching your home.

▲ The magnetic field generated by one coil affects the other, triggering a current in it

Switches

A switch works in the simplest way—by breaking the circuit mechanically. Each light in your house is connected to the power grid by its own circuit. When you turn it off, the switch moves the cables away, and the device goes off. When you turn it on, the switch reconnects the circuit, and your device comes on. For gadgets like blenders or televisions, the switch is made by a power socket, into which you must plug in your device and then turn on the switch. The device's cable acts as a second switch.

▼ This is how electric switches work

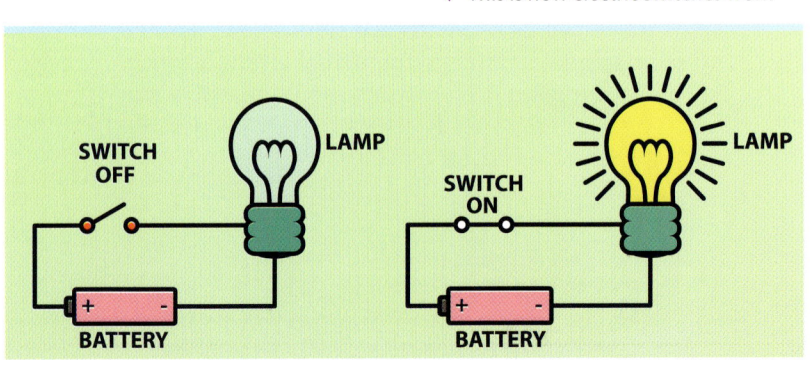

Series and Parallel

If you split a power cable, connect it to two electric devices, and then link up their cables back again, you create a **parallel circuit**. If you connect both electric devices to the same circuit, one after the other, you have made a **series circuit**. However, in a series circuit, if one device fails, it will turn the other one off too.

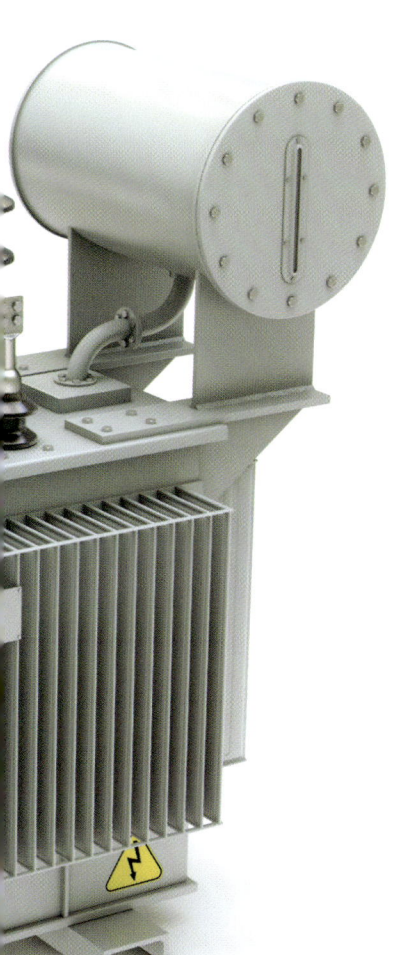

 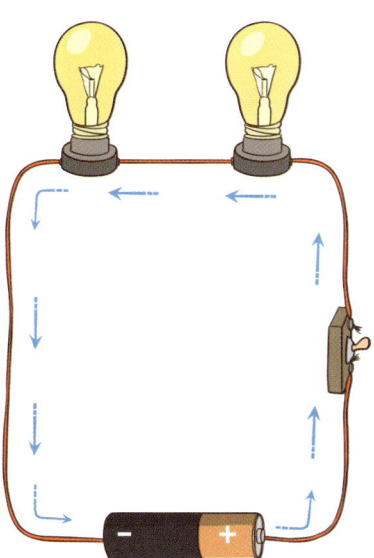

▲ *Parallel connections make sure that one device can keep running even if the other fails, as it doesn't break the circuit*

💡 Isn't It Amazing!

String lights, which have dozens of little lights in series, actually work in parallel circuits. That's why even if one light goes bad, the whole string does not go dark.

▶ *The strings are made of 22-gauge copper wire covered in coloured PVC plastic coating*

👤 In Real Life

Your home's bell is one of the simplest applications of electromagnetism. When you press the bell, electricity runs through a coil wrapped around a metal bar or horseshoe, magnetising it. It attracts another metal rod, which hits a gong. In doing so, it breaks the circuit, the magnetism stops and the rod goes back to its place.

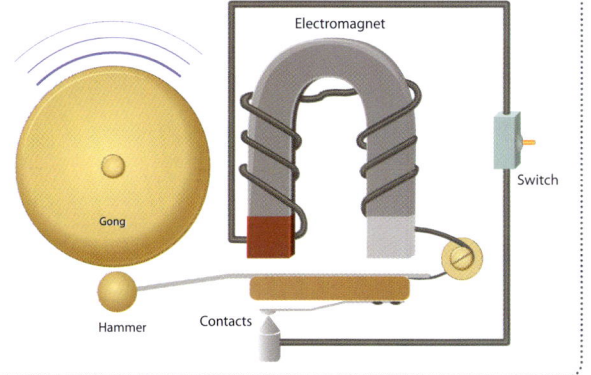

▶ *The magnetic field generated by one coil affects the other, triggering a current in it*

Magnetism

We've talked much about electricity causing a magnetic field, and the reverse. But what exactly is magnetism? Why do some materials, like iron, show it, and others, like copper, do not?

Magnetism

A magnetic field is a force produced at a right angle to the movement of a charge. Magnetic forces move within that field between its north and south poles (this field is called a dipole). The way opposite electric charges attract, opposite magnetic poles attract. And just as 'like' electric charges repel each other, like magnetic poles repel.

In most materials, electrons move in all directions, so their magnetic fields cancel each other out. These materials are called **diamagnetic**. However, in other materials such as good conductors, applying an electric charge can make all the electrons move in one direction, and so they get a magnetic field, though it does not last for long— These are **paramagnetic**. Lastly, in materials such as iron, the magnetic fields can be permanent if the current is run for a long time—These are **ferromagnetic**. Permanent magnets, like the ones seafarers use in a magnetic compass, are made of these.

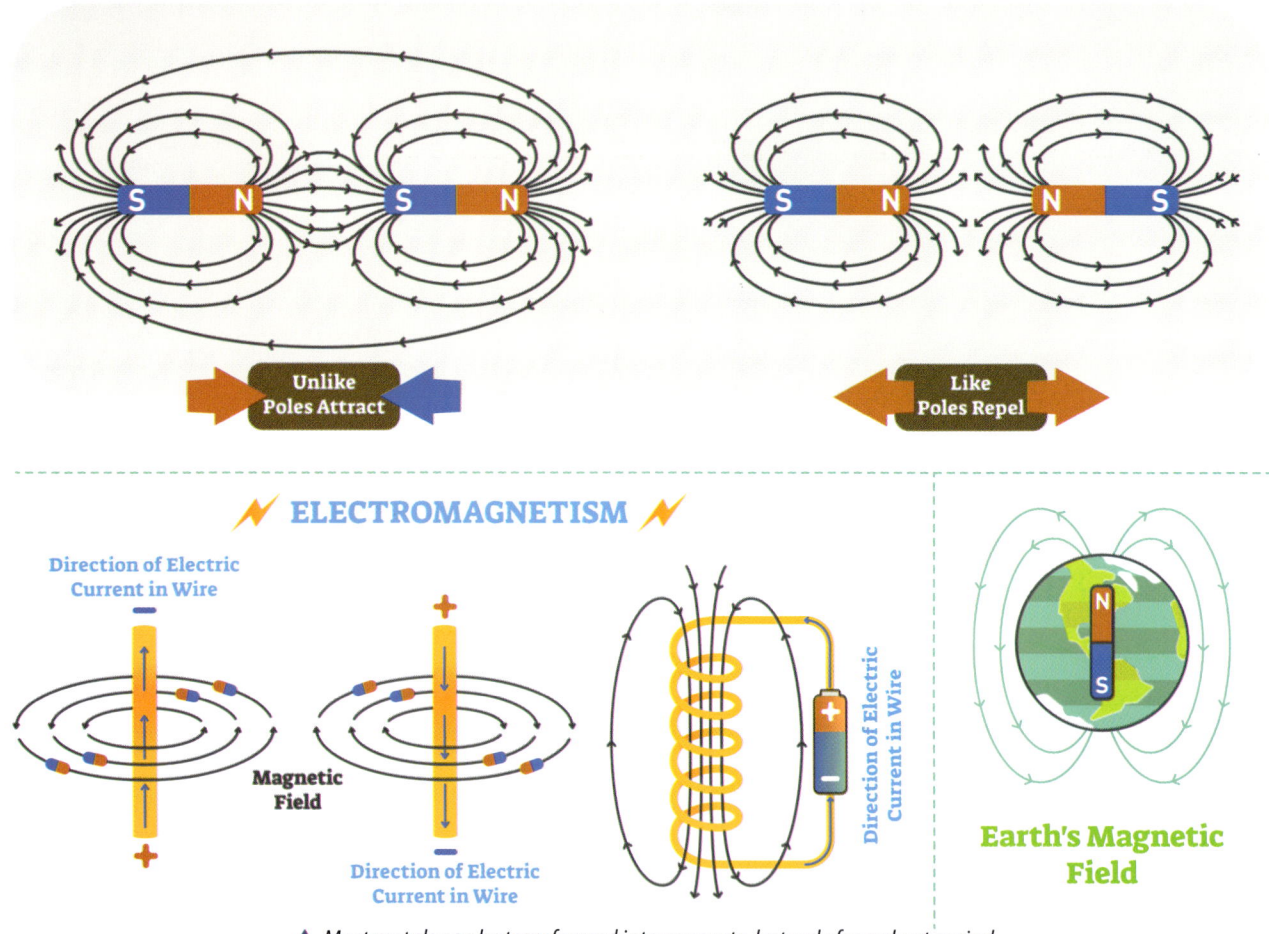

▲ Most metals can be transformed into magnets, but only for a short period

The Earth's Magnetic Field

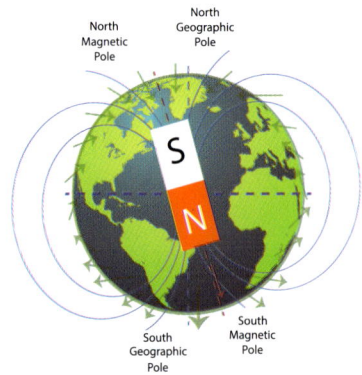

Isn't It Amazing!

Our planet's core is made of a solid iron ball surrounded by molten iron. As the Earth rotates, this molten iron (which is charged) also moves, creating a gigantic magnetic field that covers the whole planet. It is roughly the same as the Earth's axis of rotation but is off by a few hundred miles. The North Magnetic Pole is is in the Canadian Arctic moving towards Russia, while the South Magnetic Pole is located off the coast of Antarctica.

Semiconductors

We are surrounded by smart electronic devices today. If you ask your grandparents, fifty years ago the 'smartest' device out there would have been a pocket calculator, which is now reduced to an app on your phone. What made all this possible?

The answer is that these are all semiconductor devices. Once, these were large and expensive devices, able to do only the simplest of programming tasks. But as we learned more, devices became smaller and cheaper to fit more and more electronic circuits into a smaller space on a semiconductor **chip**.

What are semiconductors?

Silicon, selenium, and germanium are all examples of semiconductor materials. They have too few 'loose' electrons to be good conductors, but enough of them to not be insulators. In the last two centuries, physicists discovered that their partial conduction of electricity could be useful to regulate how it flowed, and to use them as 'gates' in a circuit. This means they can make electrons flow in one direction and stop them from another. Further, they can combine two streams of electrons into one; they can 'decide' to let one current pass instead of another, and so on. Using this, they can be programmed to do tasks like doing sums or control other electronic devices.

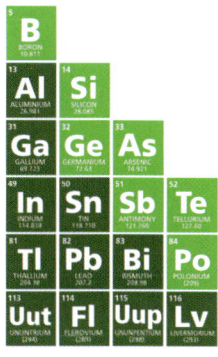

▲ *Elements above make good semiconductors.*

Doping

In the 20th century, many scientists who worked together discovered that semiconductors can be 'doped'. By doping, they mean that a pure semiconductor crystal could be deliberately adulterated with another material that increases or decreases the amount of electricity that it can conduct. If you add small amounts of phosphorus (5 electrons to spare) to silicon (4 electrons to spare), you get an **n-doped** semiconductor, which has a slight negative charge. Similarly, by adding boron (3 electrons to spare) to silicon, you get a **p-doped** semiconductor with a slight positive charge. Now, by putting the two together, you get a **p-n junction**. If you run a small current with n first and p later, the current will flow easily, but if you reverse the current, it does not go past p, as it takes up the electrons to make up for the ones it is missing. Thus, a p-n junction acts like a one-way gate.

P–N JUNCTION

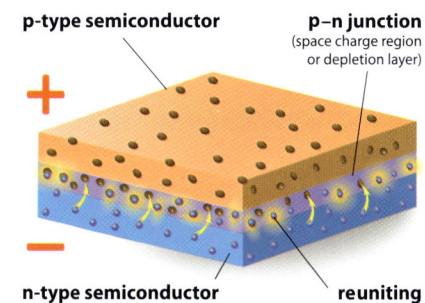

▲ *p-n junctions are used as gates in electronic circuits*

▲ *A transistor with the source, gate and drain*

Transistors

What if we make complicated junctions such as n-p-n or p-n-p? We can make another device called a transistor. This device controls how much electricity can flow through it, by using a second current to modify the conductivity of one of the semiconductors. The incoming power is called the source, and the outgoing power is called the drain. The part of the transmitter that receives the source is called the collector, while the part from which the drain leaves is called the emitter. Between them is a third connection, called the base (which receives the 'gate' current) that adjusts the conductivity. You can thus use transistors as tiny transformers to increase or decrease signal.

Renewable Energy

In the last few decades, people around the world have become concerned with what is happening to the wonderful nature and environment around us. Human activities are stuffing the air with millions of tonnes of carbon dioxide and causing climate change, plastics are polluting the ocean, and pesticides and other chemicals are killing insects and other wildlife. The generation of electricity is one of the biggest causes of climate change—from thermal power plants that emit CO_2, to the big dams that cause a lot of harm to the ecology around them. On the other hand, nuclear power is not leading to pollution, but it poses a threat if there is a leakage of radioactive material. Another problem is the fuel used for nuclear and thermal plants, which is expected to exhaust one day. That is why scientists and engineers across the world have been trying to find ways to generate electricity from a fuel source that will not run out or pollute the Earth.

⭐ Incredible Individuals

In 1962, the marine biologist Rachel Carson published the book *Silent Spring*, which warned of the dangers caused to the environment by modern industry. The book inspired many people to think of ways to reduce our impact on Earth, and was a great inspiration for people researching renewable energy.

▲ *Rachel Carson's book inspired many people to work on renewable energy*

🔍 Solar Power

This power depends on a source of energy that will eventually run out, but only after a few billion years. Light from the Sun is renewed every day and we can easily turn it into electricity. The device that does this is called a photovoltaic cell. It is made of silicon crystals. When photons from sunlight fall on the silicon crystals, the electrons in them become 'excited'. If these crystals are connected to an electrical circuit, these excited electrons start moving, forming an electric current. Solar is increasingly becoming popular as an alternative to conventional energy production.

▲ *Solar panels, made of solar cells, make the wings of satellites and give them the electricity they need*

SCIENCE | ELECTRICITY & ELECTRONICS | 107

Wind Power

People, in order to create energy, especially for running flourmills, have long been using windmills. In the 20th century, as turbine technology improved, windmills were used for generating electricity. In a place that's extremely windy, the blades of the fan would automatically move, and a turbine would then convert this motion into electricity.

Geothermal Power

▲ *Traditional windmills*

The earth releases heat from its interiors to its surface through **volcanism**. In many places (such as Iceland) this heat makes ground water escape as steam (making a geyser) or turns it **super hot** if trapped inside. A geothermal power plant captures the released steam and makes it run through a turbine to produce electricity. In other places where steam does not escape naturally, a pipe is drilled to reach the water. As the water rises, it turns into steam because the pressure falls, and is directed to turn a turbine. The steam is condensed and pumped back into the earth, where it can be heated again.

▲ *A geyser in Strokkur, Iceland*

Tidal Power

Tidal power uses the energy stored in tides as they rise and fall. Tidal power engineers build a dam that captures water when the tide rises. When the tide recedes, the gates of the dam open and the water flows out into the sea. As it flows, it turns a turbine. In other places, the natural ocean current is directly used to move a turbine.

▶ *Larger, utility-scale wind turbines can have blades with a diameter over 100 metres, which is more than a football field!*

▶ *A tidal barrage with turbines*

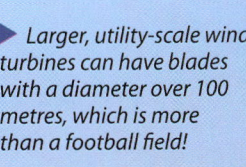

Force: Making Things Move

Force is what makes things move. It may be a giant planet revolving around giant stars, your mother dragging you out of bed to go to school, or it might be electrons jumping from one atom to another, causing a chemical reaction. It may even go right down to the fundamental particles of the Universe, pulling and pushing each other to make the vast fabric of space and time.

But science is more specific. Force, according to science, is an entity that creates motion *in a specific direction*. It is, therefore, a **vector** quantity. Your body **experiences** weight due to the force of the Earth always pulling you downwards. On the other hand, your body **possesses** mass—the total number of atoms and molecules that make you up. This is a **scalar** quantity, because you have the same mass whichever way you are headed. All measurements in physics are determined based on whether they are vectors or scalars.

Types of Force

The Universe has four fundamental forces. With these forces, you can explain almost anything that is going on.

The first of these is gravity, the force that makes two bodies attract each other.

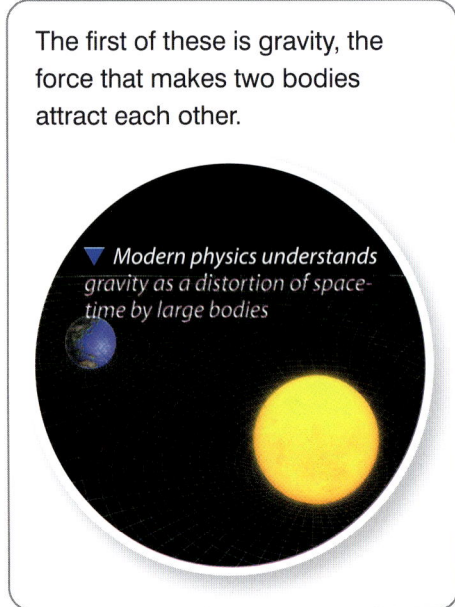

▼ *Modern physics understands gravity as a distortion of space-time by large bodies*

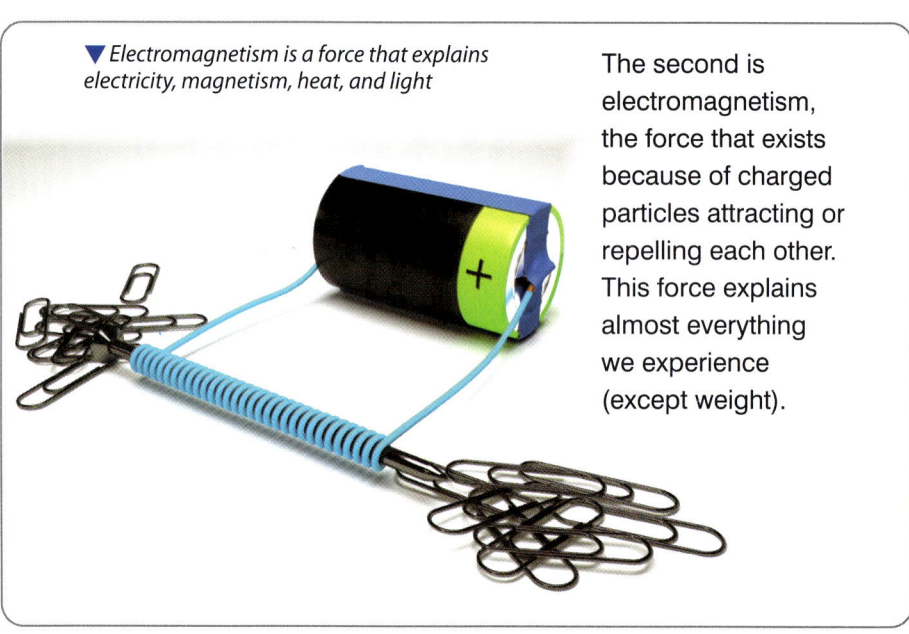

▼ *Electromagnetism is a force that explains electricity, magnetism, heat, and light*

The second is electromagnetism, the force that exists because of charged particles attracting or repelling each other. This force explains almost everything we experience (except weight).

The third force is a strong force, also called the strong nuclear interaction. This force holds protons and neutrons together in a nucleus.

▼ *The strong and weak forces work at the level of the nucleus, electromagnetic force works on atomic scales, and gravity works at the galactic level*

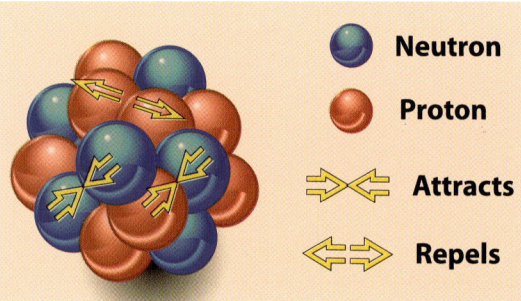

The fourth is the weak force, or the weak nuclear interaction. This also works only inside an atom's nucleus. Without this force, nuclear fusion would be difficult and stars, such as the Sun, would not exist. The continued study of these two forces will only lead to a greater understanding of natural mechanics and the universe.

Momentum

Momentum (symbol p) is what a body with some mass (symbol m) has when it has no force acting on it. When an object is standing still, that is, when it has no **velocity** (v), its momentum is zero. When it has some velocity, its momentum has a value. A small object at high speed (a ball hit by a bat) and a large object at low speed (a roadroller) may share the same momentum.

$$p = mv$$

▶ It takes a lot of force to change a roadroller's momentum

Mechanical Force

In mechanical terms, force (symbol f) is the change in momentum with respect to time (symbol t). A catcher stops a ball with a small mass, whereas it takes something huge to stop a roadroller. The force may be electrical (like charges repel, opposite charges attract), magnetic (like poles repel, opposite poles attract), or it may be a property of the density and hardness of the material (friction, elasticity, etc.).

$$f = \frac{mv}{t}$$

The value v/t gives you another fundamental idea of physics: acceleration, or the rate of change of velocity with time. Force can then be expressed as a measure of the mass of an object, and the change it undergoes in its acceleration when the object meets the force.

$$f = ma$$

▼ The dog's mass and forward acceleration stop the balls' momentum

What Makes Us Move

Force changes the momentum of an object and therefore changes it from one state of inertia to another (inertia means a body remaining in the same state, whether moving or staying still). This change of inertia can be used to make the device do work that is useful to us, such as using the force of your feet to pedal a bicycle. But what produces that force in the first place?

It is **energy**. It is the same thing that you get by eating food, or a car gets from its fuel. All the energy on our planet ultimately comes from the Sun, which gets its energy through nuclear fission. It takes a lot to explain energy, but we can share two interesting things:

- Energy is related to mass by Albert Einstein's famous Theory of Special Relativity.

- Energy can neither be created nor destroyed, but only converted from one form to another. This is the Law of Conservation of Energy.

▲ *All the energy we use ultimately comes from nuclear reactions in the Sun*

Work

The conversion of energy, from one form to another, results in some work being done. When you ride a bicycle, your body uses some of the chemical energy it got from food. Your muscles turn the chemical energy to kinetic energy, and this creates the force that pushes the pedal. In physics, the total work done (W) can be explained as the distance the bicycle travelled multiplied by the total force (f) that you applied. But remember that force is a vector. Therefore, the distance that matters is the **displacement** (symbol s), which is the linear distance between the starting point and the ending point, and not the path you have travelled.

$$W = fs$$

Work is of two types—**internal** and **external**. Your heartbeat is an example of internal work; you do external work when bicycling. In internal work, all the energy is spent in keeping the system going (like your body), while in external work, the energy spent makes the body do something, such as pushing the bike's pedals.

💡 Isn't It Amazing!

Scientists have a short way of writing extremely large numbers. So, instead of writing our planet's mass as 598,000,000,000,000,000,000,000,000 kg, we can write it as 5.98×10^{24} kg. The number written as superscript on 10 tells you the **order of magnitude**.

▶ *The Sun delivers 3.6×10^{26} kgm^2/s^3 of power every second. This unit can be further simplified as Joules per second or Watts*

WATER   SOLAR   WIND

SCIENCE | FORCE AND MOVEMENT | 111

Potential and Kinetic Energy

Kinetic energy is the energy a system has when it is moving or doing work (the energy your leg has while pedalling a bicycle). If an object is at rest then it doesn't have kinetic energy. **Potential energy** is the energy available to a system due to inertia (e.g. the unspent energy from your food), or the energy it is transferring as it does work (the energy that is now part of your bicycle's inertia of movement). Sadly, your bicycle won't have much of this kinetic energy left by the end of the journey, since most will be lost due to **friction** with the ground.

▶ The relation between work and energy. The units of both are written as Newton-metres or Joules

Power

If you look at electric batteries or lights, they are denoted by the power (symbol P) that they deliver. Something is powerful when it gives a lot of energy (which you experience as force) in a small amount of time, like a wrestler bending a bar of iron. Physicists write power as the rate at which a machine can do work (W) in each unit of time which is usually in seconds.

$$P = \frac{W}{t}$$

Cohesion refers to the forces that stop things from breaking apart. There are two main forces that hold things together.

◀ Types of energy. We often talk of energy in terms of anything that can be converted into electricity

FOSSIL NUCLEAR

In Real Life

When James Watt (1736–1819) tried to sell his improved steam engine to mills, they could not understand how it would do more work than the horses they used to pull loads. Being a clever physicist, Watt denoted the energy his engine could deliver every minute (power) in terms of the amount of work a horse could do per minute. The mill owners were impressed, and that's how we got the unit we still use: horsepower.

▲ One horsepower is how much a healthy, untired horse can draw: 33,000 pounds by a foot every minute

When Things Move in a Straight Line

Have you observed dust particles in a sunbeam? They seem to move in a completely jumbled fashion, darting about and suddenly changing direction. This motion, which seems to be random, is called Brownian motion, named after Robert Brown (1773–1858). However, it is not random. It is governed by the Laws of Motion, which were first written down by Isaac Newton after many years of observation and experimentation.

These laws form the basis of **mechanics**—the science of making things move. Every movement must have velocity and direction.

▲ Brownian motion can be explained by Newton's Laws of Motion

Newton's First Law of Motion

In simple language, this law says that an object will not change its state of motion on its own, unless some force acts upon it. An object has only two states of motion: at rest or moving in one direction. This is known as the Law of Inertia.

Imagine that you've gone to the edge of the solar system with your friends (no atmosphere, no gravity) to play cricket. Your friend bowls and you hit the ball hard. It will fly out of the solar system and to the end of the Universe. That's because the force of your hit gave it motion, and unless it crashes into something, there's no force to stop it. This won't happen on Earth because air **drag** will slow the ball down and gravity will pull it back to Earth.

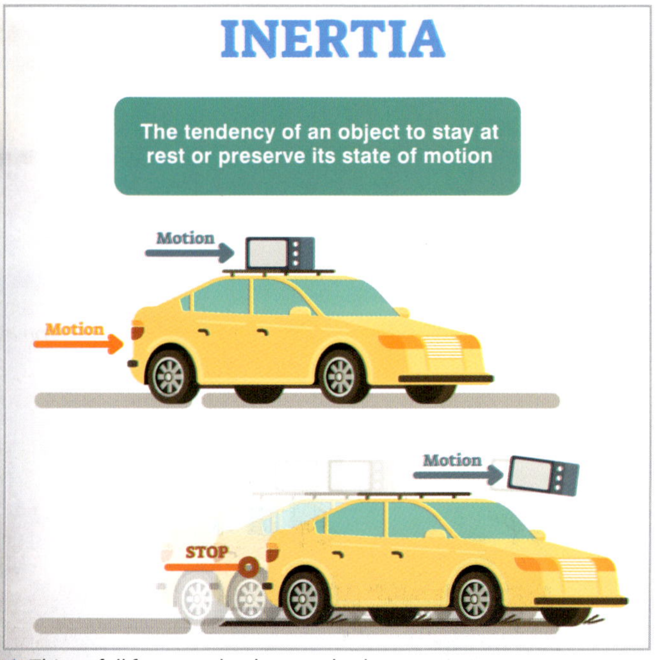

INERTIA

The tendency of an object to stay at rest or preserve its state of motion

▲ Things fall frontwards when you brake a moving car because of inertia

Newton's Second Law of Motion

This law says that the amount (magnitude) and direction of the net force (F_{net}) that acts on an object can be measured by:

1. the mass (m) of the object
2. the direction it moves in
3. the acceleration (a) it undergoes

Think of a football. When it's on the ground, it experiences several forces on it. When you kick it, your foot has to give it enough force to overcome gravity, normal force, friction force, and the drag due to air. The final acceleration of the ball is proportional to whatever is left of the force of your kick. Therefore,

$$F_{net} = ma$$

▶ *Understanding Newton's Second Law of Motion could help you win many football matches*

Newton's Third Law of Motion

According to this law, for every force, there will be another force equal to it, which acts in the opposite direction. You have seen one such force—the normal force, which stops an object from crashing through the solid it is placed on. This force makes a ball bounce off the ground or the wall. When you drag something on the ground, the friction provides resistance. Another such force is **buoyancy**, which makes things float on liquids. When you dive into a pool, you can feel the water pushing you up. Yet another is drag, the friction caused by moving through a fluid—this also acts in air, which is considered to be fluid in nature.

◀ *When you hit a ball, you will experience recoil, the equal and opposite force to the ball hitting your bat*

When Things Don't Move in a Straight Line

Though we think of motion as something that goes in a straight line, there are other kinds too. One of them is like the swaying of a clothesline, known as vibration. The movement of a swing is another kind of motion, called oscillation. The linear movement of an oscillating body is called **propagation**. When it moves forward while oscillating, we get a **wave**. The **rotation** of the Earth on its axis is circular motion; and the **revolution** of our planet around the Sun is combination of both linear and circular motions.

▲ *The pendulum of a grandfather clock oscillates, while the hands of the clock face rotate*

Vibration

Vibration is the movement of an object around a mean position. When you pull the string of a violin and let it go, the string goes back to its resting state with some force. But its momentum is so much that the string goes right past the resting point to the other end, along the same distance as you pulled on the other side. As the string swings back, its momentum makes it go past the resting point again. This to-and-fro movement is called vibration. If there were no drag due to air, this would go on endlessly.

To vibrate, there has to be a motive force pulling the object away and a resisting force pulling it back to the original state. It is often the same force, which changes direction once the vibrating entity has reached one end. In a metal string, it is the **strain** (the extent to which the atoms can be pulled apart).

◄ *The energy of a vibrating string is transmitted to us as sound waves*

Oscillation

When something moves and comes back to its place again and again, physicists say that it undergoes periodic motion. An object that vibrates with a defined time period is said to oscillate. That's how a playground swing works. At the subatomic level, everything oscillates—atoms, nuclei, electrons, quarks, and photons. The energy to oscillate comes from their electromagnetic field. Frequency is the measure of the number of oscillations a particle does in one second. It is measured in Hertz (Hz). Every particle has its own natural frequency of oscillation, which depends on the amount of energy it possesses.

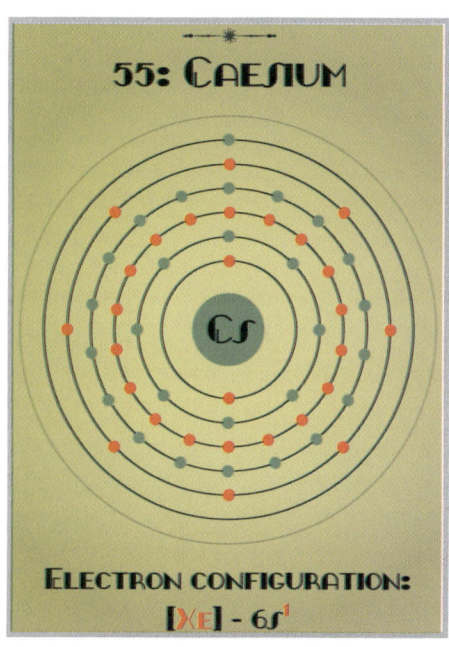

▲ *The oscillation of a Caesium-133 atom is used to define a 'second', the unit of measuring time*

SCIENCE | FORCE AND MOVEMENT | 115

Wave Motion

A wave propagates when oscillating objects also move linearly. Waves are longitudinal, when the direction of propagation and oscillation are the same. Our ears catch longitudinal waves in the air as sound. In a transverse wave, the particles oscillate perpendicular to the direction of propagation. Light and radio waves travel this way.

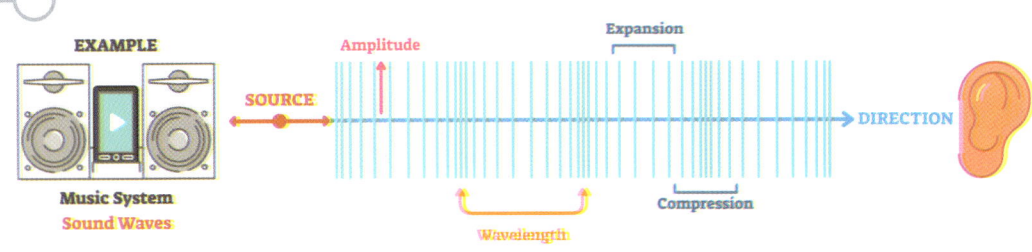

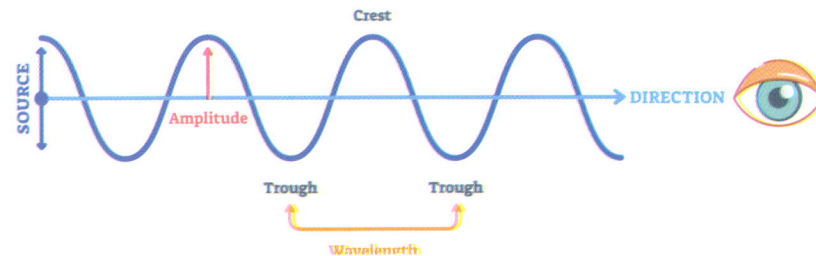

▶ Types of waves

Circular Motion

Circular motion is how a wheel or a disc moves. To calculate how fast a rotating or revolving object is moving, you must measure the angle it moves at, not the distance. This measure is called **angular velocity** and it is measured in degrees per second. As the Earth rotates, all places on the same longitude have the same angular velocity. Nevertheless, they all have different linear velocities. If you stand at the Equator, you have 24 hours to cover 40,075 km, the circumference of the Earth. At the North or South Pole though, you don't have to move at all!

▼ *The angular velocity of a point on the edge of a wheel is the same as its centre. However, its linear velocity is much faster, as it has to travel the full circumference*

In Real Life

All the members in a rock band use the power of oscillation to make music. The guitarists depend on the strain of their strings, the drummers on that of the membrane, and the singers on their own vocal chords!

▲ *Music depends on making a harmonious mix of the natural frequencies of all oscillating things*

Why Things Fall Down

When learning about gravity, you may come across a story that says that Isaac Newton discovered gravity when he was sitting under a tree and an apple fell on him. Let's talk about this discovery and how it changed the world.

> **Isn't It Amazing!**
>
> Did you know that the apple tree that inspired Newton still stands? It grows in Woolsthorpe Manor in Lincolnshire, England, which was Newton's childhood home, and is now over 350 years old.

Newton's Law of Universal Gravitation

Although we know that the Earth attracts all things to itself, Newton suggested that the reverse was also true: all things attract the Earth to themselves too. He figured out that the force of the attraction (symbol F_g) was proportional to the mass of the two bodies attracting each other (symbols m_1 and m_2), and inversely proportional to the square of the distance between them (r). Another factor is the gravitational constant (G), whose value is 6.673×10^{-11} N m²/kg².

$$F_g = \frac{G m_1 m_2}{r^2}$$

So, you could say that not only does an apple fall towards the Earth, but the Earth moves towards the apple too. But since the mass of the apple (a few grams) is nothing compared to the Earth's mass (5.97×10^{24} kg), and the distance between the Earth and the apple is only a tiny fraction as compared to the Earth's radius (6.37×10^6 m or 6370 km), the force of attraction (F_g) between the apple and the Earth depends only on the Earth. Therefore, when you do the math, $F_g = 9.8$ Newtons.

$$F_g = \frac{6.673 \times 10^{-11} \times 5.97 \times 10^{24}}{(6.37 \times 10^6)^2} = 9.8 \text{ N}$$

Now, from Newton's Laws of Motion, we know that F = mass (m) times acceleration (a). But since the mass is negligible, the acceleration due to gravity (g) is effectively a constant everywhere on Earth, that is, 9.8 m/s².

General Relativity

Einstein proposed the radical aspect of space-time. Space-time is the fabric of the Universe, made of the three dimensions of space and one of time. Everything in space is embedded in space-time but huge objects such as planets and stars can bend it around them. To imagine how this happens, get your friends to stretch a cloth flat. Place a football on it. Doesn't it bend the sheet around itself?

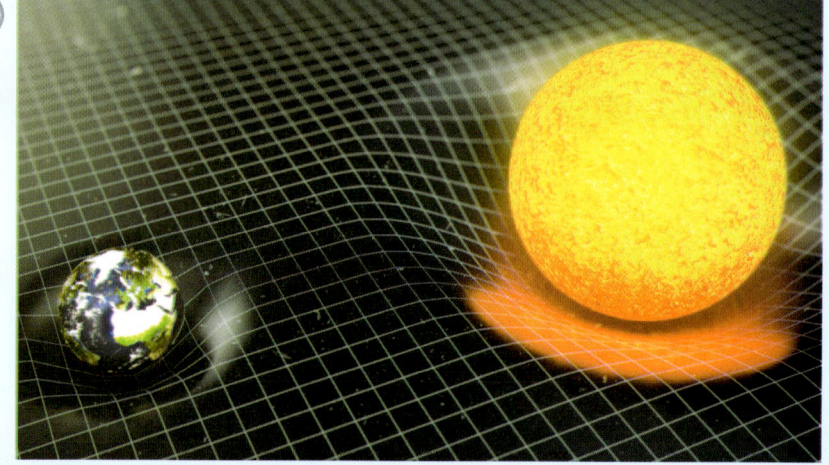

▲ The bending of space-time causes smaller objects to be drawn to the larger ones

▼ Gravity holds the solar system together

Gravitational Waves

Einstein's theory of space-time acting as a fabric means that it will have ripples going through it when something big happens (such as two stars crashing). These "ripples" are called **gravitational waves** and have the same speed as light. Unlike electromagnetic waves though, they are not known to be made of any particle till now.

▶ Gravitational waves were found by a special detector called LIGO in 2016—a hundred years after Einstein predicted them

Incredible Individuals

The Binomial theorem, laws of motion, force and mass, acceleration, inertia, universal gravitation, differential calculus, momentum, weight, vector addition, projectile motion, centripetal acceleration, circular motion, satellite motion, tidal forces, the precession of the equinoxes, and optics—one scientist discovered them all. His name is Isaac Newton, the Father of the Scientific Revolution.

▶ Newton humbly said of his discoveries, "If I have seen further, it is by standing on the shoulders of giants."

Forces of Resistance

When you pull a heavy box across the floor, why does it seem so hard to pull? This is because of friction, which is a perpendicular force resisting your forward motion. Much of friction is caused by forces of **adhesion** between the atoms and molecules of the two solids in contact.

In reality, friction between two things should be small because their surfaces are not entirely smooth, even if they appear so. That's because they have microscopic hills and valleys called asperities. But when an object has been resting, the force of gravity (mg) works with the adhesive forces to pull it down and crush the asperities. In turn, this increases the surface of contact and the adhesion becomes stronger. That's why it's harder to make an object move than to keep it moving.

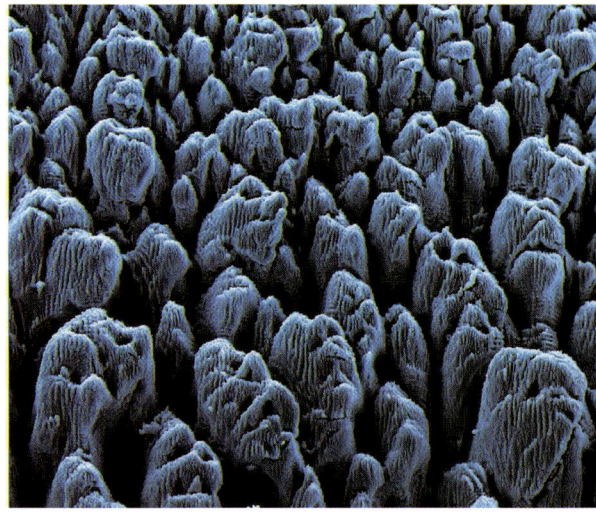

▲ The surface of silicon, seen under an electron microscope. What looks smooth and shiny to the naked eye is in fact a microscopically rough surface

Friction

As friction depends on adhesive forces, it depends on the materials in contact. Physicists use a measure called the coefficient of friction (symbol μ) to measure how two solids will interact. It is the ratio of the force required to pull (F), to the weight of the material (called load, L). Therefore, $\mu = F/L$. If the ratio is 1, it means as much force is needed to pull the load as its weight.

However, there are two coefficients of friction—one for calculating how much effort is needed to make a standing thing move (**coefficient of static friction**, symbol μ_s) and one for keeping a moving thing moving (**coefficient of kinetic friction**, symbol μ_k).

Drag

Drag is the resistance that a fluid offers to a solid object moving through it. You feel drag when walking into the wind or while swimming. It depends on the density and viscosity of the fluid, the speed at which the object is moving, the area that's exposed to the fluid, and the shape of the moving object.

In Real Life

Why can lizards stick to walls, ceilings, and even glass windows without falling? That's because their feet have hundreds of tiny hair. This increases the total surface in contact and the total van der Waals forces, and therefore increases friction.

Lubrication

Lubrication is a way to reduce friction between two solids, by introducing a liquid between them. The lubricant must have high viscosity to ensure that the friction between it and the solid surfaces does not tear it apart; otherwise, the solids will come in contact. Lubricants must also resist changing viscosity too much when they get heated in the process.

▼ A bullet train's "nose" is designed to minimise the drag it faces while moving at high speed. This is called streamlining

Engines

Humans have always dreamed of mechanical motion. During the Industrial Revolution, the science of converting heat energy into work (thermodynamics) was developed. Engineers wondered whether they could build practical engines that could actually do work, especially hauling loads of coal out of coal mines and carrying the loads into factories. Nicolas Cugnot built a steam-powered car in 1769 that could run for 20 minutes. Thomas Savery, Thomas Newcomen, James Watt, and Richard Trevithick, each one improved on the other's design of the steam engine, making them much lighter and faster. Other inventors, such as Karl Benz and Gottfried Daimler, both from Germany, worked on internal combustion engines, which were much lighter than steam engines.

Steam Power

Steam is full of energy, and if confined in a chamber, will try to push its way out. A piston is a lid, like a disc of metal, which can be used to make the chamber bigger or smaller. If the piston is attached to a rod, the force of the steam pushing against it can be converted into work. This is the idea behind a steam engine.

In the picture on the right, you see four stages of the engine at work. First, the steam is boiled and enters the piston chamber. As it enters, it pushes against the piston. As the energy is converted to mechanical energy that moves the wheel, the steam cools and is drained off. A second rod attached to the wheel controls a moving sluice. Once the piston is pushed to the end, the wheel has rotated half a circle. The rod now closes one inlet of steam and opens the inlet on the other end. Steam rushes into that side and pushes the piston back, completing one turn of the wheel. This is called a double-acting engine.

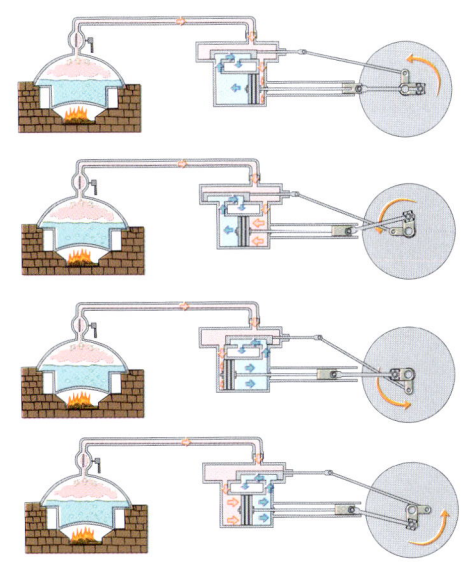

▲ *A double acting steam engine conserves power and does nearly double the work*

Internal Combustion Engine

Modern internal combustion engines have a piston chamber (cylinder) like steam engines. On the intake stroke (see 1 in the picture), the engine takes in air from the atmosphere and a small amount of fuel from the fuel tank. It compresses it in the compression stroke (2). In the power (or combustion) stroke (3), an electric spark ignites the fuel. The heat of the combustion causes the air to expand rapidly, pushing the piston forcefully. In the final exhaust stroke (4), the burnt fuel and air are removed from the cylinder.

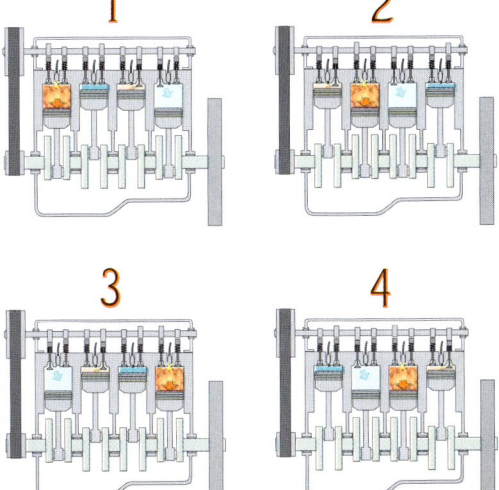

Incredible Individuals

Bertha Benz made the first long distance car journey with her sons Eugene and Richard in 1888 from Mannheim to Pforzheim in Germany. Her trip attracted large crowds and people began to see the advantages of a lightweight self-powered carriage.

▶ *Bertha Benz was the main investor in her husband Karl Benz's factory, and also invented brake pads*

▲ *Belts connect the engine's crankshaft to the axles, so that the energy from the engine can be transmitted to the wheels as mechanical force*

Machines

The word 'machine' makes you think of things with a number of gears and screws and complicated moving parts. But that's not what a machine means to physicists. To them, a machine is any device that transfers work done at one end (called the input work, W_{in}) to another end (the output work, W_{out}). Thus, in a robotic arm that's making a car, there will be a large number of tiny machines that make the whole arm, each transferring work till the end.

In an ideal machine, all the work would be transferred without loss of energy, but in the real world, there's always friction (because of solid parts touching each other) and drag (because of air). Therefore, the usefulness of a machine is measured in terms of Efficiency (η), the fraction of the input that is delivered as final work.

$$\eta = \frac{W_{out}}{W_{in}} = \frac{Energy_{out}}{Energy_{in}} = \frac{F_{out} * s_{out}}{F_{in} * s_{in}}$$

You read that work is the product of the force (F) and the length moved by the mass (displacement, s). So, if the displacement of the input can be doubled, the force can be halved. The ratio of the output force to the input force is called a mechanical advantage (MA).

$$MA = \frac{F_{out}}{F_{in}}$$

Inclined Plane

This is the simplest machine in which one end is higher than the other. It is used to raise a load (P) for a distance (s), by actually dragging it at an angle, rather than pulling or pushing it upwards directly. The work done is the work required to overcome the pull of gravity. The smaller the angle of the incline (its **gradient**), the smaller the force required to counter the pull of gravity and raise the load. This is why we feel less tired going up a gentle slope than a steep staircase.

Lever

A lever is a machine made of three parts: a load arm, an effort arm, and a fulcrum. The length of the two arms makes the most difference, as does the location of the fulcrum, which divides levers into three classes.

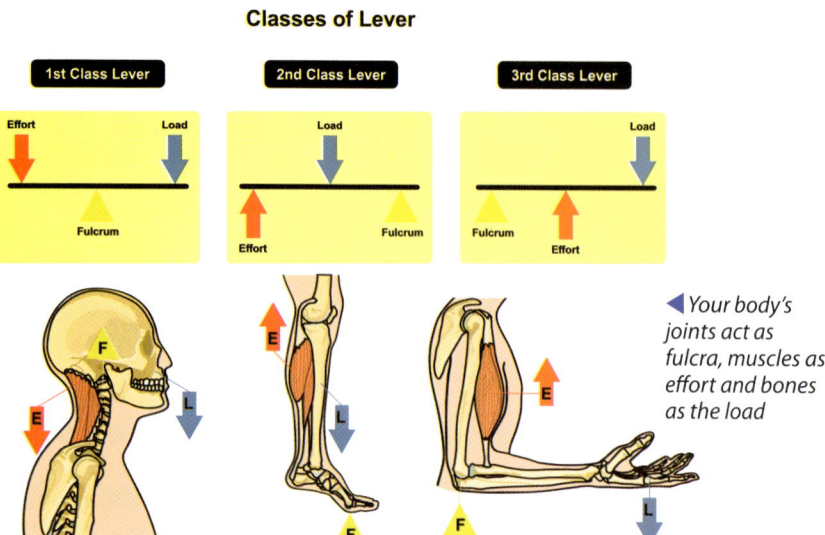

◀ Your body's joints act as fulcra, muscles as effort and bones as the load

Isn't It Amazing!

Trains have difficulty going up mountains. As they have very little friction, they can slip on the tracks if the slope is too steep. They need to ascend as gradually as possible, so the track has to be laid so that it goes round and round the mountain, with many tunnels and bridges. This also reduces the force required to counteract gravity, making them go faster.

▲ The low gradient makes the train spend very little energy climbing

Wheel and Axle

A wheel and axle convert linear motion into rotational motion, greatly minimising friction and increasing **efficiency**. The longer the radius of the wheel, the less effort you need to put in to move. You see this type of machine everywhere: in motor vehicles, in machines, in toys, and even the wheels of your suitcase!

▶ *Cranes use a wheel and axle called a windlass to convert rotational motion into linear motion*

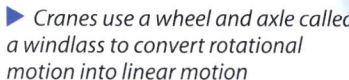

Pulley

A pulley is a wheel over which a cable runs carrying a load. The most common use of it is in an elevator, where a counterbalancing weight going down pulls the elevator car up.

◀ *By using a combination of pulleys, the length of the rope can be increased, so that the counterweight can be made lighter*

Wedge

A wedge turns the force applied in one direction by an angle. A knife is a good example of a wedge: by pressing your knife down on a carrot, you drive the two pieces away till they split. Humans have been making wedges since the Early Stone Age, in the form of stone axes and cutters.

▲ *Pizza knives combine wedges and wheels*

Screw

A screw is an inclined plane (the ribs of the screw) arranged in a spiral around an axis, to convert rotational motion to linear motion. Screws are used in presses to crush things with little force.

▶ *Screw-presses are used traditionally in Asia to press milk from coconuts*

★ Incredible Individuals

James Starley (1830–1881) and his nephew John Starley (1854–1901) perfected the modern bicycle. Through a simple combination of pulleys, wheels, and levers, it efficiently converts your input (pedalling) into motion.

◀ *All modern bicycles are based on Starleys' safety bicycle*

Density and Buoyancy

Density (symbol d) is simply a measure of how much matter there is in a unit of space. We use mass (m) as a measure of the amount of matter and volume (V) as the measure of space. Therefore, the formula for calculating density is simply:

$$d = \frac{m}{V}$$

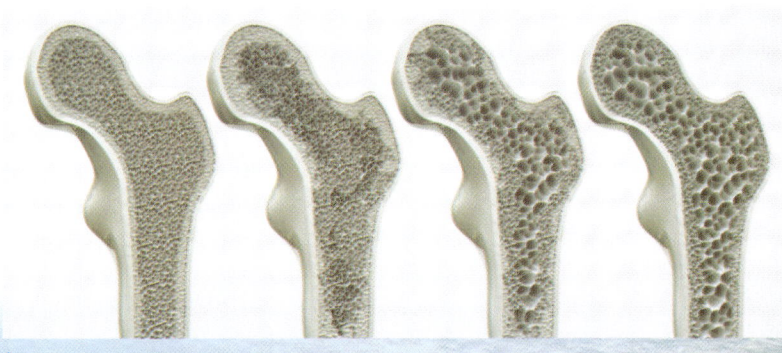
▲ As we age, our bone density reduces, making them prone to breaking

Density is expressed as kilogrammes per cubic metre (kg/m³) or grams per cubic centimetre (g/cm³). (These units are now the standard units throughout the world.) When the metric system was defined, the density of pure water at 4°C was fixed as 1 g/cm³, and the densities of all other materials are compared to it (**relative density**). Density is an important character of a substance and has a strong role in determining what that substance may be used for.

🔍 Floating and Sinking

Why do some things—such as iron nails—sink in water, while others—such as wooden nails—float? It is because of their density (d). Density increases the force on the object due to the Earth's gravity (g). The heavier mass will be pulled faster towards the Earth.

If you put an object in water, it will experience normal force that counteracts gravity, called buoyancy. Buoyancy is the resistance of the fluid to being displaced. The van der Waals forces between a liquid's atoms or molecules have to be broken by an object sinking through it (or in the case of a ship, moving horizontally). An object denser than water will have a force (m*g) strong enough to break through it, so it sinks. An object less dense (rarer) than water will not have enough force to break through, so it floats.

As gases have weaker van der Waals forces than liquid, they have lesser buoyancy and viscosity.

▶ Iron-bodied ships float because their hold is full of air (or crude oil), so that the total density is less than that of water

Isn't It Amazing!

As air is heated, its molecules move away from each other, reducing its density. The buoyancy of the cooler air below will push it upwards. This is the principle used in flying hot air balloons. Helium and hydrogen are lighter than air, so balloons filled with them also float.

▶ *Zeppelins are hydrogen balloons coupled with propellers. They were used for air transport in the early 20th century*

Specific Gravity and Purity

Relative density is the density of a substance expressed as a fraction of the density of a reference substance. When water is used, this is called **specific gravity**. This measure is used to determine whether an object is pure or contaminated, by the Archimedes Principle. If an object is put in water, it will displace water equal to its own volume. Two dense objects of the same weight will displace different volumes of water, which you can measure.

Gold is an expensive and very dense metal. It is often mixed with silver or copper for making jewellery and other things. If an object made of gold displaces more water (by volume) than a nugget of gold of the same weight, you know that it is impure.

▼ *The purity of gold objects is measured in carats. 1 carat is equal to a gold content of 4.166% in the object*

Freshwater and Seawater

Salt dissolved in water adds to its mass without changing its volume. That makes seawater, which is rich in salts, denser and therefore more buoyant than water in river deltas. Ships moving from freshwater ports to the open sea experience more buoyancy, while those moving in the reverse direction sink a bit.

◀ *Plimsoll Lines indicate how much a ship's hull may sink safely in freshwater and seawater in summer and winter. The numbers show the depth to which the ship's bottom (keel) has sunk below the surface*

Nanotechnology

As humans, our bodies are limited by nature. Without technology, we cannot stand temperatures that are too cold or too hot, nor can we fly in the sky or dive into the seas. But technology is often cumbersome and uncomfortable, such as the oxygen cylinders used by divers and mountaineers. Scientists who work with different kinds of materials are always looking to make things lighter, more flexible, and, of course, cheaper. That's where nanotechnology comes in.

The term 'nano' in nanotechnology comes from the word nanometre (nm), a unit of length one-billionth (1/1,000,000,000) of a metre; the size at which atoms and molecules exist. Nanotechnology is the science of creating materials by building them one atom or molecule at a time, while strictly controlling how they are arranged, using what we know of their chemical properties. Nanotechnology creates novel atomic structures that are not common in nature.

◀ Graphene is a form of carbon made by nanotechnology. Here you see it acting as a molecule-sized filter (black) that only allows water molecules (red and blue) through

Nanoelectronics

With every passing year, electronic devices such as computers and mobile phones are becoming more complicated than ever. There are already millions of transistors on microprocessor chips. In 2016, scientists found a way to make transistors as small as 1 nm wide. If there was a way to manufacture them on a large scale, then computers would get much tinier, much faster, and a lot more flexible than they currently are.

Another use is in creating nanometre-sized sensors. These would be tiny electrical devices that can detect pollution, heat, and movement, among other things, and transmit the information to a mobile computer. Such sensors could be sewn into clothes or even implanted under your skin, to monitor blood sugar, for example.

▶ Nanosensors sewed onto clothes could be used to detect low blood sugar levels and warn patients to eat something

 In Real Life

A lot of nanotechnology is inspired by nature. For example, lotus leaves have microscopic structures that repel water and keep the plant waterproof. Scientists have designed a vanadium dioxide nano-coating for windows that mimics the lotus leaves.

Nanomedicine

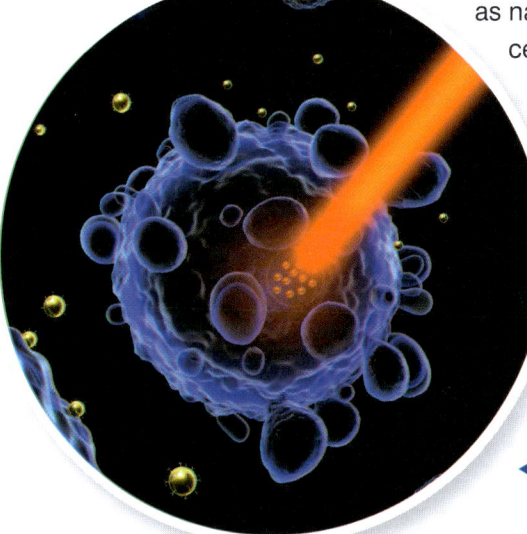

Doctors are very excited about what nanotechnology can do for medicine. One line of research uses graphene, a form of carbon which exists as thin sheets. Atoms of carbon can be laid down as nanometre-sized ribbons of graphene, to create a frame in which nerve cells (neurons) can be grown, and their axons can be made to follow a pre-decided path to meet other neurons. This way, people with brain damage who have lost the ability to do math or recognise faces could regain some ability.

Another line of research looks at using balls of gold just a few nanometres wide (nanoparticles) to kill cancer cells in combination with radiation therapy. When a patient's body is injected with these particles, cancer cells absorb them at a greater rate than normal ones. In turn, the particles make them take in more radiation than they normally would, causing them to die.

◀ One day, nanoribbons could help Alzheimer's patients regrow neurons in their brains

Nano energy

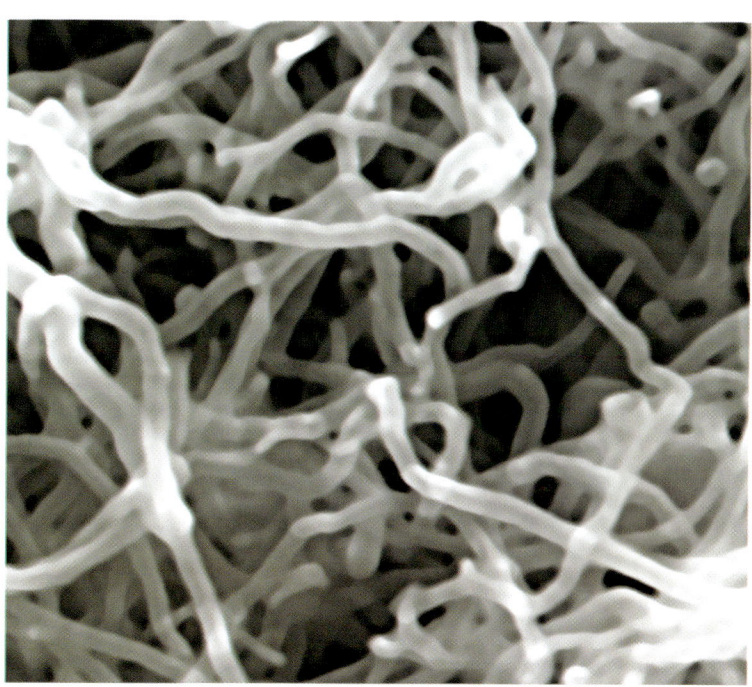

Many nanotechnologists work with graphene —a form of carbon that can be made into sheets that can then be rolled into carbon nanotubes. Nanotubes are very conductive to electricity and offer little resistance. Scientists are looking to see if they can be used to replace metal wires to make transmission of electricity cheaper, while also making electric cables lighter.

Another use of carbon nanotubes is in building sturdier yet lighter materials, such as the blades of windmills. Lighter windmill blades convert more wind energy into electricity. Using the same thought, turbine blades in other power plants can be made lighter, so that energy is not wasted in overcoming the resistance of the material due to its weight.

▲ An electron microscope picture of what carbon nanotubes look like

Other Uses

Yet another use of nanotechnology is in making paints and clothes that can resist the growth of bacteria and fungi. Nano-materials are also being used in garments to make them self-cleaning so that the use of chemical detergents can be reduced. Scientists are experimenting with nano-structures made of graphene for many things, such as building artificial organs and tools for removing pollutants from the atmosphere. Graphene structures are being made to purify sea water and polluted water, so that it can be made fit for drinking. As the human population grows, so does the demand for clean water.

▲ Nano clothes could one day keep you safe from germs while you play outside

Artificial Intelligence

What is intelligence? Scientists have suggested that there are four aspects to it, which are as follows:

1. **Perception:** The nervous system interprets the environment around us through sight, hearing, smell, taste, and touch. How these senses can be integrated by the brain is a measure of intelligence.

2. **Learning:** Perception is stored in the brain as memory—a library of everything you have perceived in the past. Learning is the making of memory. You learn facts by **rote** (such as the letters of the alphabet), and relationships by association (such as what happens to you if your mom catches you sneaking cookies).

3. **Reasoning:** This is the part that most people think is real intelligence.

    - **Inductive reasoning** relies on past actions. If you got into trouble for sneaking cookies yesterday, you could get into trouble today.
    - **Deductive reasoning** relies on current information. If there were four oranges on the table this morning, and now there are three, someone's eaten an orange.

4. **Problem Solving:** This takes the above three and sees if they work in a new situation that you have no memory of. For example, if 2 × 3 = 6 and 2 × 6 = 12, will 3 × 2 × 2 also make 12?

▲ Language and deception were thought to be unique parts of human intelligence

 ## Artificial Intelligence (AI)

If we enable a computer to master all the four powers above (Perception, Learning, Reasoning, and Problem Solving), we could call it an intelligent machine. Computers already do quite a lot—storing memory (they never forget), solving mathematical problems (way better than us), and sensing the environment (e.g. face recognition software). However, their inductive reasoning powers and the ability to solve non-mathematical problems are still limited.

However, humans have other superpowers. They understand and speak **language**, making up new sentences on the fly. AI scientists focus on getting computers to 'get' language as well as possible. That's how we have Siri and Cortana, the voice assistants in Apple and Microsoft phones and computers respectively. Humans have another power: deception, making a person believe the opposite of the truth. This is applied to computers through the Turing Test: if you cannot tell a computer apart from a human, it is intelligent.

◀ In a Turing Test, you face two screens, one that gives answers typed by a human, and one that gives answers from an AI programme. You have to guess which is which, by asking smart questions

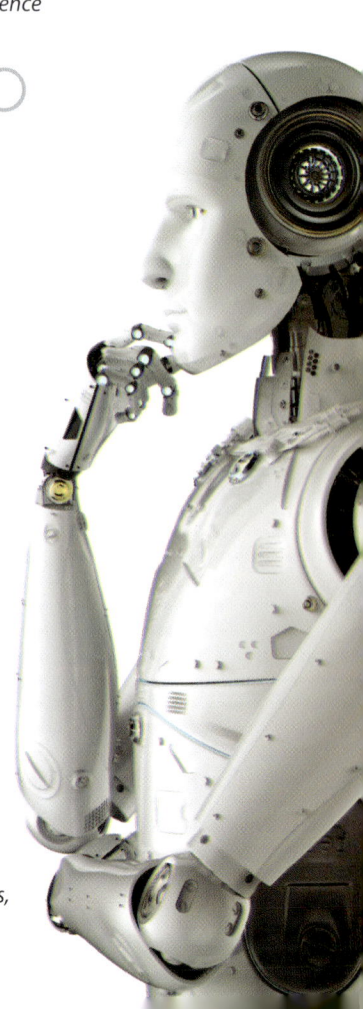

▶ Cybernetics is a field of science that combines robotics, artificial intelligence, and biotechnology to artificially enhance our body

SCIENCE | FUTURE SCIENCE & TECHNOLOGY

3D Printing

If a machine breaks down, often you have to go around hunting for a spare part or order it online and wait for days. What if you could make it yourself? That is the idea behind three-dimensional (3D) printing. Just as a printer deposits ink on paper, a 3D printer is designed to 'print' an object layer by layer.

You create a design on your computer and order a print. The printer deposits some powder onto a smooth, non-stick surface. A roller then flattens it into a thin layer. Then a printer head applies glue in the exact pattern that you designed, so that only those particles stick. The printer head rises slightly and a layer of powder is applied again and rolled over. In this manner, the machine 'prints' each layer till the whole object is complete. It sounds like a lengthy process, but it is very fast. 3D printing is now being used to make replacement teeth and bones, so patients can get them in the exact shape of the ones they have broken.

▲ 3D printing is also used to make prototype models and spare parts for machines

Laser Sintering

Sintering is the process of joining two metal surfaces together by partly melting the surfaces that need to be joined. Laser sintering uses a laser whose energy heats the metal atoms to a melting point. As a laser can be focused very precisely, it can be used in place of a glue gun in a 3D printer head, to make the metal powder particles melt and merge.

◀ Laser sintering helps make a 3D-printed metal object into a whole solid without using adhesive

Isn't It Amazing!

Here's a thought—what if spare organs for our body could be made using 3D printing, just like machine spares? Biologists are working towards making any organ we may need by directing a tiny pipette to deposit stem cells onto a scaffold, and then inducing them to differentiate into various kinds of tissues, such as muscles, blood vessels, connective tissue, and epithelium.

▶ 3D bioprinting could one day grow you a new organ from your own stem cells

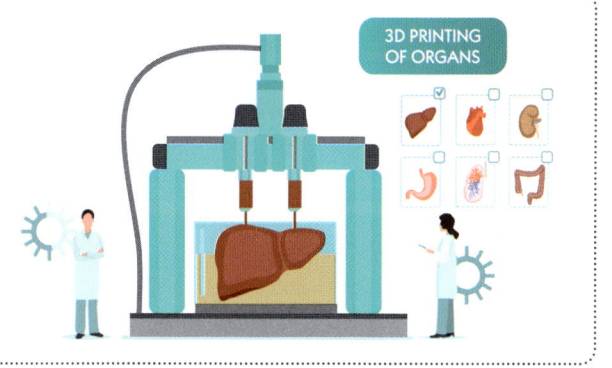

Robotics

If you have read science fiction, you must have come across several stories on robots. Robots are a kind of automaton—machines that operate by themselves. The Chinese built some of the earliest automata, including a completely mechanical orchestra. But today, if you want to be a robotics engineer, you'll have to learn several things: computing, artificial intelligence, electronics, and mechanics.

Unlike the ones in stories, most modern robots do not look like humans, except some toys. They are used for manufacturing electronic appliances, automobiles, and other goods. They are also being tried out for performing surgeries where very tiny cuts and stitches need to be made, which doctors cannot perform.

Automation

Would you consider your washing machine a robot? Once you've loaded it and switched it on, it does all the work by itself. The idea behind robots is automation—getting work done without human involvement. The Industrial Revolution of the 19th century was driven by automation. Inventors created elevators and escalators, machines that could weave cloth out of threads, and wagons that could move without being pulled by horses. Yet, we still don't consider them as robots.

◀ It may look like a box, but a washing machine is a robot too!

Industrial Robots

We think of robots as machines that can move around and use their arms and legs as we do. Modern robotics uses electricity and computer science to make large metallic 'arms' move about and do precise tasks. These robots come in two types:

1. Fixed robots: These are bolted down into one place. Such robots are used in factories to make the movements required to weld parts of a car together, or to make tiny parts for electronics such as mobile phones.

2. Mobile robots: These can move on wheels. They can go to places where it is dangerous for humans (such as deep inside a nuclear plant, outer space, or a chemical spill), and carry out either pre-programmed instructions or instructions given from a remote location by radio.

Incredible Individuals

The word 'robot' comes from the Czech word for slave labour, *robota*. It was coined by playwright Karel Čapek in *R. U. R.*, a play about artificial human beings who are slaves at first, but ultimately destroy real humans and take over the world.

▶ Poster for the play R.U.R., in which the word robot was used for the first time

SCIENCE | FUTURE SCIENCE & TECHNOLOGY

Robo-Surgery

Robotic 'fingers' can be really tiny and can move precise distances, measured in millimetres, in a way our hands cannot. This comes in use when you need to make tiny cuts and stitches when doing surgery—so surgeons love them. Instead of being nervous about making a mistake, a surgeon can sit outside the operation theatre, watching the operation on a giant screen while guiding the robot through a computer.

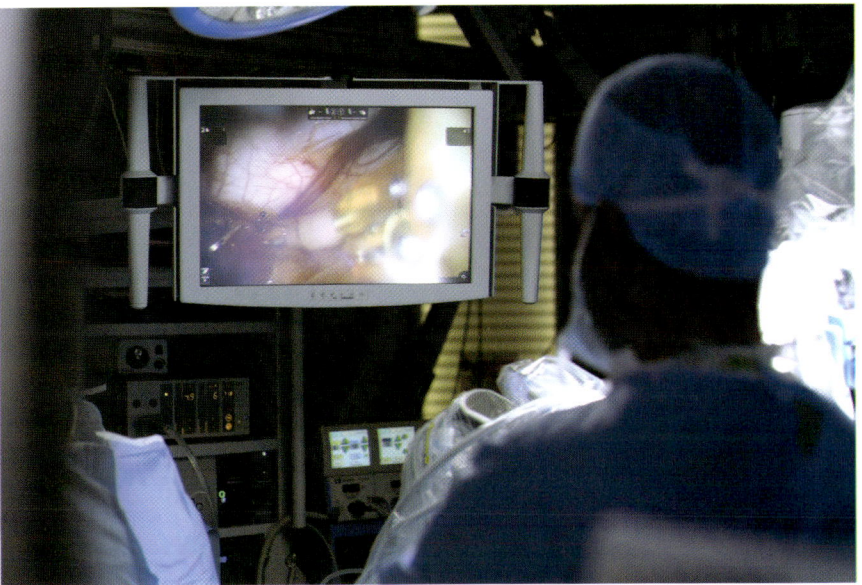

▶ Surgeons can direct robots from afar in the future, avoiding human error and achieving higher precision

▼ Industrial robots can be programmed to do repetitive yet dangerous jobs, such as high-temperature welding

Injectable Robots

Machines can be made tinier than a pinhead, which can then be injected into the blood. They can travel through the blood, find cancer cells and kill them. Or they can go right inside the cell's nucleus, locate bad DNA and 'edit' it so that you can be cured of **genetic diseases**.

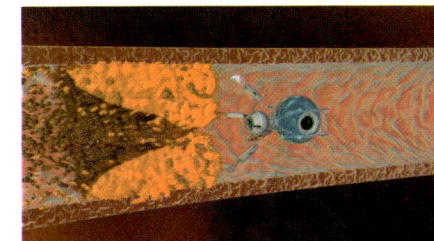

▲ Nanometre-sized robots can be used to remove arterial plaques in the future

Isn't It Amazing!

Rube Goldberg (1883–1970) was an American cartoonist who drew cartoons of complicated, convoluted machines performing simple tasks. In the field of robotics, a Rube Goldberg machine is an over-engineered machine, that is, a machine which would have done equally well with fewer parts.

▲ Example of a Rube Goldberg Machine

Genetic Engineering

Genetic engineering (GE) has been around ever since humans learned to domesticate plants and animals in the Neolithic Period (the New Stone Age). By selective breeding, ancient farmers removed **traits** that they didn't want in their domestic animals and plants. That's how wolves who were aggressive became dogs that listen to humans.

But when people talk of genetic engineering today, they mean the artificial modification of DNA in a laboratory (DNA is a molecule that carries our genes). When this DNA is injected into plants and animals, they begin to show the required traits. For example, you might have heard of BtCrops in the news. These are crops that have been modified in the lab to carry a gene that originally belongs to the bacterium *Bacillus thuringiensis* (Bt). This gene makes the plants create a protein that is toxic to insects if they eat them, but not to humans.

◀ *The idea behind genetically modified (GM) cotton is to reduce the destruction caused by the cotton weevil, and thus reduce pesticide use*

 ## Plasmids

Bacteria have small, circular molecules of DNA called plasmids. Most of the research in genetic engineering has been carried out in plasmids. Geneticists cut plasmids with a special kind of enzyme called restriction endonuclease, add new DNA to it, and stitch up the DNA using another enzyme called a DNA ligase. The plasmid is put back into bacteria and it multiplies inside them to make many copies. This way, plasmids can be modified to carry genes for human proteins.

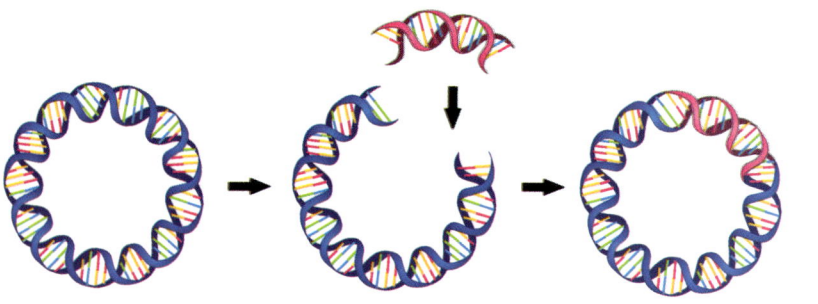

▲ *Plasmids are used to make bacteria produce biological chemicals needed by humans, like insulin*

 ## Human Genetic Engineering

You may have heard of the phrase '**designer baby**'. This is the idea that humans can genetically engineer their own cells to eliminate defective genes, or modify the genome to create 'superhumans'. Thus, babies born from such cells will have been 'designed'. However, some people fear that this could be misused to create a race of slaves or 'robotised' humans.

Isn't It Amazing!

Some diabetes patients have to take regular **insulin** injections to live normally, as their body cannot make enough insulin. Getting enough insulin from human donors would be impossible. So most injectable insulin made today comes from GM bacteria that carry the gene for human insulin in a plasmid.

▶ *Artificial insulin made by genetically engineered bacteria*

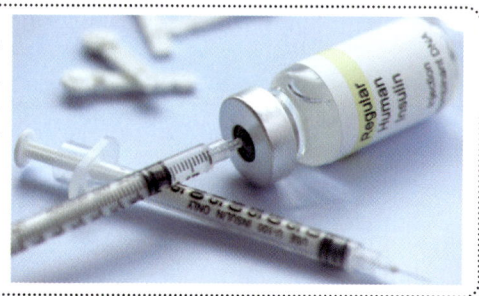

SCIENCE | FUTURE SCIENCE & TECHNOLOGY | 131

Gene Editing

This exciting new technology may help us fight cancer and other genetic diseases. Instead of using stem cells, the DNA of the defective cells can be 'edited' using an enzyme called Cas9. This enzyme recognises a kind of DNA sequence called CRISPR (Clustered Regularly Interspaced Short Palindromic Repeats). It is guided into the defective gene by a molecule called a guide RNA, whose sequence is complementary to the defective gene. The Cas9 then cuts out the CRISPR on either side of the 'bad' DNA. It carries with it a spare piece of 'good' DNA that is then stuck in place of the bad DNA. These systems have reduced the price, time, and complexity of genetic engineering.

Scientists are trying to develop injectable solutions so that every defective cell of an organ can have its DNA repaired.

▼ The double helix structure of DNA is common to all living organisms. It makes it possible to make new DNA from old

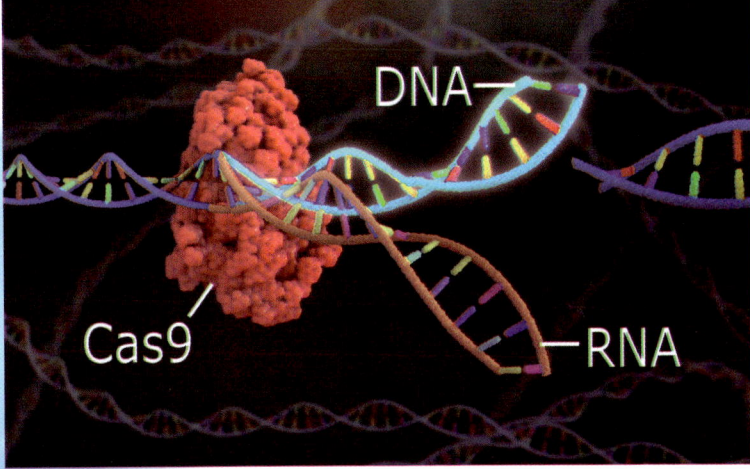

▲ How gene editing works

Incredible Individuals

In the early days of genetics, scientists did not understand that DNA could recombine at specific places. In the 1940s, Barbara McClintock (1902–92), while studying the genetics of maize, discovered that genes 'jumping' from one place to another could only explain certain changes in maize from one generation to another. This would be one of the first steps towards genetic engineering. Sadly, her work was ignored for many decades.

▲ In 1983, Barbara McClintock became the first woman to win the Nobel Prize for Medicine or Physiology solo

Photons

Sunrise: when a tiny bit of Earth comes face to face with the Sun, as our planet rotates. Birds begin to chirp, and alarms begin to go off in our homes. Everything is filled with light and a new day begins. But did you ever wonder what light really is? How does it travel so fast? How does it get to be all around us? And why are we so helpless without it?

For a very long time, people believed that light was an element of the Universe because all the light they had came from fire of some sort. For example, they saw the Sun, which gives us light during the day, as a great fireball, while the light they received at night came from lamps or logs of burning wood. Over time, scientists did experiments and theorised that light was some form of wave, that moved through an invisible substance (called ether) in space, just as waves move on the surface of the sea. Later, various experiments highlighted that light is actually made of tiny particles. These particles are called photons and have no weight at all, but have energy that can be measured. Today, several scientists believe that light is both a wave and a particle at the same time. This is called wave-particle duality.

◀ *Nuclear fusion reactions deep inside stars are the source of all the photons in our Universe*

The Speed of Light

The speed of photons travelling in a vacuum is 299,792 kilometres per second. As photons are massless, nothing heavier can travel faster than them. However, light does slow down when it enters a gas, liquid, or solid, where it interacts with the electrons of the material. The speed of light is 225,000 kilometres per second in water and 200,000 kilometres per second in glass.

Incredible Individuals

At college, Max Planck wanted to choose physics, but his professor told him that it would be futile as all the major discoveries had been made. Planck went on to study physics anyway, and ended up changing it forever with the quantum theory.

▲ *We can see objects because particles of light called 'photons' are reflected off them and enter our eyes, where they are captured by special 'vision' cells*

Quantum Theory

In 1900, the German scientist Max Planck suggested that all energy existed in fixed units called quanta. The more quanta of energy a substance has, the more energy it possesses, either as electricity, heat, light, or magnetism. For example, each quantum of electrical energy is called an electron. The more electrons a wire has, the more current it carries.

For his theory, Planck won the Nobel Prize in Physics in 1918. But what about other forms of energy such as light? In 1905, the Swiss scientist Albert Einstein suggested that light, too, is made of tiny quanta (now called photons). The more photons in a beam of light, the brighter it is. He theorised that not just energy, but even radiation itself was **quantised** in the same way.

Today, an entire field of physics called quantum theory studies how quanta of various kinds of energy behave, particularly photons. But not all photons are the same, for their energy depends on their frequency.

▲ Our modern understanding of light comes from Albert Einstein (second from left) and Max Planck (centre)

Wavelength and Frequency

Each photon 'oscillates' a number of times per second, even as it is moving forward in a beam of light. That means it travels some distance towards the left, returns to the centre, and then moves an equal distance to the right before coming back again to the centre and starting all over again. Imagine a ball tied on a string swinging sideways while you are walking forward. This vibration is called its frequency.

The frequency decides its **wavelength**, that is, the length it will travel forward for the duration of one complete vibration. The higher the frequency, the more energy the photon has, but its wavelength is shorter.

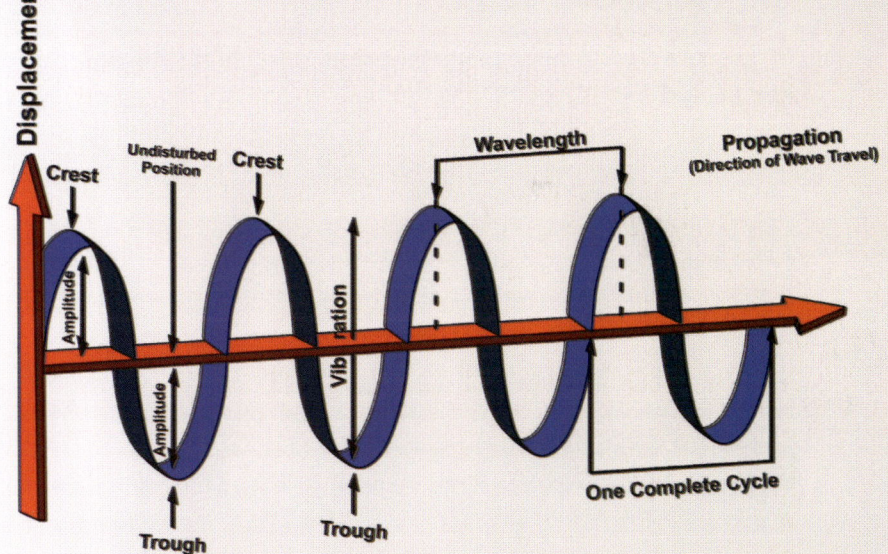
▲ Photons move as waves with a wavelength that decreases with energy

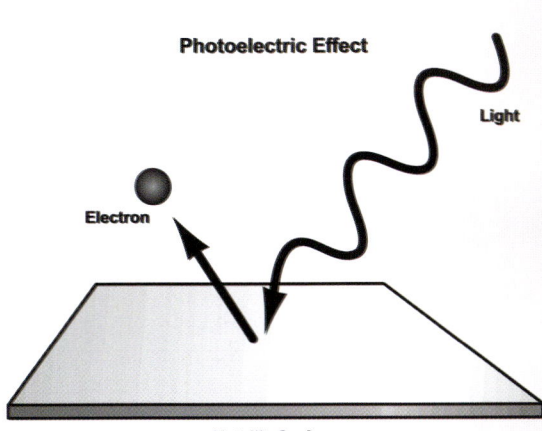
The photoelectric effect is the emission of electrons or other free carriers when light is shone onto a material

▲ The photoelectric effect led to the discovery that light is made of photons

Photoelectric Effect

Many physicists knew that some materials, such as rubidium and caesium, discharge electrons when exposed to light, though they did not know why it happens. This is called the photoelectric effect. In 1905, Albert Einstein suggested that it could be possible only if light was made of something similar to electrons, but without an **electric charge**. He proposed that light is made up of photons, which are packets of energy. This theory not only solved the mystery of the photoelectric effect, but also won Einstein the Noble Prize in 1921.

Electromagnetism

Did you know that light is only one kind of wave? It belongs to a whole class of energy particles known as the electromagnetic (EM) spectrum. This contains all kinds of waves; from those whose wavelengths are in thousands of metres to those whose wavelengths are one-quadrillionth of a metre.

Electromagnetism happens when an electric charge moves through space, creating a magnetic field at right angles to it. This phenomenon was discovered by Michael Faraday and James Clerk Maxwell. When a charged particle moves as a wave, it sets up a waving magnetic field at a right angle to it. As a result, light was also seen to be an electromagnetic wave. Following this, Planck and Einstein established that the unit of electromagnetism was a photon.

▲ Electromagnetic waves are made of two distinct fields, electric and magnetic.

Visible Light

In quantum theory, the photon is a unit of **electromagnetic energy**, and not just light. The photons that we can see with our naked eyes are called visible light. Their wavelengths range from 380 to 750 nanometres (a nanometre is one-billionth of a metre).

Why can we see these photons? Actually, we cannot see the photons themselves, but we can see the object from where these photons originate. Our eyes have special rod cells and cone cells that are sensitive to different wavelengths of light. Each of these cells respond to a certain wavelength of light that hits it. When light falls on these cells, a tiny current passes from the cell to the optical nerve. The nerve collects the information from each cell and passes it to the brain, creating a picture in your head. The brain converts each wavelength of light into a different '**colour**'. This is what you 'see'. In reality, light has no natural colour. All these colours are the same in everyone's head, so all of us can agree that the sky is blue and the Moon is white.

In Real Life

Some people lack some kinds of cells in their eyes, or have other genetic trouble, because of which they cannot see colour or differences in colour. Doctors call this **colour blindness**.

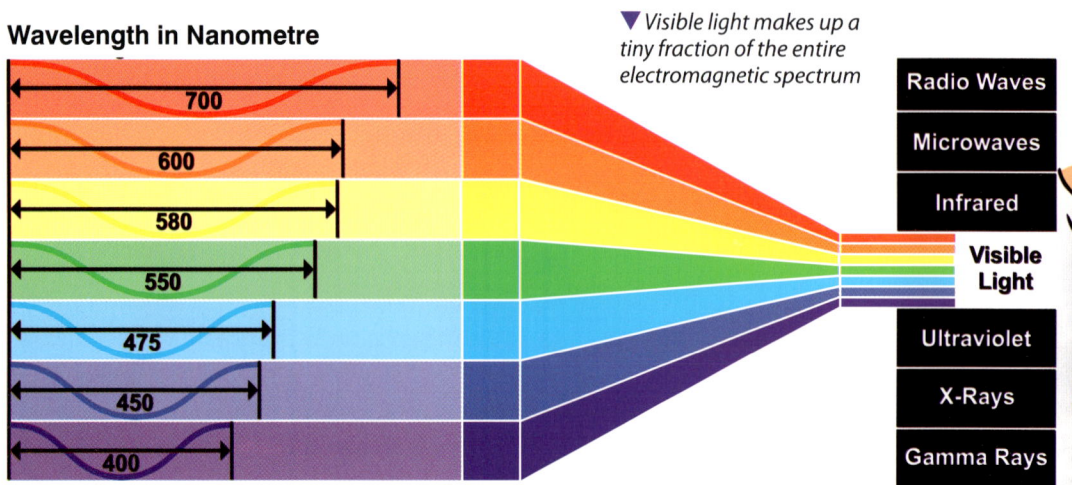

▼ Visible light makes up a tiny fraction of the entire electromagnetic spectrum

SCIENCE | LIGHT AND ENERGY

◀ A magnetic scrap lifter

🔍 Other Waves

Our eyes cannot see most of the electromagnetic waves that exist in the Universe. But we can detect them in other ways, usually using a radio antenna or other specially made **detectors**. The photons whose wavelength is smaller than visible light make up ultraviolet (UV) light. Honeybees have cone cells, which they use to see UV photons. Photons with wavelengths smaller than UV rays are called **X-rays**, and those with even smaller wavelengths are called **gamma rays**. These photons have a lot of energy in them. When they hit an atom, they can remove electrons from it and turn it into a positively charged ion. Therefore, together they are called **ionising radiation**.

Waves with lengths higher than visible light are called **infrared (IR) waves**. They are used in night vision glasses. Waves with longer wavelengths than IR waves are **radio waves**. They don't have enough energy to remove electrons from atoms, so they are called **non-ionising radiation**.

💡 Isn't It Amazing!

Ozone (triatomic oxygen or O_3) is a molecule that can absorb most ultraviolet radiation. It forms a covering above our atmosphere called the ozone layer, and stops UV rays from reaching us.

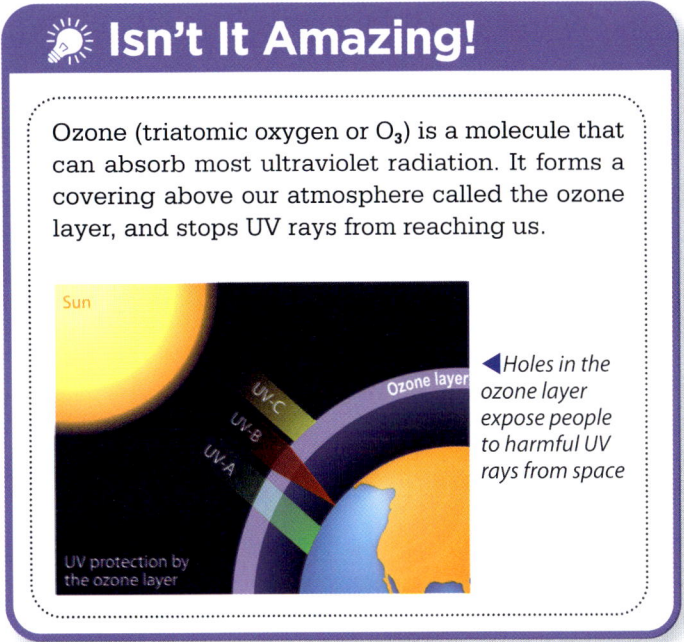

◀ Holes in the ozone layer expose people to harmful UV rays from space

Electromagnetic Spectrum

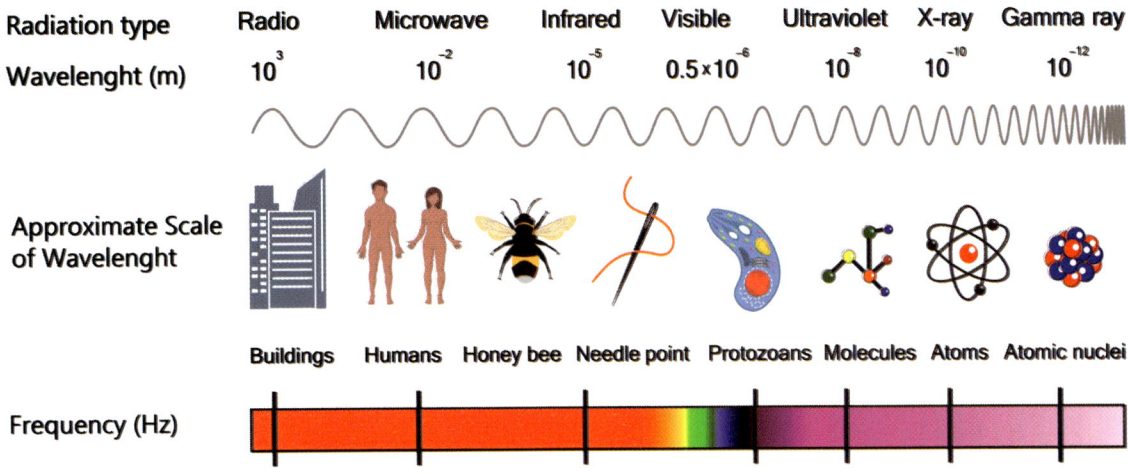

▲ Photons with shorter wavelengths than visible light have higher energy, and those with longer wavelengths have lesser energy

Energy

There are two laws that govern energy existing in the Universe. One of them, the Law of Conservation of Energy, says that energy can neither be destroyed nor created but can only be converted from one form to another. The other is the Law of Relativity, discovered by Albert Einstein, which dictates that energy can be converted into matter (and matter into energy). This is what happens deep inside the Sun, where four hydrogen atoms merge into one atom of helium and some of the matter is turned into energy in the form of photons of very high frequency. Scientists call this nuclear fusion.

Types of Energy

The Sun is the source of all the energy on our planet. Some of it is direct, like the light and heat that we get in daytime. Most of it is indirect, as we read earlier. But how many forms of energy are there, and how are they converted into each other?

Mechanical: This energy is visible in the movement of objects. We use this to do most of the work we want—from washing clothes in a machine, to running a blender or driving a car. There are two kinds of mechanical energy: kinetic energy that is present in moving things, and potential energy that is stored until needed. Sound is also a form of mechanical energy, which travels in the form of **mechanical waves** in the air.

◀ In a roller coaster, electric energy is converted to potential energy as the cars ride up. When the cars slide down, the potential energy is converted to kinetic energy under the influence of gravity

Gravitational: This energy is stored in the gravitational fields of stars and planets, which makes them move around each other. It is also the energy that is released from objects that are falling to the Earth, such as water in a dam or apple from a tree.

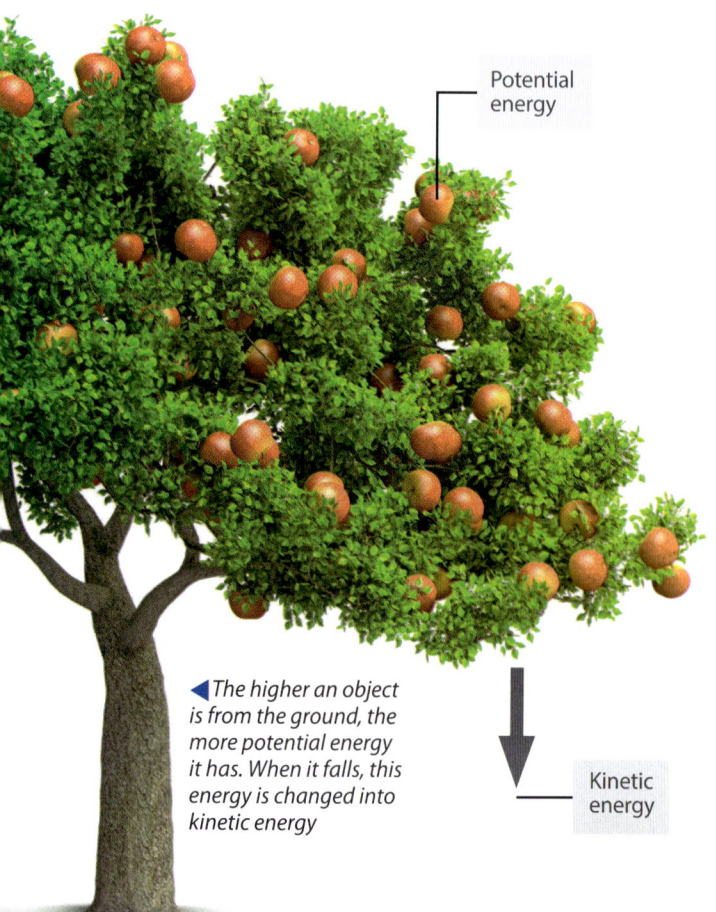

◀ The higher an object is from the ground, the more potential energy it has. When it falls, this energy is changed into kinetic energy

In Real Life

Several power plants convert energy three times to make electricity:
1. From nuclear or chemical energy into **heat energy** to turn water into steam.
2. From heat energy into mechanical energy of a rotating turbine.
3. From mechanical energy into electrical energy by electromagnetism.

▲ A lot of energy is lost to air as it is converted from one form to another in a power plant

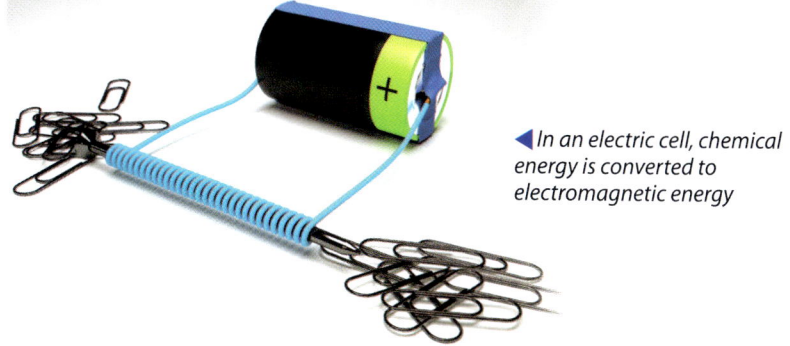

◀ In an electric cell, chemical energy is converted to electromagnetic energy

Electromagnetic: This energy is present in moving electric or magnetic fields, whether in a wire (electricity) or moving through space (radiation).

Thermal (Heat): This energy is stored in the vibrational movement of atoms, so it is really a form of mechanical energy, but at the atomic level. When a material is heated, the atoms vibrate faster and push each other away. This makes the material expand. When the material loses heat, the atoms vibrate less and therefore come closer. This is called contraction.

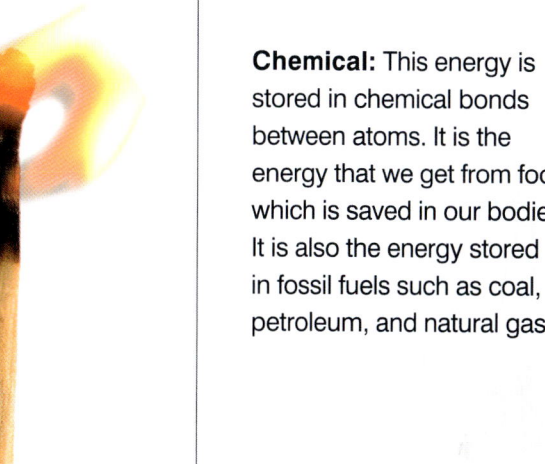

▶ A matchstick converts the chemical energy stored in its head into thermal energy when it is struck

Chemical: This energy is stored in chemical bonds between atoms. It is the energy that we get from food which is saved in our bodies. It is also the energy stored in fossil fuels such as coal, petroleum, and natural gas.

▶ Our muscles convert the chemical energy stored in food into the kinetic energy that we need to walk, run, or swim

Nuclear: This energy exists in the nuclei of atoms. When an atom is split into two in a nuclear reactor, this energy is released.

☀ Isn't It Amazing!

Our Universe is a giant sphere, which is expanding. The galaxies at the edge are accelerating away from each other faster than those at the centre. Explaining this phenomenon, scientists proposed that there might be other forms of energy that we know nothing about. Since we cannot measure them, these forms of energy are called dark energy. Our Universe is made up of 68% of dark energy and about 27% is dark matter.

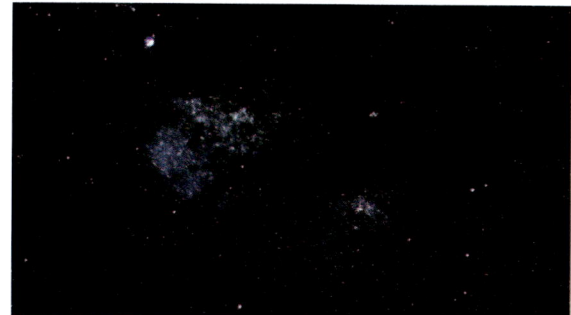

▲ Dark energy might push galaxies away from each other but it does not seem to affect anything on Earth

Optics

Did you know that the person you see in the mirror is not you but a slightly modified version of you? Because the right hand of the person in the mirror is actually your left hand and your right hand is your reflection's left hand; this is called a lateral inversion. But before we race on to that, let us understand something about reflection, refraction, and diffraction, which make up a fascinating field called Optics. This is a field whose scientific history begins with Isaac Newton, though, unlike his study of gravity, there were no apples harmed in the process.

Reflection

We've read earlier that light behaves both as a particle as well as a wave (pages 4–5). Well, if it behaves like a particle, then it should bounce like a ball when it hits a hard surface. That's exactly what happens when light is reflected on a mirror or a shiny surface. Shine is a property of metals that have loose electrons. These electrons keep photons from passing into the metal and reflect them instead. At whatever angle the photons hit the reflector, they travel away from it at the same angle. That's why when you turn a mirror, the reflection seems to move away by an opposite angle.

Absorption

Surfaces that are not very shiny, such as a cotton cloth, garden soil, and so on, will absorb light. Some photons of incoming light give up their energy to the electrons of the material they hit. You know that the energy of a photon depends on its wavelength. Each material absorbs photons of a certain wavelength and reflects the rest. The wavelength of photons reflected gives you the colour of the absorbing object. So, an object is blue if it absorbs photons of all colours but blue (that is, the range of light waves with wavelengths between 450 and 495 nanometres).

▲ *Your mirror switches your sides, so your right hand is the mirror image's left*

▼ *The sea looks blue because it transmits most wavelengths except blue, which it reflects*

Isn't It Amazing!

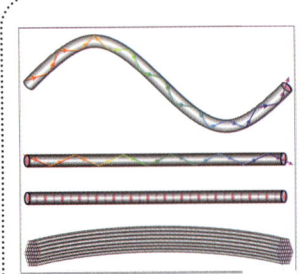

If light enters a tube whose inner surface is mirrored, the light will undergo multiple reflections until it comes out at the other end of the tube. This is called total internal reflection. This is the idea behind optical fibres, which convert computer signals (such as an email you wrote) into light rays of different wavelengths. The signals can travel at the speed of light to reach the destination.

◄ *Total internal reflection in optical fibre cables*

Transmission

Some objects, such as water and glass, neither reflect light nor absorb it. They transmit the light instead and are hence called transparent. Some objects, such as frosted glass, absorb some light and transmit the rest. These are called translucent. Objects that do not transmit any light at all are called opaque.

▼ Water (left) is transparent, while lemonade (right) is translucent

▼ Refraction makes a pencil look out of shape under water

▼ Soap bubbles diffract white light into its many colours

In Real Life

Stellar spectroscopy is the study of the spectra of starlight, that uses a special machine that looks at the wavelengths of lights coming from a star. While the spectrum of any star emits most of the wavelengths of visible light, it shows some black lines, which correspond to the light the star has absorbed (called its absorption spectrum). These lines, called Fraunhofer lines, first observed in 1802, tell you what elements the star is made of.

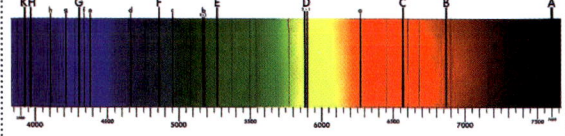

▲ The depth of the lines indicate temperature, and the wavelength shifts point to motion of the composite gases

Refraction

When you get into the bathtub, do you wonder why your body suddenly looks out of shape? Or why things look bigger or smaller when you look through mum's or dad's glasses? That's because water and glass bend light. When light travelling through air enters a denser medium, it loses speed, as the photons encounter resistance from the material's electrons. The speed of light in water is three-fourths its speed in air. This also causes a change in the angle of light which physicists call refraction. Refraction is used to build contact lenses that correct eyesight.

Diffraction

Ever blown soap bubbles and seen rainbow colours when light shines on them? That's because the bubbles diffract light. Diffraction happens when white light (that is light of all wavelengths) is refracted by a medium (like glass or water). As the photons slow down, they travel at different speeds according to their energy, so they bend at different angles. This means that photons of different wavelengths (colours) get separated.

Different crystalline solids will diffract light in different patterns. These patterns of diffraction are used by scientists to figure out the chemical composition of a substance.

Lenses and Prisms

A lens is a block of glass through which light is made to pass. Lenses can be concave or convex. They use the power of refraction to make light either converge at a point (convex lenses) or diverge (concave lenses). A lens affects the view of an object behind it. Convex lenses are used in many instruments to focus light onto a point that needs to be lighted up, as well as in contact lenses and eyeglasses which help long-sighted people see better. In a camera, a **convex lens** shrinks the wide world into a small space. Concave lenses are used in flashlights and projectors to increase the area that can be lighted, and also in spectacles which help short-sighted people see better. In a movie projector, the **concave lens** does the reverse of the camera.

Convex & Concave Lenses

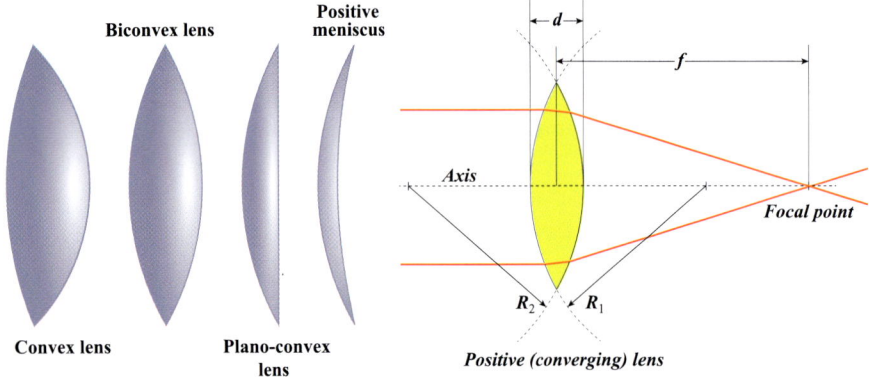

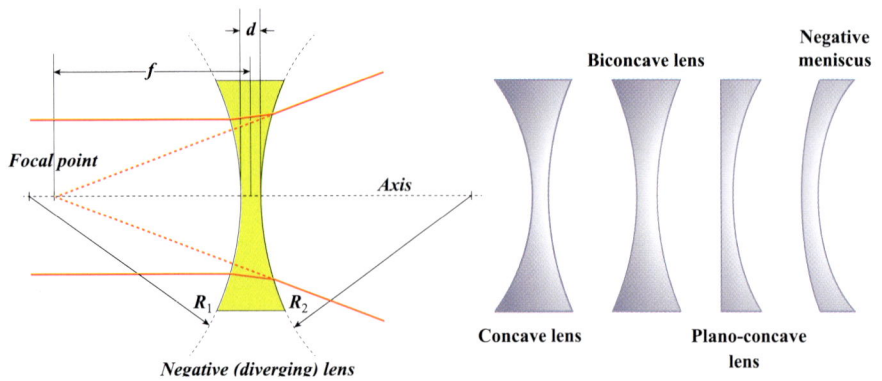

▲ Convex lenses focus light onto a focal point while concave lenses expand the area the light can cover

Isn't It Amazing!

There is a lens in your eye too. It is made of transparent proteins and is known as the crystalline lens. But unlike a glass lens, the thickness of the eye lens can be increased or decreased, allowing you to focus on a faraway object or a near one. In some people, the ability of the lens becomes limited, due to which they need to wear glasses of the correct **power**.

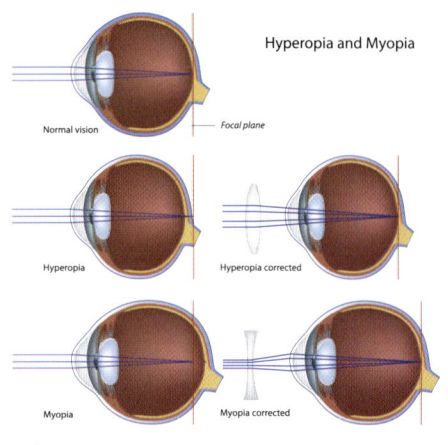

▲ Long-sightedness (far-sightedness or hyperopia) is corrected by convex lenses, while short-sightedness (near-sightedness or myopia) is corrected by concave lenses

Microscopes

The simplest microscope is a magnifying glass. It is a lens that is convex on both sides (**biconvex**), which projects light onto an object. As the light is reflected from the object, it comes back to your eyes in the form of an **image** which looks larger than it actually is. This is called **optical magnification**. If the image appears ten times larger than the object, it is said to be magnified 10 times.

▶ A magnifying glass is also called a simple microscope

In a compound microscope, the idea is taken further by using more than one lens. A condenser lens collects light from outside (either sunlight or an electric light) and focuses it onto the object in the slide. As the light passes through the object, it falls on the first convex lens, which scientists call the 'objective'. This lens focuses the image onto the second lens, called the 'eyepiece'. This adds more magnification before the image reaches your eye. The thickness of the objective lens determines its **optical resolution**. High resolution means that the distance between the two objects the microscope can 'see' as separate ones is really small. Anything below the resolution will appear unclear. If the eyepiece magnification is more than that of the objective, you get empty magnification, that is, the image is larger but not better resolved.

◀ Light from the condenser focused onto the objective lens of a microscope

Prisms

A prism is a device that makes refraction happen twice. The first is when light waves enter from air into the prism, and the photons of different wavelengths separate. The second is when light leaves the prism back into the air, and the photons speed up again but are separated so much that they now exit as separate waves. Prisms are used together with light filters to get a beam of light of a single wavelength. They can also be used to turn a beam of light by an angle. This is the principle used in a submarine's **periscope**.

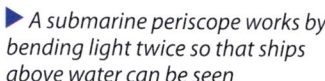
▶ A submarine periscope works by bending light twice so that ships above water can be seen

Heat Transfer

Let's now turn our focus towards heat. Heat is a form of energy that is stored in the movement of atoms and molecules. The hotter they are, the more kinetic energy they have. Because of this, heat can also travel and therefore make other things hot, because it moves from a place of high temperature to a place of lower temperature. If this did not happen, our Universe would be a cold dead place. Here we will look at how heat can be used to do a lot of our work.

▲ *Radiation is the method by which the Sun's heat is transmitted to our planet*

 ## Conduction

Ever wondered why a saucepan is stirred with a wooden spoon while cooking? That's because wood is a poor conductor of heat, that is, heat does not travel along the molecules of wood. On the other hand, it travels fast among the atoms of a metallic spoon, until the spoon becomes as hot as the sauce. This is called conduction of heat.

Metals have atoms arranged in neat rows and columns. When a metal atom gets heated, it begins to vibrate faster, converting heat into kinetic energy. As it vibrates, it crashes into the next atom, transferring some of the energy to it, so the next atom also begins to vibrate. In this way, all the atoms begin to vibrate, and the entire metal spoon becomes hot. Metals are therefore good conductors of heat. On the other hand, the molecules in wood are not arranged in a regular way at all and they all vibrate out of sync with each other. Hence, heat cannot travel in any one direction, and the spoon takes much longer to become hot.

▲ *A wooden ladle helps you stir chocolate while it melts without burning your hand*

💡 Isn't It Amazing!

What happens if you put a flask with a shiny outer surface into one with a shiny inner surface and create a vacuum between them? There can be no heat transfer by conduction or convection, and the surfaces reflect the light, so radiation is also ruled out. This is the principle of the vacuum flask, which was invented by James Dewar.

Convection

Shell some peas and boil them in a saucepan. Do you notice that they bounce up and down as the water heats up? This is because of a form of heat transfer called convection, which occurs in liquids and gases. When water molecules are heated by the gas or electric coil at the bottom of the pan, they begin to move around faster and rise to the top. They push the colder water to the bottom, which then gets heated and moves up. This sets up a round motion in the water called a **convection current**. Convection currents allow for uniform heating and cooking of food in a pan or a steamer.

▲ Convection currents in a boiler make peas jump up and fall down

Radiation

Radiation transfers heat even in a vacuum through photons whose energy is very high. In an electric radiator, which is used in many homes to heat rooms during winter, the electrons moving through the machine collide with the atoms it is made of, making them eject photons. These photons hit the molecules in the air and heat them, thus heating the room. Radiation is also how the Earth receives heat from the Sun.

▼ The three different kinds of heat transfer

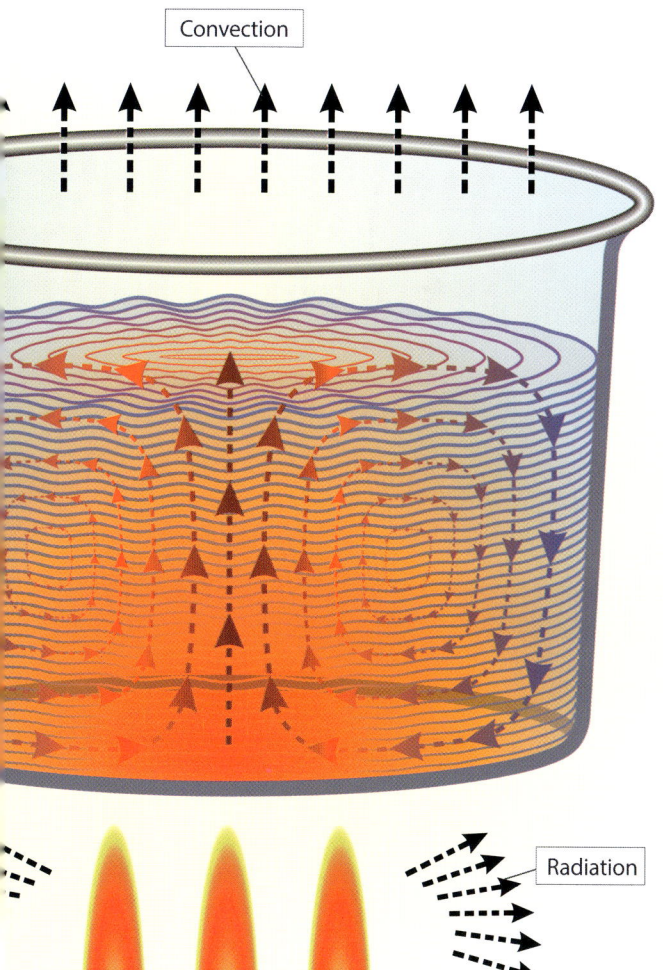

▲ Radiators heat rooms in winters by converting electricity into electromagnetic waves

SPACE

Throughout history, the vastness and magnificence of the night sky has captivated humanity's imagination and led to a deep yearning to unravel its mysteries. The universe is awe-inspiring, with its galaxies, comets, and shooting stars all begging for explanation and further exploration.

One of the most captivating celestial entities is the star—these luminous bodies of gas have been admired by civilizations since ancient times. However, despite their long-standing fascination, the truth remains elusive. How many stars are there in the universe? Are they evenly distributed, or clustered together in galaxies? Exactly how far are these marvelous points of light from us? Through the study of stars, astronomers seek to uncover not only the secrets of our universe but also the mysteries surrounding the very existence of life itself.

The field of astronomy, one of the oldest sciences, has been explored and expanded over time. Ancient civilizations, including the Babylonians, marveled at the stars and set forth an astronomical foundation that has been built upon ever since. Greek philosophers like Pythagoras and Ptolemy examined the mysteries of the skies, contributing greatly to our understanding of the cosmos. The advent of the telescope in the 17th century transformed the field and launched an era of groundbreaking discoveries.

Today, astronomy continues to push forward the limits of our understanding. By incorporating advancements in science and technology, we continue to unravel the mysteries of the universe, from our place within the solar system to the furthest reaches of outer space. From mapping new planets to detecting gravitational waves, the insights we gain from studying the cosmos have widened our scientific knowledge and expanded our imaginations.

The insatiable human desire for exploration and knowledge has inspired our greatest discoveries, and space exploration has only furthered our understanding. Since the invention of the telescope over four centuries ago, our advancements in technology have given us unprecedented opportunities to explore and examine the cosmos. As our observations and knowledge continue to grow, we are increasingly awed by the expansive, ever-changing tapestry of celestial phenomena before us.

▼ *Stargazing—an act of observing the stars in the night sky, with or without a telescope.*

Creation of the Universe

Our universe is about 13.8 billion years old. Everything that exists in time and space—including all objects, energy, over hundred billion galaxies containing hundreds of billions of stars, the solar system, the planets, etc., are all part of what we call the universe. The universe is so vast that it really cannot be measured. We can only imagine how big it is by understanding that some celestial objects are so very far away in the universe that light travelling from them takes billions of years to reach Earth!

What is the Big Bang Model?

The Big Bang model is a theory about how the universe was formed and how it evolved. In fact, among the many theories on this subject, the Big Bang is the most popular. The essence of this theory is that the universe emerged from a state of very high temperature and density. This caused a violent collision on an extremely large scale, which is why the model is called the Big Bang. The theory was based on the observation that several other galaxies were moving away from the Milky Way galaxy in different directions and there seemed to be an ancient force responsible for this. Scientists estimate that the Big Bang happened nearly 13.8 billion years ago when the universe came into being.

Who thought of the Big Bang Model?

In 1927, a Belgian priest and astronomer, Georges Lemaître made a very important discovery—he independently proposed that the universe is expanding. In 1922, Russian mathematician Aleksandr Friedmann had also arrived at this conclusion. Lemaître claimed that the universe began as a single point, that is, it had a finite beginning. It later expanded into its current vastness. He also said that it could keep growing. His formulation of the modern Big Bang theory was based on the work of Albert Einstein. Two years later, American astronomer Edwin Hubble confirmed Lemaître's theory that the universe was, in fact, expanding. He observed that galaxies were moving away from Earth and that the galaxies that were farther away were moving at a faster rate than those nearby. This meant that if things were moving away from each other, then perhaps a long time ago they existed close to each other.

▲ The moon crater 'Fridman' is named after Aleksandr Friedmann

▲ Georges Lemaître also had a namesake in the lunar crater 'Lemaître'

 The Theory

According to the Big Bang Theory, the universe started off as a hot and extremely dense point, about a few millimetres wide. Approximately 13.8 billion years ago, this tiny point (or **singularity**) exploded in a violent bang from which all of matter, energy, space, and time were created.

Different theories state that immediately after the Big Bang, there probably was a colossal sea of protons, electrons, neutrons, and other particles. With time, the universe continued to cool, resulting in the decay and recombination of various particles. Protons and electrons may have combined to form neutral hydrogen. The universe may have been opaque before the recombination, due to the scattering of light by the free electrons. Once neutral **atoms** were formed, it became transparent. The atoms joined together and after a very long time formed stars and galaxies. The initial few stars were responsible for creating bigger atoms and also for groups of atoms known as **molecules**. This led to the birth of several more stars. Simultaneously, galaxies were banging against each other and coming together. During this process of formation and dying of stars, things like asteroids, comets, planets, and black holes were created.

▼ The universe is a vast unending expanse of celestial matter and objects

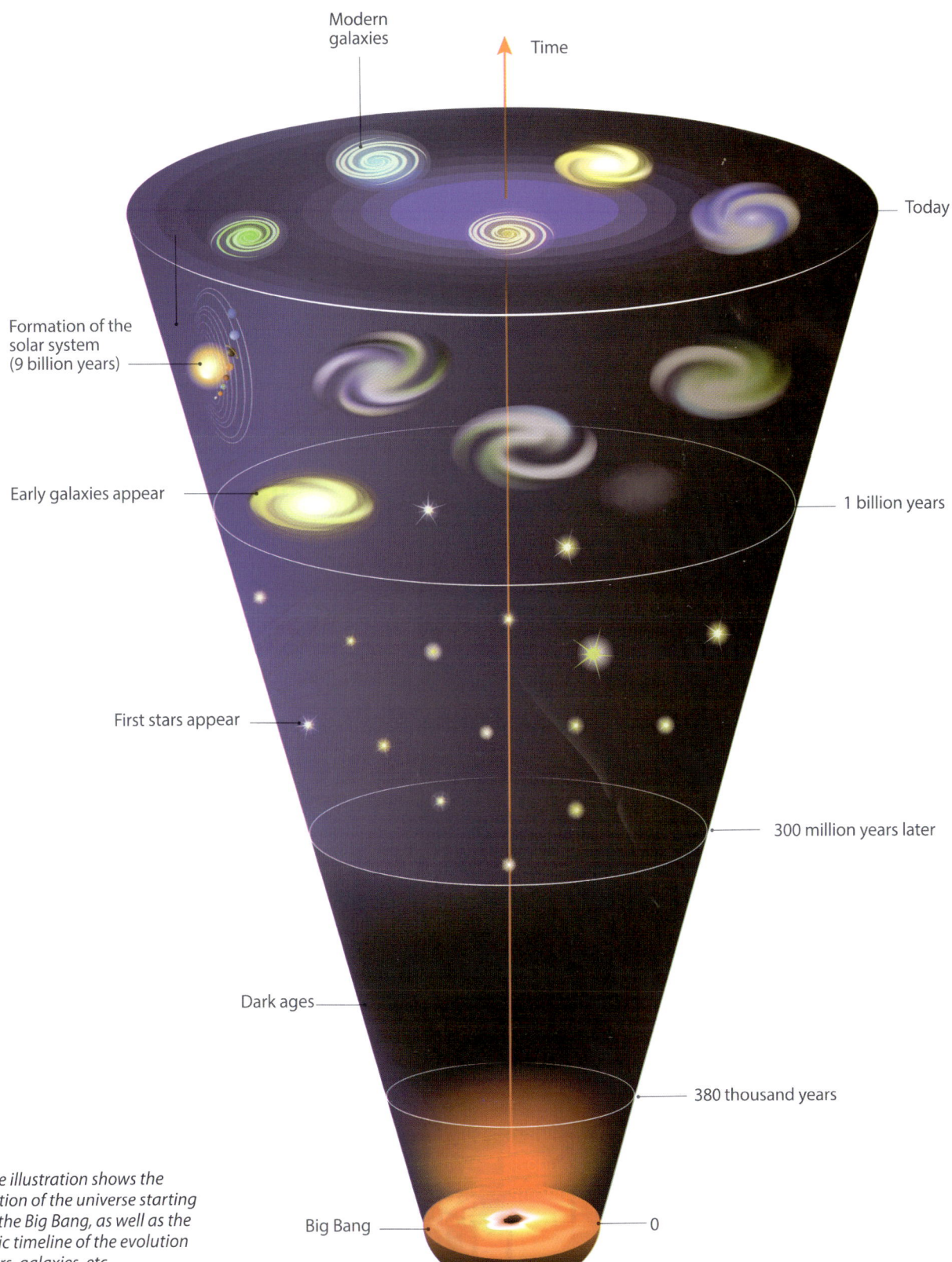

▶ The illustration shows the evolution of the universe starting from the Big Bang, as well as the cosmic timeline of the evolution of stars, galaxies, etc.

⭐ Incredible Individuals

While Friedmann (1888–1925) and Hubble (1889–1953) proposed the Big Bang theory, it was George Gamow (1904–1968) who took up the task of coming up with a practicable model for this theory. Though Friedmann's theory was brilliant, it was not known by many. Those who had heard it did not believe it. But Gamow and his doctoral student Ralph Alpher (1921–2007) had faith in the theory. At the time, Ralph Alpher was a mathematics student who was working on describing how the universe evolved. Furthermore, the CMB radiation was first noticed accidentally, in 1965, by Arno Penzias (1933–present) and Robert Wilson (1936–present) at the Bell Telephone Laboratories in New Jersey, USA. So, the Big Bang model was the brainchild of several people.

All about Galaxies

Galaxies are home to stars and other celestial objects. It was only in the early 20th century that the existence of galaxies other than the Milky Way was recognised. Before that, early astronomers labelled them as nebulas, since they appeared to look like hazy clouds. Galaxies are present in every part of space, as observed through powerful telescopes. They differ in shape, structure, and the level of activity within them.

What is a Galaxy?

A galaxy comprises a large group of hundreds of billions of stars and **interstellar** matter (gas and dust) bound together by gravity. Almost all the large galaxies are also believed to have gigantic black holes at their centres. Galaxies exist in a variety of shapes and sizes ranging from dim dwarf-sized objects to bright, massive, spiral-shaped ones. Almost all galaxies seem to have been formed immediately after the universe came into existence. These beautiful formations are generally found in clusters, some of which form a larger cluster and span hundreds of millions of **light years** across the universe. A light year is the distance travelled by light in one year, at a speed of 3,00,000 km/s.

Types of Galaxies

There are three main classifications of galaxies—elliptical, spiral, and irregular, as seen in the diagram. Some spiral galaxies are called 'barred spirals'.

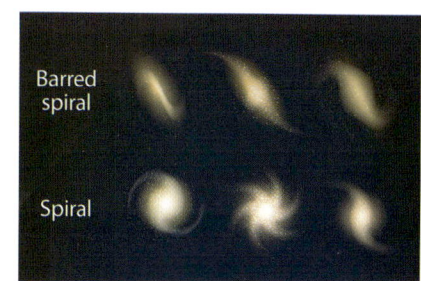
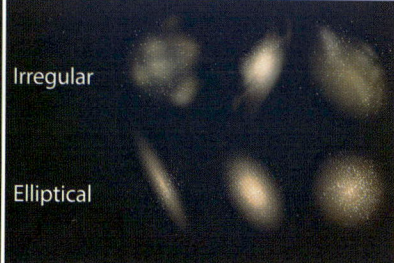

▶ Types of galaxies, The Milky Way is a large barred spiral galaxy.

Elliptical Galaxies

These galaxies are round, oval, or more like an elongated sphere. Sometimes, they may be so stretched that they look like a cigar. These galaxies generally contain many old stars, but not much dust and other interstellar matter. Like the stars in the discs of spiral galaxies, their stars also orbit around the galactic centre, but in a more disorderly way. Not many stars have been known to have formed in elliptical galaxies. The largest known galaxies in the universe are giant elliptical ones which can be as big as two million light years long. The smaller of these galaxies are known as dwarf elliptical galaxies. Virgo A (or M87) is an example of a giant elliptical galaxy found close to the centre of the Virgo cluster of galaxies.

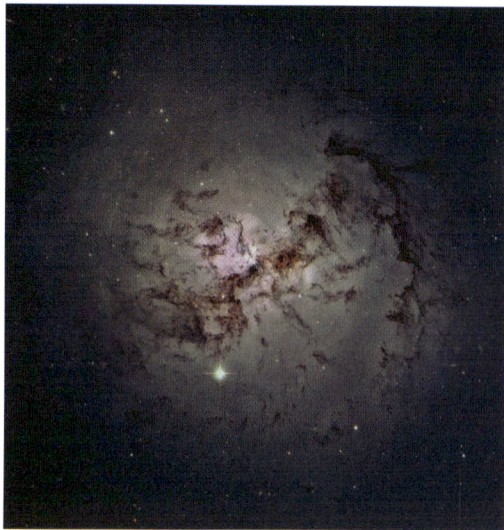

▲ Seen here are the dust lanes and star clusters of the NGC 1316 giant elliptical galaxy in the Fornax constellation

▲ The Messier 59 is an elliptical galaxy. It is also one of the largest elliptical galaxies in the Virgo galaxy cluster

Spiral Galaxies

Spiral galaxies comprise a flat disc with a bulging centre. These galaxies have long spiral arms that wind towards the centre. The disc comprises stars, planets, dust, and gas, which rotate or spin around the galactic centre in a regular manner, at hundreds of kilometres per second. This spinning motion may result in the matter in the disc taking the shape of a spiral, like a pinwheel.

While many new stars are born in spiral galaxies, the older stars are generally located in the bulging centre of the galactic disc. These discs have a halo around them and astronomers believe that they comprise unknown dark matter.

One type of spiral galaxy is known as 'barred spirals' since the bulge at the centre looks stretched like a bar and the spiral arms come out from the ends of the bar. The Milky Way is a large barred spiral galaxy and is home to our solar system. It is one from a group of galaxies known as the Local Group.

◀ An infrared picture of M74—a spiral galaxy—as seen by NASA's Spitzer Infrared Array Camera

▶ A barred spiral galaxy—NGC 1672 in the constellation of Dorado

Irregular Galaxies

Galaxies which do not have any distinct shape, such as spiral, elliptical, or lenticular (resembling lenses), are irregular galaxies. Irregular galaxies—such as the Large and Small Magellanic Clouds—are uneven or out of shape as they are generally under the gravitational influence of other nearby galaxies. Since they are packed with lots of gas and dust, irregular galaxies are a fertile ground for the formation of new stars.

◀ An image of an irregular galaxy—NGC 1427A

In Real Life

One of the most important things needed to support and sustain life on Earth and in the universe is water. Water in its solid state (ice), exists in abundance in the universe and is found in interstellar dust clouds as well as in the orangish-red fields of Mars. However, that by itself is not enough to support life. Water, in its liquid state, acts as a crucial lubricant for the molecular or chemical processes for all forms of life such as human beings, plants, and animals. Hence, astronomers always look for signs of water in its liquid state in the universe to see if alien life exists elsewhere.

Incredible Individuals

In 1950, Arthur Allen Hoag (1921–1999), an American astronomer, discovered one of the rarest kinds of galaxies, a type of ring galaxy consisting of a symmetrical central core made up of older stars, surrounded by a bright ring of young blue stars with no apparent connection between the two. It came to be known as the Hoag's Object. These rare galaxies comprise less than 0.1 per cent of all observed galaxies in the universe.

Amazing Celestial Oddities
Black Holes and Auroras

The mysteries of the universe are unending. Here are two more that are mindboggling; one is the blackest object to be found in deep space, and the other is a celebratory vibrant show of lights seen on Earth!

What are Black Holes?

What can be darker than space itself? Well the darkest objects to be found in the depths of our universe are also some of the weirdest and strangest things—black holes! A black hole is an area with such tremendous gravity or pull that nothing—not even light—can escape from it. Usually, black holes are formed when a star dies. When the fuel in a star gets depleted or finished, it starts to disintegrate and cave in on itself, resulting in a huge bang. All the matter remaining after the explosion—which is much, much more than the mass of the Sun—falls into a really tiny point. This point where a large amount of mass is trapped is called a singularity. It has a huge impact even though it is small.

A black hole's 'surface' is known as its event horizon that defines the boundary where the velocity needed to escape the hole exceeds the speed of light.

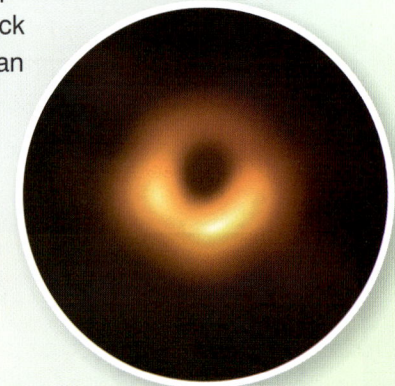
▲ The first-ever image of a supermassive black hole and its shadow in the centre of Messier 87. It was captured by the Event Horizon Telescope (EHT)—an international collaboration of radio telescopes

The Aura of Auroras

If you are lucky enough to find yourself near the North Pole or the South Pole, you may want to check out the amazing and exquisite light shows in the sky. These lights are known as auroras. The lights near the North Pole are called Aurora Borealis or the Northern Lights and the ones near the South Pole are referred to as Aurora Australis or the Southern Lights.

What Causes Auroras?

Auroras are mostly seen during the night, but they are effects created by the Sun. Besides heat and light, the Sun is responsible for sending us small particles and a lot of other energy.

Auroras are caused by charged particles that travel between the Sun and Earth along magnetic fields.

Sometimes, due to **solar winds** and storms, the amount of energy sent by the Sun varies. During one particular type of solar storm, called a coronal mass ejection, the Sun ejects a large bubble of electrified gas which can travel at great speeds through space. When a solar storm like this approaches us on Earth, the energy and small particles move down into Earth's atmosphere along the magnetic field lines at the North Pole and South Pole.

When the particles reach Earth's atmosphere, they engage with the gases in it, and this results in amazing displays of bright lights in the sky.

▲ The Northern Lights during winter in Tromso, Norway, in front of a *fjord*

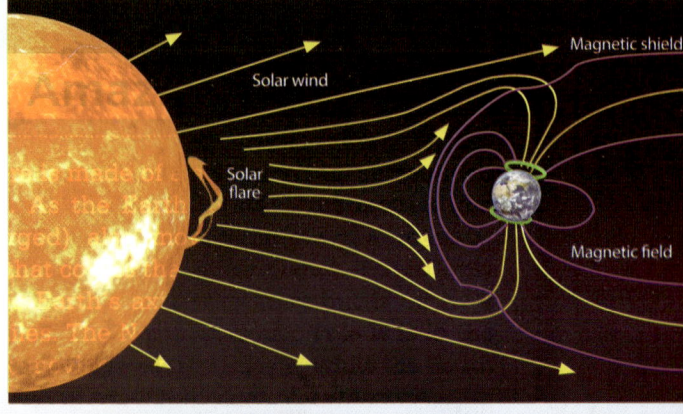
▲ Auroras are named after the Roman goddess of dawn, who traveled from east to west, announcing the coming of the Sun

Amazing Asteroids

Besides the planets, the Moon, and the stars, there are several smaller celestial objects in space called 'small bodies'. These include asteroids, meteoroids, and comets.

 ## What is an Asteroid?

An asteroid is a small, rock-like object which orbits the Sun, just like planets. But unlike planets, asteroids are much smaller. They are sometimes called minor planets.

A majority of the several hundred thousand asteroids in our solar system are found in the asteroid belt. It is a flat ring-like region between Mars and Jupiter. Some asteroids are also found in the orbital path of planets like Earth.

Where did Asteroids Originate From?

Asteroids are leftover pieces from the time when the solar system was formed around 4.6 billion years ago! The solar system began with the collapse of a huge cloud of gas and dust, which condensed to form the Sun, planets and their moons. Asteroids are the remains in the asteroid belt that never made it to the Sun, nor could they transform into planets or any other celestial bodies.

 ## Are all Asteroids Identical?

Asteroids are different from each other and were created in different places and at different distances from the Sun. Most have a sharp and uneven shape. Some asteroids are hundreds of kilometres in diameter, but many are the size of a small stone. Asteroids are made up of various types of rock, clay or metal, like nickel and iron. They provide important information regarding our planets and the Sun.

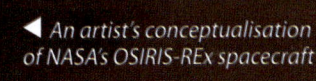

◀ An artist's conceptualisation of NASA's OSIRIS-REx spacecraft

In Real Life

Many space missions have been sent by NASA to observe asteroids.

1998: The NEAR Shoemaker spacecraft went to Eros, an asteroid near Earth.

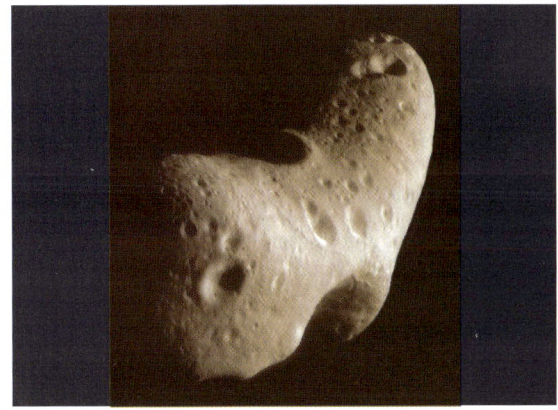

▲ The Eros asteroid was named after the god of love from Greek mythology.

2011: The second-largest object in the asteroid belt—Vesta, a small planet, was orbited and studied by the Dawn spacecraft.

◀ Vesta was named after the virgin goddess of home and hearth from the Roman mythology

2012: Nasa's Dawn space probe orbited and studied the dwarf planet Ceres, the largest object in the asteroid belt.

▶ Ceres was the first asteroid to be discovered in 1801

2016: The OSIRIS-REx spacecraft was launched by NASA to study Bennu, which is an asteroid near Earth. The objective was also to bring a sample of it back to our planet for study.

Meteoroids, Meteors, & Meteorites

Meteoroids, meteors, and meteorites are all related to the 'shooting stars' we sometimes see streaking across the night sky. We call the same celestial objects by different names, depending on where they are.

⭐ What are Meteoroids and Meteors?

When one asteroid bangs into another, it may break into pieces. These pieces are called meteoroids. A meteoroid is a small rocky or metallic natural object that enters Earth's atmosphere. When a meteoroid falls to Earth with great speed, there is a resistance (or drag) of the air on the rock, which heats it up.

As it falls and comes closer to Earth and passes through our atmosphere, it starts to vaporise (becomes gaseous), and a streak of light is seen, which is the hot air left behind by the burning piece of rock. This is a meteor, a streak of light in the sky. Meteors are not really stars, but due to their appearance and streaks of light, they are also known as 'shooting stars'! Meteors are sometimes confused with comets due to the light they both seem to emit. However, Comets are made of ice and dust, not rock.

⭐ Meteorites

Most meteoroids get vaporised by the time they enter Earth's atmosphere, however, some of these rocks do not disintegrate. Instead, they reach the surface of Earth and are known as meteorites. Most meteorites are the size of a small pebble, but some rare ones can also be the size of a large boulder. Since meteorites originate from asteroids, they are useful to scientists, who can gain more information about these ancient rock-like objects.

◀ The image shows the difference between asteroids, meteoroids, meteors, and meteorites

👤 In Real Life

The Hoba is the largest meteorite found on Earth. Found in 1920 in Namibia, Africa, it weighs approximately 53,977 kg! It is an ataxite, an iron meteorite which contains more than 16 per cent nickel.

▼ The Hoba fell to Earth less than 80,000 years ago and has never been moved

SPACE | OUR UNIVERSE

▲ Meteor showers occur when Earth passes through a trail of debris left by a comet or an asteroid.

⭐ It's Raining Meteors!

When many meteors fall to Earth at the same time, they are referred to as a meteor shower. Meteors fall at a speed which is 32 times faster than that of a speeding bullet!

A meteor shower is generally named after the constellation from which it appears to be coming. Scientists have estimated that there are nearly 21 meteor showers that occur annually. Listed below are some of the major meteor showers, their constellations, and the months when they can be viewed.

Quadrantids (originally Quadrans Muralis, now Bootes constellation): December/January

Lyrids (Lyra constellation): April

Perseids (Perseus constellation): August

Orionids (Orion constellation): October

Leonids (Lyra constellation): November

Geminids (Gemini constellation): December

💡 Isn't It Amazing!

More than 45,000 kg of space debris falls on Earth every day. Meteors enter Earth's atmosphere at unbelievably high speeds ranging from over 40,000 km per hour to 2,57,495 km per hour.

In the year 1908, an object as large as a residential building fell from the sky and exploded in the air above Siberia. Known as the Tunguska event, named after a river, this object razed trees in an area spanning nearly 2,072 square kilometres. Luckily, no human being or creature was killed or hurt, but it is one of the most significant events of this kind to ever be recorded in human history. Scientists are not sure of the object's origins and whether it was a comet or an asteroid.

▲ No impact crater was found at the explosion site of the Tunguska event.

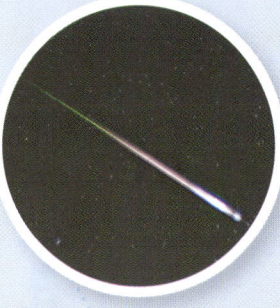
▶ An image of a meteor during the 2009 Leonid meteor shower

Satellites: Natural and Artificial

We are all familiar with the word 'satellite' and we know that there are both natural and artificial satellites. Natural satellites, like Earth's Moon, are not created by people, unlike artificial satellites. Natural satellites can exist in a variety of shapes, sizes, and types. They are generally solid bodies and very few of them have atmospheres. They were most probably created from the gas and dust moving around planets in the early days of the solar system. Artificial satellites, on the other hand, are made by human beings and have some specific uses.

What is a Satellite?

A moon, planet, or a machine that orbits a planet or star is known as a satellite. Our Earth orbits the Sun and the Moon orbits Earth, hence both are examples of natural satellites.

The word 'satellite' is more commonly used to refer to machines that are launched into space and move around Earth or any other celestial body in space. These are man-made or artificial satellites. They aid scientists in their studies and help them get more information about our universe, solar system, oceans, land, and atmosphere. Artificial satellites are also useful since they are able to take photographs of deep space objects and other phenomena and send them back to Earth. For example, pictures of our planet taken from space help meteorologists forecast the weather and predict natural disasters like hurricanes.

Other types of satellites are used for communication purposes, like those which beam TV and phone signals across the world or those which help us get important and useful information like our exact location.

◄ *The Moon is Earth's natural satellite. It takes 27 days to complete one orbit around Earth*

Moons of the Solar System

Our solar system consists of hundreds of moons. Some asteroids have also been found to have small moons. While Earth has only one moon or natural satellite, some other planets have many more, while others have none.

The two planets closest to the Sun are Mercury and Venus. They do not have any moons. Mercury is so very close to the Sun and its gravity, that it would, most probably, not be able to hold on to its moon. The moon would either crash into Mercury or get into an orbit around the Sun, eventually getting sucked into it.

Mars, on the other hand, has two moons. Jupiter, the outer giant planet can boast of 79 moons (53 of them have names, while the others are yet to be officially named)! It also has the biggest moon in the solar system, called Ganymede. Jupiter's moons are so large that they can be viewed with a pair of binoculars on a clear, dark night.

Saturn currently has 53 named moons and may have another nine which are still to be confirmed. If they are confirmed, the Ringed Planet will have 62 moons in all. Coming to Uranus; this planet has 27 confirmed moons so far, some of which are partially made of ice. Neptune, till date, has been found to have 13 moons and may have one more, but it is not yet confirmed.

▶ *The image shows the moons of the solar system and their comparative sizes to each other and to Earth*

Matter & Antimatter

In our universe, anything that has mass, takes up space, and has volume is called matter. This means that ordinary or regular matter is something we can see, feel, touch, and even taste. Antimatter is the opposite. It is matter made up of antiparticles that have properties opposite those of normal matter. Antiparticles are subatomic particles having the same mass as a given particle, but with an opposite electric charge. To understand antimatter, let us first take another look at what matter is.

What is Matter?

Everything around us—all solids, liquids, and gases comprise atoms which are the main ingredients of all matter. At the centre of each atom is a nucleus which comprises two different particles—protons and neutrons. The nucleus is surrounded by smaller particles called electrons. So basically, all matter is made up mainly of neutrons, protons, and electrons. Both protons and electrons have an electric charge. Protons are positively charged, and electrons are negatively charged.

When there are two opposite charges—negative and positive—they attract each other, but when the charge is the same, they repel each other.

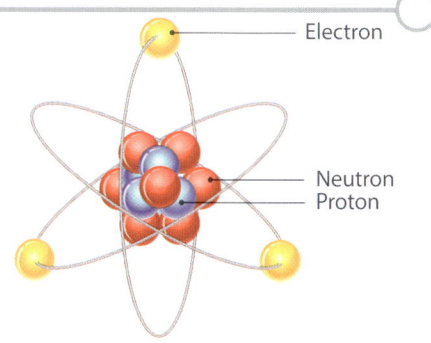

▲ An illustration of the structure of an atom made up of protons, neutrons and electrons. Protons and neutrons make up the nucleus of the atom

What is Antimatter?

Antimatter is almost the same as regular matter, but it comprises antiprotons, antineutrons, and antielectrons or positrons. The main difference between the particles of matter versus antimatter is that, in the latter, the corresponding antiparticles have the reverse charge. Anti protons, therefore, are negatively charged, and antielectrons have a positive charge.

So, what happens when particles and antiparticles collide with each other? When an electron and a positron come into contact with each other, the two get destroyed, leaving behind gamma rays or radiation. To put it another way, the mass of the particles is converted into pure energy. Matter and antimatter, therefore, cannot exist close together for more than a small fraction of a second because they will crash against each other and release energy.

▲ An artist's rendition of flying antimatter particles reacting with matter particles in a nebula

💡 Isn't It Amazing!

Hydrogen atoms are available in plenty in the universe. These atoms are also the simplest of all the other elements in the universe. The very first anti-atom or antimatter counterpart of a regular atom was created in 1995 by physicists at CERN—the European Organisation for Nuclear Research in Geneva. It was the anti-hydrogen atom. Unlike hydrogen, anti-hydrogen is rare and difficult to produce.

▶ The Globe of the Science and Innovation Centre at CERN in Geneva is 27 meters high and 40 meters in diameter

The Life Cycle of Stars

Stars take different paths in their evolutionary cycles. Their life cycles are determined by their mass. We can roughly classify stars into two types—average stars and massive stars. The greater the mass, the shorter the life cycle.

Massive star

Main Sequence Stars

Like babies need their food to grow into adults, young stars or protostars develop into main sequence stars by gathering mass from the clouds where they are born. This is the main phase of a star when it actively generates energy. A star can glow and remain in this stage for a few million years to billions of years, depending on its mass and rate of conversion of mass into energy. Generally, very high-mass stars have a faster rate of converting mass into energy and hence they have a shorter lifespan. For example, a very luminous high-mass star in its main phase can burn energy 1000 times faster than the Sun. Its lifespan will be shorter in comparison to a low-mass star.

Red supergiant

Supernova

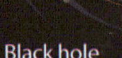

Isn't It Amazing!

One sugar cube of neutron star material would weigh about 1 trillion kilograms on Earth—almost as much as a mountain!

Black hole

Neutron star

Stellar Black Holes

Stellar black holes are created when the core of a really massive dying star (having 20 times the mass of the Sun), collapses upon itself, causing a supernova. A black hole is a place in space where the pull of gravity is so strong (because matter is squeezed into such a minute space) that even light cannot get out. Since light cannot escape, black holes are invisible and cannot be seen directly. They can only be viewed through space telescopes with special tools.

When the core of a high-mass star collapses, it crushes electrons and protons to form neutrons, creating a neutron star. A neutron star is one of the densest objects that can be viewed directly by astronomers. Imagine an object the size of the Sun pressed into the size of a planet like Earth! Due to this, the gravitation on its surface is tremendous. A neutron star also has a very powerful magnetic field.

▼ Neutron stars live up to around 100,000 to 10 billion year

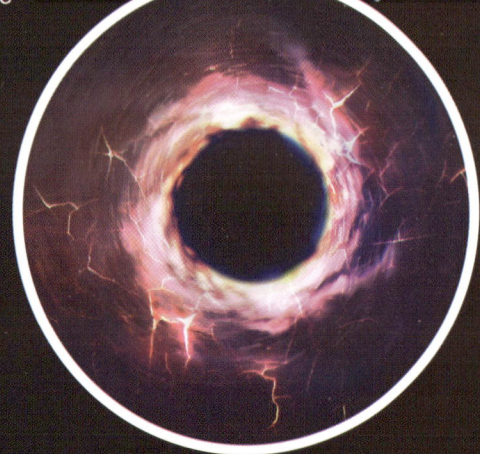

▲ One black hole can pack more than thrice the mass of the Sun into the diameter of a city!

SPACE — STARS AND GALAXIES

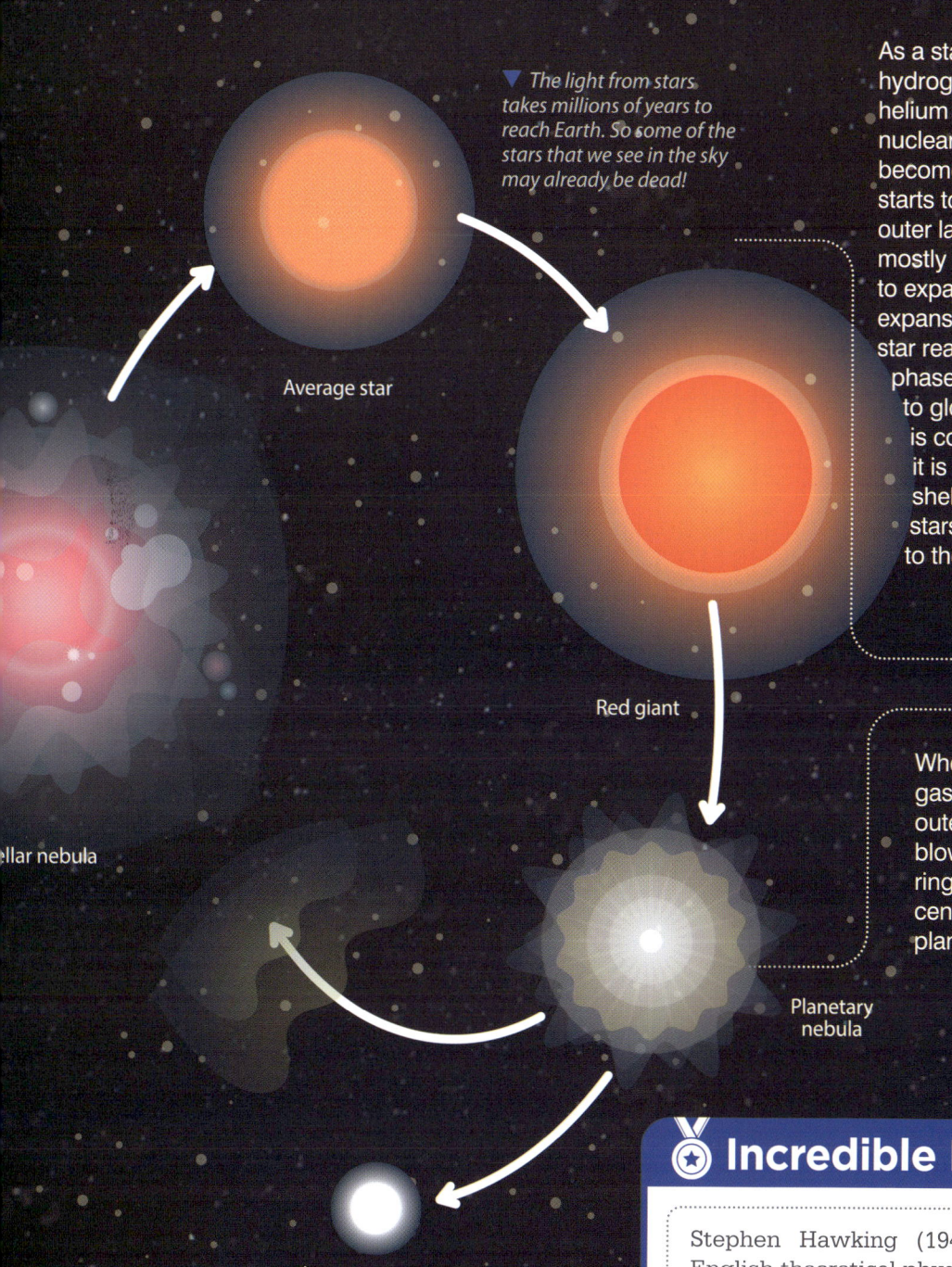

▼ The light from stars takes millions of years to reach Earth. So some of the stars that we see in the sky may already be dead!

Average star

Red giant

Planetary nebula

White dwarf

As a star continues to glow and hydrogen is converted into helium at its core through nuclear fusion, the centre becomes unstable and starts to contract. The outer layer of the star (still mostly hydrogen), begins to expand. When this expansion happens, the star reaches the red giant phase, i.e. it cools and starts to glow red. It is red since it is cooler than the protostar and it is a giant because its outer shell has expanded. Almost all stars evolve the same way up to the red giant stage.

▲ Red giant star- the fate of the Sun in about 5 billion years

When all the hydrogen gas contained in the outer shell of a star blows away, it forms a ring around the core or centre and is called a planetary nebula.

▲ Planetary nebulae were so named because early astronomers thought they looked like planets through a small telescope

In the case of stars like the Sun, when only the hot stellar core is left behind and the outer layers have all gone, the burning and dense core is called a white dwarf star. This is the fate of only those stars with a mass up to 1.4 times the mass of the Sun. Did you know that the Sun will become a white dwarf billions of years later?

▲ White dwarf stars will live longer than their host galaxies

🎖 Incredible Individuals

Stephen Hawking (1942–2018) was a much-admired English theoretical physicist of the late 20th and early 21st century. His best-selling book published in 1988 (also a motion picture)—*A Brief History of Time: From the Big Bang to Black Holes*—made him a celebrity. Hawking's main work revolved around the study of black holes, the remains from the collapse of giant stars. He also worked in the areas of general relativity, thermodynamics, and quantum mechanics in his attempt to understand how the universe was formed.

His achievements are all the more praiseworthy due to his battle with a degenerative muscular disease, which damaged his nerves and muscle system. The illness left him without the ability to write and he could barely speak. It forced him to be confined to a motorised wheelchair. Despite these setbacks, Hawking continued to pursue his pioneering work in the field of astronomy and popularised the subject.

▶ Doctors told Stephen Hawking that he wouldn't live past his early 20s

Nebulas: The Birthplace of Stars

Stars are born within nebulas found in interstellar space (region between stars). Astronomers have studied different nebulas in the Milky Way galaxy using powerful telescopes. They look like beautiful, delicate paintings with a vibrant array of colours.

▼ *The cloud associated with the Rosette nebula, a stellar nursery about 5,000 light years away from Earth*

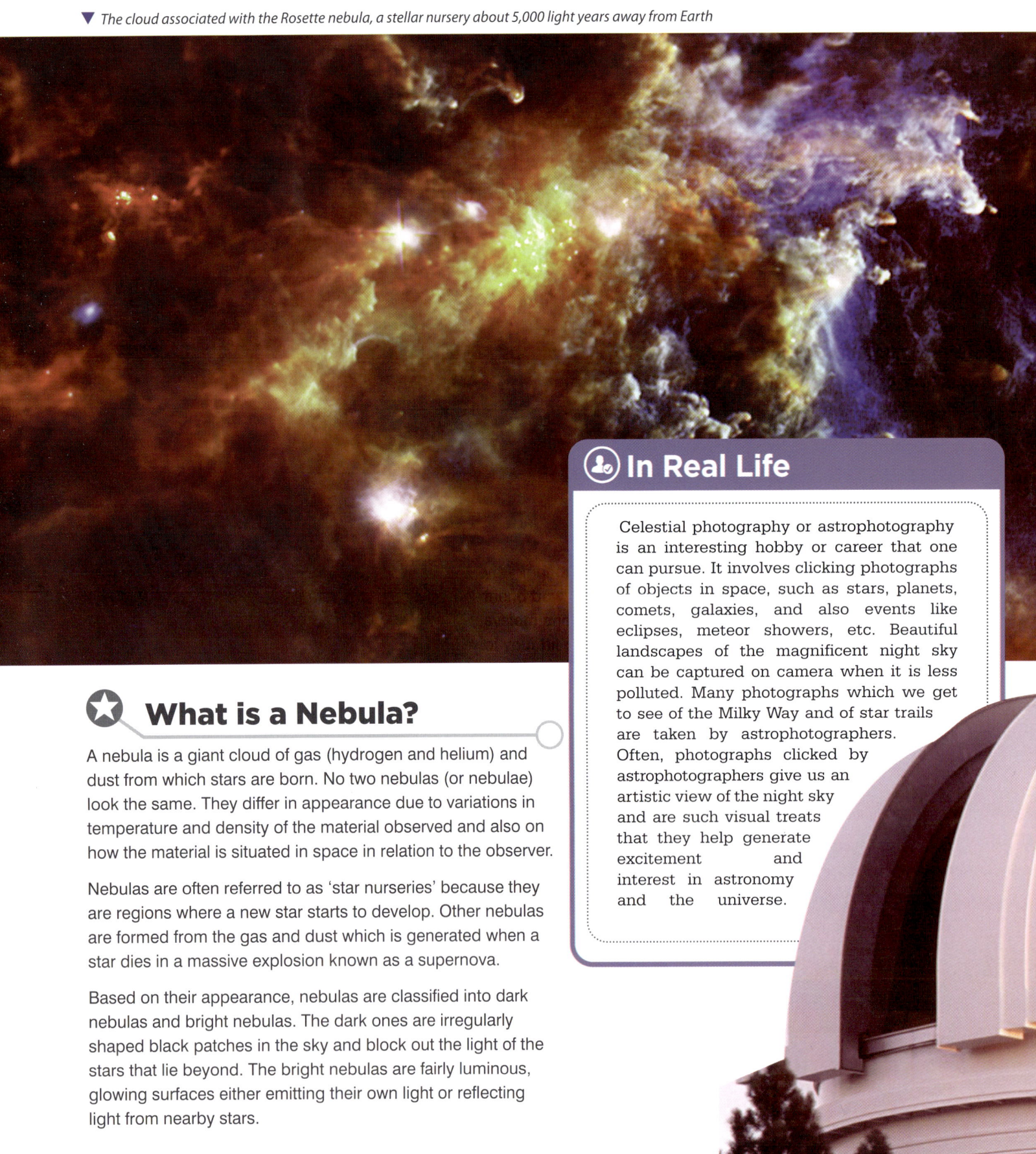

What is a Nebula?

A nebula is a giant cloud of gas (hydrogen and helium) and dust from which stars are born. No two nebulas (or nebulae) look the same. They differ in appearance due to variations in temperature and density of the material observed and also on how the material is situated in space in relation to the observer.

Nebulas are often referred to as 'star nurseries' because they are regions where a new star starts to develop. Other nebulas are formed from the gas and dust which is generated when a star dies in a massive explosion known as a supernova.

Based on their appearance, nebulas are classified into dark nebulas and bright nebulas. The dark ones are irregularly shaped black patches in the sky and block out the light of the stars that lie beyond. The bright nebulas are fairly luminous, glowing surfaces either emitting their own light or reflecting light from nearby stars.

In Real Life

Celestial photography or astrophotography is an interesting hobby or career that one can pursue. It involves clicking photographs of objects in space, such as stars, planets, comets, galaxies, and also events like eclipses, meteor showers, etc. Beautiful landscapes of the magnificent night sky can be captured on camera when it is less polluted. Many photographs which we get to see of the Milky Way and of star trails are taken by astrophotographers. Often, photographs clicked by astrophotographers give us an artistic view of the night sky and are such visual treats that they help generate excitement and interest in astronomy and the universe.

The Veil Nebula

National Aeronautics and Space Administration's Hubble Space Telescope discovered the Veil nebula, an exquisite remnant of one of the best-known supernovas caused by the explosion of a massive star 20 times bigger than the Sun. The star exploded between 10,000 and 20,000 years ago. The nebula gets its name from its elegant and beautiful structure and resides in the constellation of Cygnus, the Swan, about 2,400 light years away.

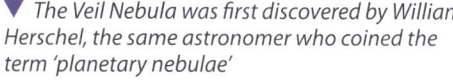
▼ The Veil Nebula was first discovered by William Herschel, the same astronomer who coined the term 'planetary nebulae'

★ The Orion Nebula

One of the earliest observed nebulas was the Orion nebula, located in the sword of the hunter's figure in the constellation of Orion. The nebula was discovered in 1610, two years after the invention of the telescope, by French scholar Nicolas-Claude Fabri de Peiresc. It was the first nebula to be photographed in 1880 by Henry Draper in US. The Orion Nebula is approximately 1,350 light years away from Earth and contains hundreds of very hot young stars clustered around four massive stars known as the Trapezium.

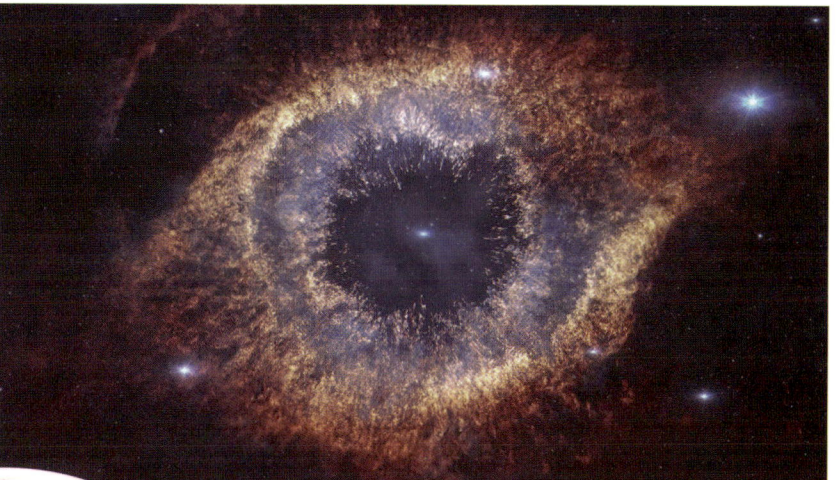
▲ The Helix Nebula is nicknamed the 'Eye of God' because of its striking appearance

▲ The Orion Nebula is easy to find, even in moderate light-pollution

The Helix Nebula

The Helix nebula is closest to Earth and is the largest known planetary nebula which is located in the constellation of Aquarius. It is nearly 700 light years away, so it would take a human being travelling at the speed of light about 700 years to reach there!

The Crab Nebula

In 1054, Chinese astronomers recorded a bright supernova that gave rise to the Crab Nebula. The nebula, however, was first discovered by English astronomer John Bevis in 1731. It gets its name from the fact that its shape resembles a crab and it is filled with mysterious, thin thread-like structures. This nebula is about 6,500 light years away in the constellation Taurus.

◄ The Palomar Observatory in California is home to the famous Hale Telescope, that has proved instrumental in cosmological research

What's a Supernova?

High-mass stars die in a huge explosion called a supernova and finally end up either as neutron stars or as black holes. Supernovas are extremely important for scientists to study because they tell us more about how the universe was formed.

Another Star Bites the Dust

Supernovas are a class of violently exploding stars whose luminosity, after eruption, suddenly increases several million times. The term supernova comes from nova (meaning 'new' in Latin). Supernovas are characterised by a tremendous, rapid brightening which lasts for a few weeks, and then slowly dims down. A supernova explosion is catastrophic for a star and ends its active or energy-generating life. Massive amounts of matter, equal to the material of several Suns, may get blown into space when a star 'goes supernova'.

▶ A supernova close enough to Earth could cause a mass extinction

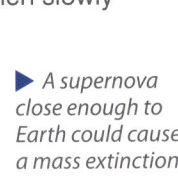 Supernova of a Single Star

There are two types of supernova. One occurs at the end of a single star's lifetime, when the star begins to cool down and runs out of its nuclear fuel, resulting in some of its mass flowing into its core, or in other words, the force of gravity takes over. The star cannot withstand its own gravitational force and collapses. This cave-in happens in a matter of 15 seconds and is so fast that it causes tremendous shock waves, resulting in the explosion of the outer part of the star. This leaves behind a dense core and an expanding cloud of dust and gas. If the star is a supergiant, its supernova can also create and leave behind the densest object in the universe—a black hole.

◀ Stellar mass black holes are known as collapsars

Supernova of a Binary Star System

Another type of supernova takes place in a binary system of stars when two stars orbit the same point and at least one of those stars is a white dwarf. If one white dwarf strikes against the other or if one of them sucks out or gobbles up too much matter from the nearby star, the white dwarf explodes, causing a supernova.

It is easier to spot and see supernovas in other galaxies rather than in our own Milky Way galaxy, since dust obstructs our view.

◀ An illustration showing a white dwarf pulling matter from a companion star

Incredible Individuals

In August 2018, NASA awarded its highest honour, the Distinguished Public Service Medal, to astronomer Yervant Terzian (1939–2019). He was honoured with this recognition for his dedicated contribution and impact on education, public service, and scientific research. He has played a huge role in inspiring young students as well as the public at large. Much to his credit, Terzian had been part of eight NASA committees, including the Hubble Space Telescope Fellowship Committee. He is famous for his studies of stellar evolution and the discovery of regions of hydrogen gas between galaxies. This discovery indicated the presence of unseen matter in intergalactic space. He has authored and co-authored over 235 scientific publications!

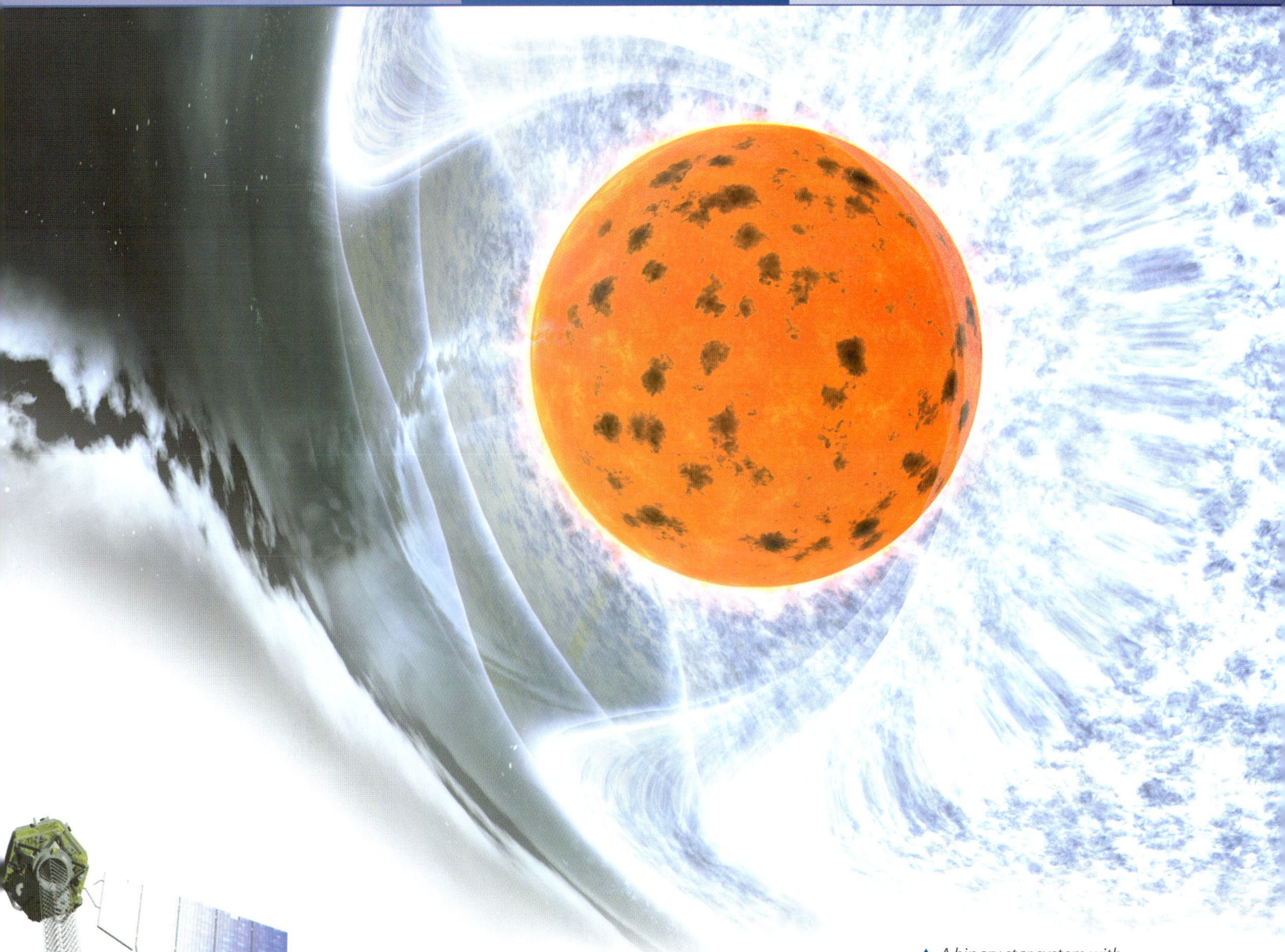

▲ *A binary star system with a red dwarf and a blue giant*

Star Dust

Supernovas can lead us to a lot of important information. Supernovas involving white dwarfs are used to measure distances in space. Studying these stellar explosions also helped scientists in learning that stars are like factories of the universe, manufacturing vital chemicals within their cores like carbon, nitrogen, and oxygen—all life-forming elements that make up our universe.

Massive stars create elements like gold, silver, uranium, and platinum, which also aid the universe in creating generations of stars, planets, etc. Human beings carry some remains of these explosions in their bodies. In fact, everything in the universe is created from scattered star dust!

Studying Supernovas

Scientists at NASA use different types of telescopes to study supernovas. For example, the NuSTAR (Nuclear Spectroscopic Telescope Array) mission uses X-ray vision to investigate the universe.

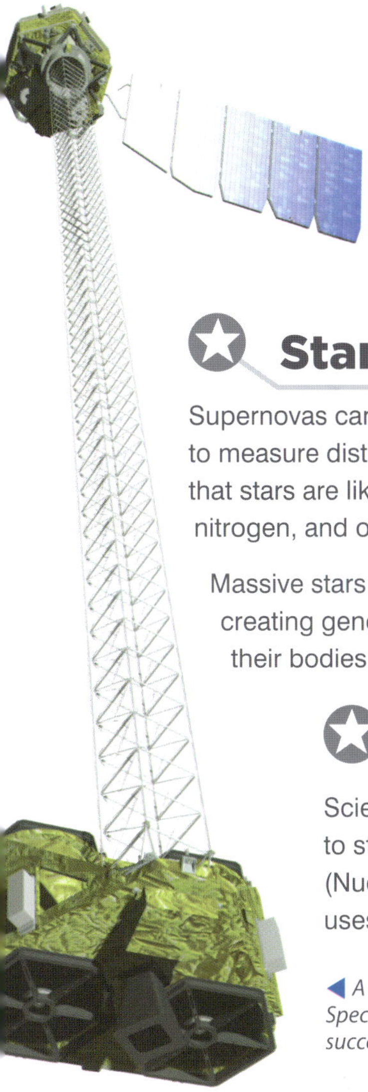

◀ *A visual representation of the NuSTAR (Nuclear Spectroscopic Telescope Array). The telescope was successfully launched on 13 June 2012*

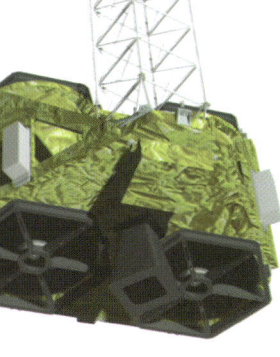

> **Isn't It Amazing!**
>
> Supernovas cast off or eject matter into space at a speed of 15,000 to 40,000 kilometres per second.

Stargazers

The theories about the laws of nature and how celestial bodies exist and function are numerous and as vast as our universe. Over centuries, with improvements in technology and the invention of sophisticated equipment like powerful space telescopes, better cameras, etc., more accurate studies have been possible than in the early days before such equipment was invented.

 **1546–1601**

 **1730–1817**

 **1738–1822**

Tycho Brahe

Brahe was a Danish astronomer known for developing astronomical instruments and measuring and fixing the accurate positions of 777 stars.

1572: His discovery of a 'new star' brighter than Venus led him to upturn the then prevalent theory of inner and continuous harmony of the whole universe. This harmony was ruled by the stars, which were thought to be perfect and unchanging. Brahe's study of the dramatic changes in stars challenged this age-old law.

1573: He published his observations of the new star in *De Nova Stella*.

Charles Messier

He was a French astronomer who worked under Joseph-Nicolas Delisle, another noted French astronomer.

1758–1759: He was the first in France to spot the Halley's Comet and thus began his passion to look for new comets. He was responsible for locating 13 comets.

1760: He started making a list of nebulas to help differentiate them from comets. Many of them are referred to by using his catalogue system. He was the first to compile such a catalogue.

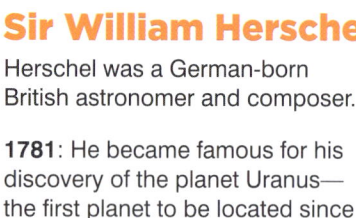

Sir William Herschel

Herschel was a German-born British astronomer and composer.

1781: He became famous for his discovery of the planet Uranus—the first planet to be located since prehistoric times.

1784–1785: He first suggested that nebulas are composed of stars and developed the theory of stellar evolution.

SPACE — STARS AND GALAXIES

Edward Emerson Barnard

Barnard was a leading American astronomer of his time and a pioneer in celestial photography.

1889: He started photographing the Milky Way with a more technologically advanced camera, which helped reveal new data.

1892: He discovered 16 comets and Jupiter's fifth satellite.

1916: He discovered the star (Barnard's Star) that has the greatest known **proper motion** (motion of an individual star relative to other stars).

1919: He published a catalogue on dark nebulas.

Hans Albrecht Bethe

Bethe was a German-born American theoretical physicist who helped shape quantum physics.

1938: He studied and provided conclusive answers to the problem of energy generation in stars and explained how stars could burn for billions of years by specifying and analysing the nuclear reactions responsible for this.

1967: He was awarded the Nobel Prize based on his 1939 paper on energy generation in stars which helped create the field of nuclear **astrophysics**.

 1857–1923  1900–1979  1906–2005   1910–1995

Cecilia Payne-Gaposchkin

Cecilia was a British-born American astronomer who discovered that stars are mainly made of hydrogen and helium. She also established that stars could be classified according to their temperatures.

1925: She published a thesis on stellar atmospheres.

1930: She studied the luminosity of stars and published a book titled *Stars of High Luminosity*.

Subrahmanyan Chandrasekhar

1931: Chandrasekhar said that a star with mass more than 1.44 times that of the Sun does not, in fact, form a white dwarf. Instead, it continues to collapse, blowing off its gaseous covering in a supernova explosion and becoming a neutron star. An even bigger star continues to collapse and becomes a black hole. His calculations contributed to our understanding of supernovas, neutron stars and black holes.

1983: He won the Nobel Prize in Physics for his theories on the evolution of stars.

Constellations in the Sky

Since ancient times, human beings have gazed at the stars and looked to them for help in navigating across the mighty oceans. Stars were also used to predict the seasons and prepare plans for sowing seeds and harvesting crops. In order to easily recognise and gather information from this 'celestial calendar' in the skies, stars (brighter ones in particular) were grouped together as constellations and named according to their apparent shapes.

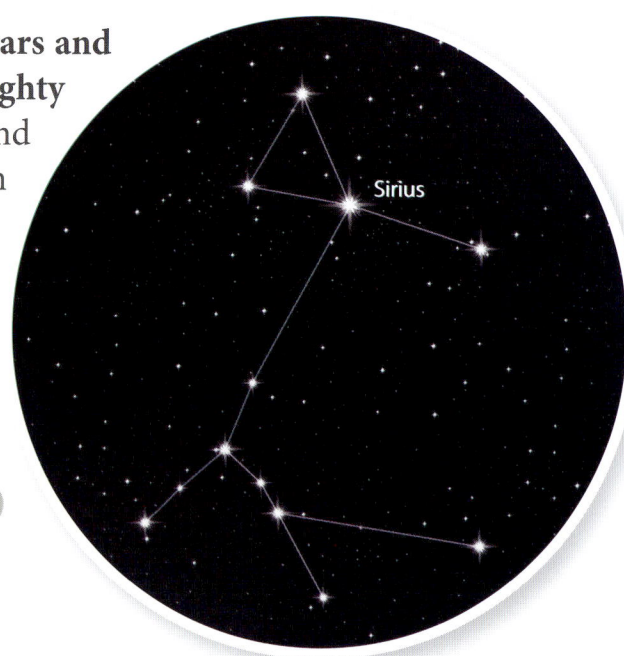

▲ *The Canis Major constellation with Sirius, its brightest star*

What is a Constellation?

In astronomy, a constellation is defined as a group of stars. They are not exactly real; in order to easily pick out the different stars in the night sky, people made up patterns of stars and named these patterns according to the apparent shapes that they took. These patterns might display objects, creatures, or mythical people. So, these star groups or constellations are named after those apparent shapes. For example, there are groups of stars which seem to take the shape of a big bear or a lion and a hunter.

Importance of Constellations

Constellations help in locating stars and mapping the night sky. For example, if you know enough about constellations, you might spot Orion one evening, by identifying three of the bright stars that form the Hunter's belt. Remember that Canis Minor and Canis Major are nearby. Without constellations, finding a speck of a star in the vastness of the night sky would be very difficult.

Constellations are also known to play a role in farming, agriculture, and navigation. Earlier, when there were no calendars, constellations and stars were the only way to identify the harvesting and sowing seasons. Besides, the position of the North Star allowed travellers to find their exact location and travel across the globe.

How many Constellations are there?

Officially, there are a total of 88 constellations, out of which 48 were identified by the ancient Greeks. Since some of the main constellations include more than one form or creature, the total number of shapes and images formed in these constellations is more than 88 and includes 9 birds, 2 insects, 19 mammals, 10 water creatures, 1 constellation shaped like a historical figure's hair, a serpent, a flying horse, a dragon, 2 centaurs (a mythological creature that is half-man and half-horse), 1 river, 29 inanimate objects, and 14 men and women.

Christening the Constellations

In ancient times, people named constellations after mythological creatures or characters, or even objects. Some were named after religious beliefs. Most of these star patterns do not exactly represent the names that were given to them. The names are suggestive. They were meant to be indicative, not representative.

▲ *Ursa Major or the Great Bear constellation. Ancient Greeks associated the constellation with the nymph Callisto, who was positioned in heaven by Zeus in the form of a bear*

Spotting Constellations

Some constellations are seasonal, but some can be seen year-round and appear to be fixed in place. The constellations that people can view also depend on the place and time when they are being viewed. Do you ever wonder why this is the case and why constellations appear to rise and set?

Which Constellations can you Spot?

▲ *An old illustration depicting the constellations visible from the northern hemisphere and the southern hemisphere*

People in different parts of the world are able to view different constellations, depending on whether they live above the Equator or below it. All places above the Equator are part of the northern hemisphere, and all places below it are part of the southern hemisphere.

People living above the Equator will only be able to see the constellations that appear in the sky above the northern hemisphere. Similarly, people living below the Equator will only be able to see the constellations that appear in the sky above the southern hemisphere. If you live near the Equator, then you will be able to view some constellations from both the hemispheres.

Why do Stars Seem to Move Across the Sky?

Sometimes, stars seem to move across the night sky. To understand why it appears so and why everyone on Earth cannot see all constellations, we need to understand Earth's motions—its rotation on its own axis and its revolution around the Sun.

As Earth rotates, one side of it faces the Sun and the other side faces away from the Sun. So, the side facing the Sun receives light causing day, while the side facing away from the Sun does not receive light causing night. Though stars are always present in the sky, they are visible only at night, when Earth is facing away from the Sun's glare.

Earth's revolution around the Sun causes the seasons, such as monsoon, summer, and winter. Both aspects—the seasons and night and day, cause people in different parts of Earth to view different parts of the night sky during different seasons. This makes people think that stars are moving when, in fact, it is Earth that is moving.

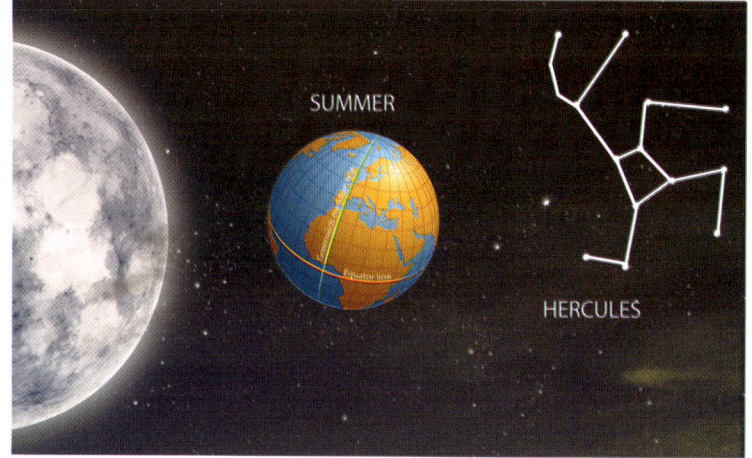

▲ *Earth's rotation and revolution make stars appear to move across the skies, and hence not everyone can see all constellations all the time*

Constellations in the Northern Hemisphere

Each of the two hemispheres have different celestial objects and constellations for you to marvel at. Some stars and constellations can be seen more clearly from the northern hemisphere. In the southern hemisphere, they would be quite low on the horizon, or not visible at all. The star map in the centre shows the constellations of the northern hemisphere.

◀ *A star map showing the constellations with their perceived shapes*

⭐ Polaris and the Three Circumpolar Constellations

One of the most popular and well-recognised patterns in the northern sky is that of the seven bright stars which form the Big Dipper, part of the Ursa Major or Great Bear constellation. The two stars (Dubhe and Merak) at the end of the bowl of the Big Dipper are also known as the pointer stars. If you draw a straight line through them, they will point you to Polaris or the North Star. It is located in the tail of the Little Bear or at the end of the Little Dipper in the Ursa Minor (Small Bear) constellation close by. If you extend that straight line from Polaris, you will see a constellation which looks like a 'W'. That is the constellation of Cassiopeia. Ursa Major, Ursa Minor, and Cassiopeia are circumpolar constellations. The extremely bright Polaris is one of the most striking sights in the northern skies. Incidentally, Ursa Minor is the third largest constellation in the sky.

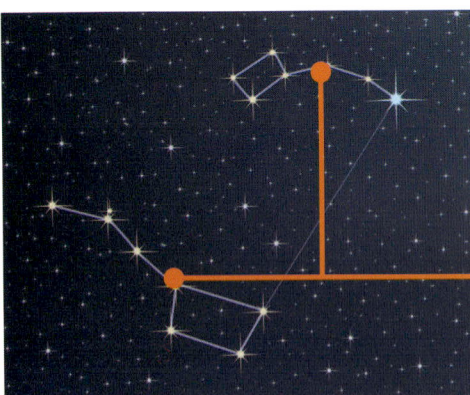

▲ Ursa Minor
▼ Ursa Major

Mythology: The Big Bear and Little Bear originate from a Greek myth. The Greeks considered the two bears to be Callisto and her son Arcas. They were turned into bears by Zeus. They could also be referring to the two bears who saved the life of baby Zeus from his cannibalistic father. The long tails of the bears were said to have been the result of Zeus swinging them far up in the sky.

▶ *Constellations of the northern hemisphere*

Andromeda

▲ The Andromeda constellation

From Cassiopeia, if you look down to the right, you will find the Andromeda galaxy and close to it you will be able to identify a huge rectangle, which is the constellation Pegasus. Follow the left star at the base of the rectangle and you will be able to spot the Andromeda constellation. Alpheratz, which means 'the horse's navel' in Arabic, is the brightest star in this constellation. If you are lucky, you may even be able to spot a fuzzy oval in the sky, which is the amazing Andromeda Galaxy, the large galaxy closest to Earth.

Mythology: Andromeda represents the princess of Ethiopia who, according to the Greeks, was saved from a sea monster by Perseus.

Isn't It Amazing!

It is believed that the luminosity of the Antares star—the brightest star in the Scorpius constellation in the Southern hemisphere—is 10,000 times greater than the Sun's luminosity.

▲ The Cepheus constellation

Cepheus

This constellation represents a king and is a dimmer constellation compared to many others. However, it is easily recognisable, being shaped like a stick house. In August and September, you will find Cepheus located on the upper right side of Polaris. The top of the roof generally points towards the Pole Star. If you are able to locate the more well-known Cassiopeia constellation, then you can spot Cepheus, which is a close neighbour. Alderamin is the brightest star in this constellation.

Mythology: It is named after the King of Ethiopia and father of Andromeda. He was forced to sacrifice his daughter to a sea monster.

Constellations in the Southern Hemisphere

No study of the constellations is complete without observing those in the sky above the southern hemisphere. When viewed from the south, northern constellations will appear upside down. Also, the northern circumpolar constellations like the Big Dipper, Cassiopeia, etc., become seasonal and Polaris cannot be seen at all.

Even if you think you know your constellations well, it isn't easy to spot them after a change in hemispheres. For instance, in the southern hemisphere, the Summer Triangle becomes the Winter Triangle and similarly, some of the other constellations point in different directions, compared to how you would see them in the northern hemisphere.

★ Canis Major and Sirius

If you look high up into the north-eastern sky, you will be able to find Canis Major to the right (south-east) of Orion. Also known as the Greater Dog, Canis Major can proudly boast of a star called Sirius, which is the brightest star in the dark sky. It is also the fifth-nearest to Earth. The Canis Major dwarf galaxy is also part of the Canis Major constellation and is the dwarf galaxy nearest to Earth. A dwarf galaxy is small when compared to other galaxies like the Andromeda or Milky Way. It consists of about a hundred million or a couple billion stars. On the other hand, the Milky Way galaxy consists of about 200–400 billion stars.

Mythology: Canis Major was considered to be Orion's hunting dog.

▲ *Canis Major with Sirius, the brightest star in the night sky*

★ Carina and Canopus

The second brightest star, Canopus is also found in the south in the constellation of Carina. You can spot Canopus by looking at an angle of 35° from Sirius. It can generally be viewed from October to May and is almost always seen when Sirius is visible. Earlier, Carina was part of a larger constellation called the Argo Navis. It was divided into three different constellations—Carina, Puppis, and Vela—by French astronomer Nicolas Louis de Lacaille.

Mythology: Carina was earlier a part of the Argo Navis constellation, named after the ship Argo. In an old Greek myth, Jason and the Argonauts went on this ship to rescue the Golden Fleece.

◄ *Carina or the Keel constellation*

Crux or the Southern Cross

The Southern Cross is the most familiar and well-known pattern in the southern hemisphere. It is the most striking feature of the Crux constellation with its five bright stars roughly forming the shape of a cross. Crux is the smallest constellation amongst all the constellations. Two of its brighter stars are Acrux and Gacrux, which point towards the southern celestial pole. A dark nebula, the Coalsack Nebula is also part of this constellation.

◀ *Crux or the Southern Cross*

Alpha Centauri: The Nearest Star System

It will be well worth your while to visit the southern hemisphere in order to see the closest star system to Earth, the Alpha Centauri. It also happens to be the third brightest star system in the night sky. Being circumpolar, you can see Alpha Centauri all through the year if you live south of the Equator. Sometimes in May, Alpha Centauri can be seen a few degrees above the southern horizon. It is part of the constellation Centaurus.

▲ *The Alpha Centauri star system is about 4.3 light years from Earth*

▲ *Constellations in the southern hemisphere*

In Real Life

Interestingly, the five stars of the Crux appear on the flags of countries like New Zealand, Papua New Guinea, Samoa, Australia, and Brazil. They are also part of the national anthems of the latter two countries.

▶ *The Australian and Papua New Guinean flags depict stars from the Southern Cross*

A Brief History

Astronomy was one of the first few natural sciences to develop. However, unlike other such sciences, it had reached a high level of refinement and achievement by the second half of the first millennium BCE. It has been one of the most enduring traditions across the world for almost 4,000 years.

⭐ Astronomy in Ancient Times

The Nebra Sky Disc is the oldest known representation of the cosmos. It is the earliest record of astronomical observations depicting the Sun, a lunar crescent and stars. In the Bronze Age, this was a kind of astronomical clock or tool used in agriculture for finding out the correct time for sowing and harvesting. The 1600 bronze tool has a diameter of about 30 centimetres and weighs approximately 2 kg.

Early recordings of astronomical phenomena are also found in the ancient Babylonian, Chinese, Central American, and North European cultures. These ancient cultures tried to measure time; trace the movements of the Sun, the Moon, and the stars; track the regularity in the occurrence of sunrises, sunsets, and other celestial events through structures they built. The rock formation of Stonehenge in the UK is evidence of this. Native Americans also left behind rock drawings (petroglyphs) of astronomical phenomena.

▲ *The Nebra Sky Disc was discovered in 1999 in Germany, by treasure hunters using a metal detector. It depicts the Sun or a full Moon, stars, and a crescent Moon*

▲ Stonehenge

⭐ Timeline of Astronomy

The history of astronomy is long, and spread across many nations. Many cultures learned from each other to make advances in this field.

3114 BCE

Ancient Mayans note the 18.6 year cycle of Earth's Moon rising and setting. They prepare a calendar charting the movements of the planets, the Moon and the Sun.

▶ *A Mayan astronomer is depicted within the pages of the Madrid Codex, a Mayan book about almanacs and horoscopes*

585–470 BCE

Ancient Greeks build on the knowledge of the Mayans to predict eclipses. Specifically, Thales uses this knowledge and predicts a solar eclipse. A Greek philosopher named Anaxagoras provides an accurate explanation of eclipses. He describes the Sun and how the Moon reflects light from the Sun.

▶ *Anaxagoras also tried to explain the occurrence of meteors and rainbows. He described the Sun as a large, fiery mass*

SPACE | ASTRONOMY

400 BCE
The ancient Babylonians learn to record the position of celestial bodies by dividing the heavens into twelve 30-degree segments under the Zodiac system.

387 BCE
A famous Greek philosopher Plato starts a school called the Academy. Plato proposes that planets follow perfectly circular orbits and that all celestial bodies move around Earth.

▶ A part of a much larger fresco depicting the School of Athens; Plato and Aristotle are depicted here

350 BCE
Aristotle, another well-known Greek philosopher and scientist, plays a key role in the development of Western thought. He publishes *On the Heavens,* which is the oldest existing source clearly mentioning that Earth is a sphere and gives valid reasons to support his claim. He arrives at this conclusion by observing Earth's circular shadow on the Moon during a lunar eclipse.

◀ Aristotle's theories were groundbreaking at the time, and were used until around the 1500s CE

270 BCE
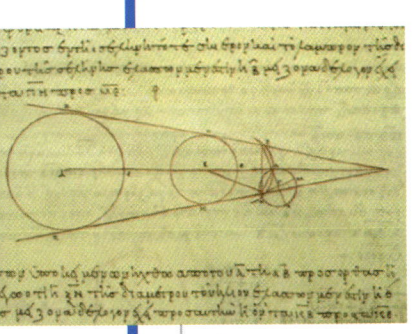

Greek astronomer Aristarchus of Samos proposes a system where the Sun is the central figure around which Earth and the other planets move. This is called the **heliocentric model** of the solar system. This leads to the geocentric versus heliocentric debate.

▲ A Greek copy of Aristarchus's notes on the relative sizes of the Sun, Earth, and the Moon

330 BCE
Heraclides, a Greek philosopher and astronomer and the first to suggest the rotation of Earth, proposes the very first model of our solar system. In this model, he puts the planets in order and places Earth at the very centre of the model. This is the obsolete **geocentric model** of the solar system.

▲ Heraclides was a pupil of Plato

240 BCE
Greek philosophers Eratosthenes (known for the oldest surviving record measuring Earth's size) and Aristarchus use simple geometry to calculate the size of Earth, the Moon, and the Sun, as well as the distances between the planets nearby. They estimate the size of the universe relative to Earth.

▲ The illustration depicts Eratosthenes's time as a teacher in Alexandria

130 BCE
Hipparchus, a Greek astronomer and mathematician, prepares the first star catalogue and constructs a celestial globe with the stars and constellations arranged on it.

45 BCE

Julius Caesar introduces the Julian calendar, similar to the one we use today, to the Roman Empire. It is a purely solar calendar and includes leap years.

▲ Caesar took the help of Greek mathematicians and astronomers for the calendar

⭐ Incredible Individuals

While working on the Julian calendar, the Alexandrian astronomer Sosigenes miscalculated the length of the year by 11 minutes and 14 seconds. Over the centuries, this seemingly minor mistake had led to a 10-day deviation. So, as a reformative step, Pope Gregory XIII introduced the Gregorian calendar (which we use till date) in 1582.

Renaissance & Astronomy

The Renaissance period (14th–16th century) saw a rebirth of European culture, art, politics, economics, and science. This era was also characterised by a heightened interest in the study of everything related to ancient Greece and Rome, and the discovery of new territories and continents. Astronomy too played a key role as important advances in science were made and new theories about the universe were put forth by astronomers. Great artists, scientists, thinkers, authors, and statesmen flourished during this time.

⭐ Nicolaus Copernicus (1473–1543)

Although Copernicus, the father of modern astronomy, wasn't the first to challenge Ptolemy's geocentric theory, he reinvented the heliocentric model. He was the first person to publish his claim, thereby challenging the doctrine of the Church.

Copernicus concluded that Earth and all the planets in the solar system revolve around the Sun. He also proposed that Earth rotates daily on its axis, and what human beings see in the night skies depends on Earth's motion. Copernicus did not have the equipment to validate his theories, and he was proved correct much later in the 1600s by astronomers like Galileo Galilei.

▲ An oil painting by Jan Matejko depicts Nicolaus Copernicus looking at the skies from the balcony of a cathedral. It is titled 'Conversations with God'

💡 Isn't It Amazing!

It is indeed amazing that Copernicus made many of his astronomical observations with the naked eye! He passed away more than 50 years before Galileo Galilei first observed the skies using a telescope he had made.

▲ Tycho Brahe's wealth totaled to 1% of Denmark's wealth

⭐ Tycho Brahe (1546–1601)

Danish astronomer Tycho Brahe was the first 'true' observer of the skies—he built the Danish Observatory using **sextants** instead of a telescope (which had not yet been invented). A sextant is an instrument used to determine the angle between the horizon and a celestial object like a star, the Sun, or the Moon. He showed that the Sun was much farther than the Moon from Earth by using **trigonometry**, a branch of mathematics concerned with functions of angles and their application to calculations.

⭐ Johannes Kepler (1571–1630)

A German astronomer named Johannes Kepler supported Copernicus's heliocentric model in his book, *The Cosmographic Mystery*. He became one of the first figures in the field of astronomy to offer public support to the theories proposed by Copernicus.

Kepler was a student of Tycho Brahe. The two worked together briefly before Brahe's death in 1601. Brahe's database and his observation of an exploding star (a supernova) made Kepler realise that planets and other bodies moved in ellipses. This became his first law of planetary motion out of the three. Till his discovery, it was believed that planets travelled in a circular path instead of an oval path.

▶ Johannes Kepler was a mathematician as well as an optician

Galileo Galilei (1564–1642)

Italian scientist Galileo Galilei was the pioneer of modern 'observational' astronomy. In the early 1600s, he made path-breaking discoveries using extremely powerful telescopes made by him, which were based on a model invented in the Netherlands around the time. Based on his observations of Venus, he accepted and explained the heliocentric model of the universe. This went against the prevalent theory of the geocentric system.

▲ *Galilei shows the chief magistrate of Venice how to use a telescope*

Galilei made revolutionary astronomical discoveries that went against the assumptions made by people before him. For example, while many believed that the Moon's surface is smooth, he rightly claimed it to be uneven. Galilei also made observations about the puzzling appearance of Saturn and its atmosphere, which later turned out to be its rings, and also explained the nature of sunspots. He claimed that Venus goes through phases like Earth's Moon and was also responsible for the discovery of four of Jupiter's moons.

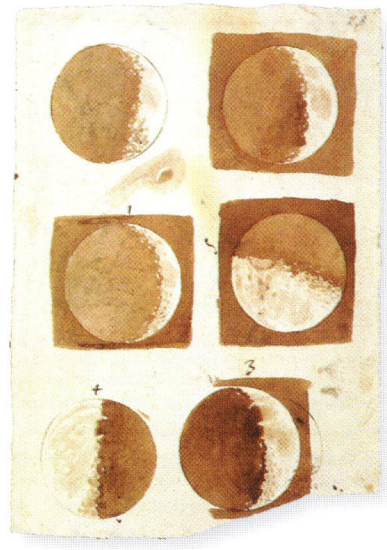

▲ *Galilei drew the Moon's phases and discovered that it had an uneven surface using a powerful telescope magnified up to 20 times*

The latter two observations implied that there existed more than one centres of motion in the cosmos and that the planets revolved around the Sun. It was a decisive moment in the world of science and astronomy.

These discoveries went against the belief of the Roman Catholic Church, which believed that Earth was the central body in the solar system. So Galilei was sentenced to life imprisonment. He died due to an illness while under house arrest.

▲ *The Vatican did not admit that Galileo was right until 1992*

▼ *Galilei facing the Roman Catholic Church during an inquisition*

Modern Astronomy

The period between the 18th and 20th centuries was marked by the discovery of the outer planets of the solar system as well as discoveries in stellar and galactic areas. From the late 19th century onwards, astronomy also included **astrophysics**. While astronomy is the science that measures the positions and characteristics of heavenly bodies, the application of the laws and theories of physics to understand astronomy is called astrophysics. Scientists also research gases and dust particles found close to and in between the stars, and nuclear reactions that provide the energy radiated by stars. Cosmology—the study of the origins of the universe—was another area of interest and focus in this period.

▲ The Hubble Space Telescope was launched in 1990. It is still in operation today

▲ Cassini is credited with introducing Indian Astronomy to Europe

▲ Newton was knighted by Queen Anne of England in 1705, becoming Sir Isaac Newton

Gian Domenico Cassini (1625–1712)

Italian-born French astronomer, Gian Domenico Cassini, amongst others, discovered a dark gap—the Cassini Division—between the A and B rings of Saturn, in 1675. He also discovered four moons of Saturn—Iapetus, Rhea, Tethys, and Dione. His primary focus was the Sun, but later with the use of powerful telescopes, he also studied the planets. He was the first to notice the shadows cast by Jupiter's moons as they travelled between Jupiter and the Sun. He measured the planet's rotational period after observing the spots on its surface and discovered the flattened poles. Cassini was also the first to record observations of the zodiacal light. Although he did not accept new ideas and theories easily, he is still remembered as one of the important astronomers of the 17th and 18th centuries.

Sir Isaac Newton (1643–1727)

English physicist and mathematician, Sir Isaac Newton is one of the greatest scientists in history. Newton developed the three laws of motion (which became the foundation for physics), the theory of gravity, and a new branch of mathematics called calculus. He also advanced the science of optics, contributing significantly towards reflecting telescopes; worked on **diffraction**; and came up with the theory of light.

👤 In Real Life

Despite astronomy having developed into an advanced science, one of its major pitfalls is that it is an 'observational' science rather than one based on scientific experiments. A majority of the measurements have to be undertaken at great distances from the objects being studied, without any control over their temperature, pressure, or chemical composition. The only exceptions being meteorites (pieces of asteroids which land on Earth); lunar surface soil and rock samples; comet and asteroid dust samples brought back by robotic spacecrafts; and interplanetary dust particles in and above the stratosphere—which can be tested in a laboratory environment.

▲ In 1720, Halley succeeded John Flamsteed as Astronomer Royal

▲ Laplace is sometimes referred to as French Newton

▲ Lagrange played a major role in the development of the metric system of weights and measures

⭐ Edmond Halley (1656–1742)

An English mathematician and astronomer, Edmond Halley was the first to calculate the orbit of a comet, that was later named after him. He also played a key role in the publication of Newton's *Mathematical Principles of Natural Philosophy*.

In 1678, he published a star catalogue comprising locations of southern stars determined using a telescope. The first work of its type to be published, it helped establish him as a reputed astronomer.

⭐ Pierre-Simon, marquis de Laplace (1749–1827)

French mathematician, astronomer, and physicist, Laplace was known for his contributions in exploring the stability of the solar system. Some observed that there are disturbances in the solar system which are caused by the fact that all planets are attracted by the Sun. However, they are also attracted—though by a smaller degree—by all the other planets. New mathematical methodology was developed in the 18th century to provide a more efficient rationale for such disturbances. Laplace and Joseph-Louis Lagrange (1736–1813) played an important role in showing that the solar system was actually quite stable.

The International Space Station

The International Space Station (ISS) is the largest space laboratory in low Earth orbit. It was launched by the USA and Russia along with the help of experts from Europe, Japan, and Canada. Brazil and 11 members of the ESA helped in its construction.

 ## The Origins of ISS

President Ronald Reagan had given NASA the go-ahead for this initiative in the 1980s. In the 1990s, it was redesigned to reduce costs. In 1993, USA and Russia decided to combine their individual space station plans and amalgamate their technologies, expertise, and modules with contributions from the ESA and Japan.

The construction of the ISS started in November 1998, with the launch of the Russian control module Zarya and the US-built Unity connecting node. They were linked in orbit by American space shuttle astronauts. Thereafter, constant additions were made, including a control centre, complex laboratories, equipment, and habitats. The ISS was completely functional by May 2009.

 ## Assembling the ISS

Besides the Russian modules, other elements were added over the years. Some were brought to the ISS by space shuttles and assembled by astronauts during a spacewalk, also known as an Extravehicular Activity (EVA), in orbit. Space shuttles and the Soyuz spacecraft served to transport astronauts back and forth. A Soyuz remained there at all times as a rescue vehicle. In 2006, a pair of solar wings and a thermal radiator were added.

The ISS has a 16-metre-long, Canadian-built Canadarm2, which is a large robotic arm that serves as a crane and is used for a variety of tasks. The ISS has six docking ports that allow six spacecrafts to visit the station simultaneously. In November 2000, the ISS welcomed its first resident crew, American astronaut William Shepherd and Russian cosmonauts Sergey Krikalyov and Yuri Gidzenko. Since then, the ISS has been constantly occupied and has had over 200 astronauts from 20 countries visit it.

▼ A photograph of the International Space Station seen from Atlantis STS-135, after undocking in May 2010

Isn't It Amazing!

Here are some interesting facts about the ISS:
- The crew lives and works on the ISS while travelling at about 8 kmps.
- In 24 hours, ISS orbits Earth 16 times; it witnesses 16 sunrises and sunsets.
- The living and working space of the ISS—which is larger than a six-bedroom house—consists of six sleeping quarters, two bathrooms, and even a gym.
- The ISS measures approximately 108 metres end to end, just 91 centimetres less than a full-length American football field.
- More than 50 computers on-board control the systems.

Incredible Individuals

American biochemist and astronaut, Peggy Whitson was the first woman commander of the ISS and holds the record for spending the maximum time in space amongst American astronauts. She spent 665 days in space!

◀ NASA's Peggy Whitson conducted four spacewalks as a member of Expeditions 50, 51, and 52 on the ISS and contributed to hundreds of experiments

The Hubble Space Telescope

Hubble Space Telescope is named after the foremost observational cosmologist of the 20th century, Edwin Hubble. This telescope was designed and built by the European Space Agency and National Aeronautics and Space Administration. It was deployed on 25 April 1990.

▲ A replica of the Hubble Space Telescope is displayed in Edwin Hubble's hometown in Missouri

▲ The Hubble Space Telescope was deployed from the cargo bay of the space shuttle Discovery

⭐ The Hubble Telescope's Activities

The Hubble Space Telescope has played an important role in:
- Helping estimate the age of the universe, which is believed to be almost 14 billion years old
- Detecting black holes
- Revealing faraway galaxies
- Discovering dark energy—a force causing the universe to expand at a galloping rate
- Capturing strong explosions of energy during the collapse of gigantic stars
- Studying the atmosphere of planets outside the solar system, which revolve around stars.

▲ More than 1.3 million observations have been made by the Hubble Space Telescope

⭐ Instruments and Equipment on Hubble

Hubble uses cutting-edge technology and very specialised equipment. For example, its Fine Guidance Sensors—which lock onto stars as Hubble orbits Earth—are part of its Pointing Control System and help the telescope aim precisely in the correct direction. In fact, the Hubble telescope has the ability to lock on to a target object located about 1.6 km away by moving no more than the width of a human hair!

Hubble's mirrors collect 40,000 times more light than the human eye. It uses five main scientific instruments including the Wide Field Camera 3 and spectrographs (which split light into its individual wavelengths). The Wide Field Camera 3 can see three types of light—near-ultraviolet, visible, and near-infrared. The first and the third types cannot be seen by people.

🏅 Incredible Individuals

German-born British astronomer, Sir William Herschel (1738–1822) started off as a musician. A book on telescope construction got him interested in astronomy. He wanted to observe distant celestial objects, for which he required powerful telescopes with large mirrors to collect sufficient light. He was compelled to make his own mirrors. His contribution to developing the telescope in the 18th century was crucial.

▶ British astronomer William Herschel was the one to discover the planet Uranus

💡 Isn't It Amazing!

Hubble does not travel to the stars, planets, or galaxies, instead it takes pictures of them as it whirls around Earth at about 27,300 kmph.

More than 15,000 scientific papers have been published using Hubble's data, making it one of the most productive scientific instruments ever built.

Satellites

An object that moves around a larger object is known as a satellite. There could be a natural satellite like the Moon that moves around Earth, or an artificial satellite such as a man-made machine. Both types of satellites orbit a larger astronomical body. Generally, natural satellites orbit a planet. Sir Isaac Newton was the first to suggest the idea of an artificial satellite in orbital flight, in 1687. Let us take a look at artificial satellites in Earth's orbit.

▲ A satellite can travel the entire circumference of Earth about 14 times in a day

▶ Moon is the largest natural satellite in the Solar System relative to the size of its planet

⭐ Where Do Satellites Orbit?

Artificial satellites like space stations, space shuttle orbiters, etc., can be crewed, or unmanned and controlled by robotics. Since the launch of the first artificial satellite, Sputnik 1, over 8,900 satellites have been launched into Earth's orbit by more than 40 different countries. Currently, there are over 2,787 satellites orbiting Earth, while the rest have exceeded their useful lives and become space debris. Other satellites have also sent into orbit around Venus, Mars, Jupiter, Saturn, Earth's Moon, and also the asteroid Eros.

👤 In Real Life

Global environmental changes are a matter of grave concern in the 21st century. These include the effects of global warming, ozone depletion, and widespread changes in land cover due to human activities such as **biomass burning**. Satellites have proved to be very useful in monitoring these activities on Earth. Satellite pictures enable scientists to 'view' Earth and understand the actual extent and impact of such activities on our planet. Data from satellites helps differentiate between environmental changes caused by human beings versus those caused by nature. NASA's Mission to Planet Earth programme is one such study of Earth from space.

▲ Deforestation has caused the depletion of rainforests in Brazil

⭐ Why are Satellites Important?

Satellites vary greatly in size, design, and function. Information about Earth's surface, atmosphere, and astronomical observations are mainly collected through scientific satellites. Weather satellites broadcast photographs and information related to cloud patterns and measure other meteorological conditions that help predict the weather. Relays made by communication satellites enable us to tune in to and make phone calls, receive radio and television programmes, and also access the internet from different parts of the planet. Some satellites help in navigation to determine the positions of ships and airplanes. The **Global Positioning System (GPS)** also uses navigation satellites. It is a space-based radio-navigation system that helps us find our location regardless of where we are in the world. Military satellites carry out military observation and surveillance.

▲ Many cars and phones today have GPS navigation systems that help people find their destinations

The Future of Space Exploration

Over the years, humans have made incredible progress in space exploration. The 21st century is also called the Age of Information and Technology. The study of space has become even more exciting in this century, thanks to innovations in space travel and exploration.

Private Spaceflights

Private companies have played a part in spaceflights since 1962, when NASA launched its first privately-made satellite. Today, companies like SpaceX and Boeing have started competing for big government contracts.

On February 6, 2018, SpaceX successfully launched an operational rocket named Falcon Heavy into space. It carried a Tesla Roadster, which is an electric sports car. Starman, a mannequin dressed in a spacesuit, sat in the driver's seat of the car. Falcon Heavy became the most powerful operational launch vehicle in the world.

Blue Origin and Virgin Galactic are some other examples of private companies that have ventured into space tourism. Blue Origin's upgraded New Shepard spacecraft shows amazing views of Earth. It went on its tenth test flight in January 2019. This marks another step towards sending paying tourists into suborbital space.

State-of-the-art Spacecrafts

The new NASA missions are getting more advanced with state-of-the-art technologies. For example, the design of NASA's Orion crew exploration vehicle is along the lines of the earlier Apollo missions, but with upgraded systems that use modern technology. The new capsules will be large enough to accommodate four crew members and have three times the volume capacity. The Orion capsules are supposed to be safer and more reliable than the space shuttle.

An added innovation is that they are built to be reused up to ten times and will use the same method of parachuting back to Earth, but will land on dry land, instead of an ocean splashdown. Having launched Orion in an unmanned test flight in December 2014, NASA aims to send a crewed mission on it in 2021. Such new-age space vehicles herald a new period in space exploration—one which will take human beings farther than they have ever been before, including in close proximity to the Moon and Mars!

◄ *Launched by SpaceX, Falcon Heavy's side boosters land on Landing Zone 1 (LZ1) and Landing Zone 2 (LZ2) during a demo mission*

In Real Life

The Falcon Heavy launch generated excitement amongst the general public and space industry. Along with broadcasts of Starman, the launch was viewed 40 million times on SpaceX's YouTube channel. The company has since then bagged its first competitive contract from the US Air Force.

▲ *Maiden launch of SpaceX's Falcon Heavy in February 2018*

All about Astronauts

An astronaut is a person who travels into outer space, but the term is commonly used for persons on US spacecrafts. The Chinese call them taikonauts or *yuhangyuans*, which in Chinese means 'space navigator'. Read on to know more about their brave journeys.

 ## Who can Become an Astronaut?

People who apply to become astronauts undergo a strict selection process. Experienced test and jet aircraft pilots, and those with advanced scientific, medical, or engineering prowess are eligible. In the US, astronauts are classified into shuttle pilots and mission commanders, mission specialists, and educator mission specialists.
In Russia, they have two categories: mission commanders, who are usually pilots, and flight engineers.

 ## How do Astronauts Prepare to Go into Space?

Astronauts undertake two to four years of rigorous physical and mental training and should be able to live in isolated and confined spaces for long periods. They undergo training in technical, safety, and survival techniques as well as handling emergencies. They are also trained in systems, robotics, spacecraft operations, space engineering activities, etc. Some of them working on the **International Space Station (ISS)** need to learn Russian to communicate with the Russian Mission Control Centre. The ISS was set up in low-Earth orbit mainly by the USA and Russia, with help and components from a multinational association.

▼ *Spacesuits protect astronauts from the hazards of being out in space. They are also known as Extravehicular Mobility Units*

⭐ Simulations and Mock-ups

To prepare for space, astronauts often practice on life-sized models called 'mock-ups'. In the USA, the Space Vehicle Mock-up Facility serves this purpose.

At the facility, astronauts practice and learn to navigate themselves in a weightless condition called **microgravity** or zero gravity. The KC-135 (also called the Weightless Wonder or, humorously, the Vomit Comet) provides US astronauts with a zero-gravity environment for 20-25 seconds. Two other types of facilities help them practice moving large objects in space that have a tendency to float away, and practice spacewalks and rehearse on a full-sized model of a space vehicle while underwater.

⭐ What do Astronauts Eat?

Earlier, astronauts had to eat unappetising edible cubes, freeze-dried powders, and semi-liquids packaged in aluminium tubes. Freeze-dried foods were difficult to rehydrate and crumbs were dangerous since they could float off and destroy instruments on board. Since then, food eaten in space has improved considerably and astronauts today have a more appetising menu consisting of food items that can be prepared easily. Salt and pepper are only available in liquid forms since the powder form would pose a threat to both astronauts and the spacecraft.

▲ Astronauts float in space due to zero gravity, which leads to weightlessness

◀ A meal in space—astronauts eating floating tomatoes and hamburgers in the service module

⭐ Why do Astronauts Wear Spacesuits?

Spacesuits protect astronauts from harmful radiation and extreme temperatures experienced in space. They shield them against dangerous and fast-moving space dust particles that can injure them. The Primary Life Support Subsystem supplies oxygen for breathing and removes exhaled carbon dioxide. The visors protect the astronauts' eyes from harsh sunlight. A Liquid Cooling and Ventilation Garment keeps astronauts cool during a spacewalk.

👤 In Real Life

In space, flour tortillas are considered to be a better food choice than bread. This takes care of the problem of bread crumbs floating around. Meals and menus are planned in advance, and nutritionists ensure that the astronauts get their required daily intake of calories.

▶ A spacesuit weighs approximately 127 kg

The First Humans in Space

The Soviet Union sent the first human beings to outer space. This was a huge milestone for them and for the entire space industry. Let us take a look at some of these pioneers.

Yuri Gagarin: First Man in Space

Yuri Gagarin (1934–1968), the son of a carpenter, initially studied at a trade school near Moscow. He later took up flying and graduated from the Soviet Air Force cadet school in 1957.

Gagarin made headlines on 12 April 1961, when he blasted into space aboard the Vostok 1 spacecraft at 9:07 am, Moscow time, orbited Earth at a speed of 27,400 kilometres per hour and reached a height of 301 kilometres. He spent 108 minutes in orbit before returning to Earth. Gagarin ejected from the vehicle and landed by parachute. He became a worldwide hero and was awarded the Order of Lenin amongst other recognitions and titles.

▲ At the Paris International Air Show (1965), Yuri Gagarin greets NASA's Gemini 4 astronauts Edward White II and James McDivitt

Valentina Tereshkova: First Woman in Space

After Gagarin's success, Soviet Chief Designer Sergey Korolyov wanted to send a woman to space. Earlier, it was assumed that the best candidates were military pilots, as they were accustomed to the stress of space flight, however, they were exclusively male. Since the Vostok spaceship was mostly automated, piloting was no longer a requirement, but parachuting skills were essential since Vostok cosmonauts were required to use and manoeuvre a parachute to help them land safely on Earth when they were ejected from the capsule.

For this reason, in 1962, Valentina Tereshkova was selected from among 400 female applicants. While Tereshkova had little formal education, she was an experienced and skilled parachutist. She became the first woman in space aboard the Vostok 6 on 16 June 1963. In three days, Tereshkova orbited Earth 48 times and successfully landed back on Earth on 19 June. No other Russian woman went into space until 19 years later.

Incredible Individuals

When NASA opened up its astronaut selection process to women in 1976, Sally Ride was one of the 8,000 applicants. Women were being considered and selected as Mission Specialists for the first time. In June 1983, Ride blasted off into orbit on the Challenger orbiter, becoming the first American woman to go into space.

▲ Sally Ride was amongst the first six female astronauts to be recruited in the 1978 batch by NASA

▲ Major of the Soviet Air Forces, Valentina Tereshkova was the first woman in space

The First Human Beings to Reach the Moon

On 20 July 1969, Neil Armstrong, Buzz Aldrin, and Michael Collins created history by becoming the first astronauts to reach the Moon aboard the Apollo 11. Armstrong stepped onto the lunar surface—the first person to do so—with the famous words, "That's one small step for [a] man, one giant leap for mankind." Aldrin and Armstrong spent over two hours on the Moon collecting surface samples and clicking photographs. After spending 21 hours and 36 minutes on the Moon, they returned to Earth in a splashdown in the Pacific.

Neil Armstrong

Neil Armstrong (1930–2012) qualified as a pilot at 16 and served in the Korean War. After completing his degree in aeronautical engineering in 1955, he worked with NACA as a civilian research pilot, and later worked for NASA. He tested many supersonic fighters, including the X-15 rocket plane.

In 1966, as commander pilot of the Gemini 8, along with David Scott, he managed the first manual space docking with another unstaffed rocket. A glitch made the spacecraft go into an uncontrollable spin, but Armstrong recovered control and managed an emergency landing in the Pacific Ocean.

Edwin 'Buzz' Aldrin

Buzz Aldrin graduated from the US Military Academy in New York, became an air force pilot and served 66 combat missions in the Korean war. He did his PhD in **astronautics** from MIT. In 1963, he was the first person with a doctorate to be recruited by NASA.

His work on docking and rendezvous techniques for space vehicles led to the success of the Gemini and Apollo programmes and is still being used. Aldrin started underwater training to mimic spacewalking and completed five and a half hours on three spacewalks. He wrote several memoirs and books and was awarded the Presidential Medal of Freedom and the Congressional Gold Medal.

In Real Life

All the crew members of Apollo 11 spent 21 days in isolation to prevent contamination by lunar microbes. After their successful return, the crew did a 21-nation tour and were hailed globally!

▲ *Commander of the Apollo 11 flight Neil Armstrong*

▲ *Lunar module (Eagle) pilot Buzz Aldrin*

Milestones in Space Exploration

The United States of America and Soviet Union were the key players in space exploration from 1957 till the end of the Cold War in 1991. After the disintegration of USSR, Russia, and US became collaborators on space missions and projects, for instance, the ISS. Major milestones in space aviation and exploration are listed below.

1957
October: The Soviet Union launched the first artificial satellite, Sputnik, into space. In November of the same year they sent the first living creature, a dog, into space aboard Sputnik 2.

1958
January: First satellite launched by USA—Explorer 1.

1960
August: Soviet Union's Sputnik 5 carried two dogs (Strelka and Belka)—the first living beings to survive a journey into space.

▲ The space capsule of Sputnik 5 in a museum

1961
April: Yuri Gagarin, a Russian cosmonaut, became the first human in space.

May: Alan Shepard became the first American to go into space.

1962
February: John Glenn became the first American to orbit Earth.

June: Russia sent the first woman into space—Valentina Tereshkova.

1965
March: Cosmonaut Alexei Leonov undertook the first spacewalk.

June: Ed White became the first American to undertake a spacewalk.

July: NASA's Mariner 4 transmitted the first photographs of Mars.

1971
April: Salyut 1, the first-ever space station was launched by the Russians.

November: The Mariner 9 probe became the first craft to orbit another planet—Mars.

1970
September: Soviet craft Luna 16 was launched and was the first automatic spacecraft to bring back soil samples from the Moon.

1969
July: The first humans landed on the Moon—Neil Armstrong and Buzz Aldrin.

1968
December: NASA launched Apollo 8; later, its crew members became the first men to orbit the Moon.

▲ The Apollo 8 crew in training

1966
February: Soviet Union's Luna 9 became the first spacecraft to land on the Moon.

June: Surveyor 1 became the first American spacecraft to land on the Moon.

▲ The Luna 9 mission proved that landers would not sink into the dust on the Moon

▶ The Skylab space station prior to launch

1973
May: Skylab, the first American space station was launched—it was the first manned research lab in space.

1975
May: USA's Apollo 18 and the Soviet Soyuz 19 launched in the Apollo-Soyuz Test Project—the first joint US-Soviet space project.

1976
September: Water frost discovered on Mars by American probe Viking 2.

1977
August and September: The USA launched interplanetary probes Voyager 2 and then Voyager 1.

1979
March and August: Voyager 1 and 2 began sending images of Jupiter and its moons.

1981
April: The first space shuttle, Columbia was launched. In February 2003, on its 28th mission into space, minutes before it was to land, it broke apart, killing all 7 astronauts on board.

▲ Crew members of space shuttle Columbia died when it crumbled over Texas in February 2003

1986
January: Voyager 2 began transmitting images from Uranus.

February: The core section of the Soviet space station Mir was launched.

1990
August: NASA's Magellan, the first planetary spacecraft launched from the space shuttle, began mapping the surface of Venus using radar equipment. Also, the Hubble Space Telescope was deployed by space shuttle Discovery.

1992
May: NASA's space shuttle Endeavour began her maiden voyage.

▲ Space shuttle Endeavour flew its final mission in 2011

2000
February: USA's Near Earth Asteroid Rendezvous (NEAR) spacecraft began transmitting images of the asteroid Eros. A year later, NEAR landed on its surface.

1998
November: The first segment of the International Space Station (ISS), built in collaboration with the space agencies of USA, Russia, Europe, Japan, and Canada, was launched.

1997
July: The Mars Pathfinder, an American robotic spacecraft, arrived on Mars and later began transmitting images.

1995
February: American astronaut Eileen Collins became the first female space shuttle pilot. In 1999 she became the space shuttle's first female commander.

▲ Eileen Collins seated at the flight desk commander's station

2001
April: American Dennis Tito paid the Russian space programme $20,000,000 to become the first tourist in space.

◀ Dennis Tito (extreme left) was the first private citizen to visit the International Space Station

2003
August: The Spitzer Telescope, the largest-diameter infrared telescope in space, was launched by NASA.

2005
July: A planned collision of a NASA spacecraft with a comet took place, to help study the building blocks of life on Earth.

Also, space shuttle Discovery (STS-114) was launched with seven astronauts aboard—it was USA's first 'Return to Flight' mission after the 2003 Columbia disaster.

2006
January: NASA's spacecraft Stardust returned to Earth with the first dust ever collected from a comet.

2007
August: NASA launched its Phoenix Mars Lander, which discovered chunks of ice on the planet.

2012
May: SpaceX launched its Dragon C2+ mission to send supplies to the International Space Station.

August: NASA's Voyager 1 probe, launched in 1977, entered interstellar space.

2010
March: NASA's MESSENGER (Mercury Surface, Space Environment, Geochemistry, and Ranging mission) became the first spacecraft to orbit Mercury.

November: Curiosity, the biggest, most advanced robot ever sent to explore another planet, was launched by NASA. It landed on Mars in August 2012. Curiosity was launched in November 2011.

2010
December: SpaceX (Space Exploration Technologies Corporation), a private American aerospace company, launched a spacecraft into orbit and returned it safely to Earth. It became the first non-governmental organisation to do so.

2009
March: NASA launched the Kepler spacecraft to look for exoplanets.

June: NASA launched the Lunar Crater Observation and Sensing Satellite (LCROSS) to confirm the presence or absence of ice on the Moon. In November they discovered a significant amount of ice near the Moon's south pole.

2013
November: The Mars Orbiter Mission or Mangalyaan was launched successfully by the Department of Space–Indian Space Research Organisation (ISRO). At a cost of ₹4.5 billion, it is one of the cheapest interplanetary space missions ever. USA, Russia, and Europe are the only others who have sent missions to Mars, and much to the credit of India, it succeeded in its first attempt.

2015
March: NASA's Dawn spacecraft became the first to orbit a dwarf planet, Ceres.

July: NASA's New Horizons, which had conducted a six-month-long study of Pluto and its moons, came closest to the planet.

2018
June: Japanese mission Hayabusa 2 arrived at the Ryugu asteroid. In September of the same year, it stationed the first rovers to operate on an asteroid. It will bring back asteroid samples to Earth in 2020.

2019
January: China's Chang'e-4 robotic spacecraft was the first to land successfully on the far side of the Moon (side facing away from Earth).

September: India's Chandrayaan-2 Moon lander, Vikram, made a hard landing on the lunar surface. It was targeted to make a soft landing on the Moon's south pole but ISRO lost communication with it moments before its landing.

Word Check

Accelerator: In a car, the accelerator is a pedal at the feet of the driver. Pressing it makes the car go faster.

Aeronautics (also aeronautical/astronautical engineering): It is the science of designing, building, operating, and testing aircrafts or vehicles that are used to travel in Earth's atmosphere or in outer space.

Alloys: In the making of metals, alloys are formed by mixing two or more pure metals. This creates new types of metals that are suitable for different technologies.

AM: This stands for Amplitude Modulation, a method in which sound is coded on to radio waves for transmission.

Anaesthetic: It is a drug that numbs a part of your body (local anaesthetic) or puts your whole body to sleep (general anaesthetic).

Analgesic: It is a painkiller.

Anatomy: It is the study of the internal structure of living things.

Angular Velocity: The velocity with which an object traverses an arc of a circle.

Anode: It is the positively charged electrode by which the electrons leave an electrical device.

Anode reaction: The chemical reaction in a cell that gives off electrons.

Appendectomy: It is the surgical removal of the appendix, a small pouch-like organ in the lower right side of your abdomen.

Astronomical map: It is a scientifically drawn chart of stars, galaxies, surfaces of planets, and the Moon in the night sky.

Bay: It is a small body of water surrounded by land on three sides.

Biconvex Lens: A lens in which both surfaces are curved outwards, as in a magnifying glass.

Big Bang model: It is the theory of the evolution of the universe that states that the universe emerged from a state of extremely high temperature and density, which occurred around 13.8 billion years ago.

Bipedal: Using two legs for walking.

Buoyancy: The force exerted by a fluid resisting the force of gravity.

Burro: It is a small donkey.

Carburettor: It is the part of the engine where fuel and air combine and burn. The carburettor also controls the flow of air into the engine and the engine's speed.

Cathode: It is the negatively charged electrode by which electrons enter an electrical device.

Cathode reaction: The chemical reaction in a cell that takes up electrons.

Centrifuge: A machine used to separate undissolved solids from a liquid by spinning.

Chemical Reaction: An exchange of electrons between two elements or compounds.

Circumpolar constellations: They are the constellations that never set below the horizon when seen from a particular location on Earth.

Climate Sceptic: A person who does not believe that climate change is being caused by human actions.

Clutch: It is the part that connects the engine to the wheels.

Coefficient of Kinetic Friction: A measure of how much force will be needed to overcome friction between two substances moving in opposite directions.

Coefficient of Static Friction: A measure of how much force will be needed to overcome friction between two substances resting on each other.

Concave Lens: A lens in which one or both surfaces are curved inwards.

Conquistador: It is a title used to describe a leader in the Spanish conquest of the Americas.

Constellations: They refer to the groups of stars that form an imagined pattern in the sky. These constellations are imagined by those who named them to form conspicuous configurations of objects or creatures in the sky.

Convection Current: The circular movement of atoms or molecules in a liquid or gas caused by the heating of one side.

Convex Lens: A lens in which one or both surfaces are curved outwards.

Cro-Magnon: It is an erect and tall race of ancient humans of France. They were among the earliest *Homo sapiens* on Earth.

c.: This is an abbreviation for the word 'circa', which means about or approximately.

Current: The movement of electrons across an electric potential.

Deductive Reasoning: A decision based on current circumstances as well as memory.

Designer Baby: A human whose genome has been modified artificially to eliminate disease traits or to enhance intelligence, strength, etc.

Detector: An electronic device

INVENTIONS & DISCOVERIES | SCIENCE | SPACE — WORD CHECK

that creates a current when an electromagnetic wave falls on it.

Diamagnetic: Materials that cannot be magnetised at all.

Dielectric: A substance that does not allow current to pass.

Displacement: The difference between the initial and final locations of an object.

Dissect: It is a process by which a person methodically cuts open a dead creature (plant, animal, or human) to study its insides.

ECG: It is the abbreviation for electrocardiogram. It is a test that records your heartbeat to see if it is functioning well.

EEG: It is the abbreviation for electroencephalogram. It is a test for examining abnormalities in your brain.

Efficiency: The fraction of the input energy that a system delivers as work.

Electric Charge: A property of matter that makes it react to an electromagnetic field.

Electromagnetic Energy: The energy of a moving electric charge or magnetic field.

Electromagnetic rays: A number of visible and invisible rays that include X-rays, all the colours of light, microwaves, infrared rays, gamma rays, and many others.

Electromagnetism: An electric field created by a moving magnet, or a magnetic field created by a moving electron.

Electron: It is an elementary particle that is negatively charged. The two other elementary particles are protons, which carry a positive charge, and neutrons, which carry no charge at all. Together these three elementary particles form an atom.

Estuary: It refers to the widening arms of a river, where they meet the sea.

Exoplanet: Also known as extrasolar planets, they are planets that orbit a star other than the Sun.

Experiences: The effect of an external force upon an object.

External Work: The work done by a system on the environment.

Ferromagnetic: Materials that can be magnetised permanently.

FM: Frequency Modulation is a way of imposing sound on to radio waves so they can be transmitted over the radio.

Friction Force: The force needed to overcome friction.

Friction: The resistance offered to motion by electromagnetic attraction between objects.

Gamma rays, X-rays, and infrared rays: They are different types of electromagnetic rays; they are like light rays, but are invisible to our eyes.

Gamma Rays: Very high energy electromagnetic waves with wavelengths smaller than X-rays, emitted from nuclear reactions.

Gear shift: In vehicles, gears are used to manage speed and direction with maximum efficiency. A gear shift is the mechanism by which a driver can change gears to change speed or direction.

Genetic Disease: A disease caused by changes in a person's DNA, because of which their bodies don't work correctly.

Geocentric model: According to this theory, Earth lies at the centre of the solar system or universe. It has now been debunked.

Geostationary: It refers to the orbit of a satellite that keeps up with the spin of Earth; thus, it remains above the same spot in comparison to our planet.

Global Positioning System (GPS): It is a space-based radio-navigation system that broadcasts highly accurate navigation pulses to users on or near Earth.

Gradient: The ratio of the rise of a plane and its horizontal length.

Gravitational Waves: Disturbances in space-time caused by the movement of astronomical bodies.

Gulf: It is a part of the sea that is surrounded by land on three sides.
It is larger than a bay.

Heliocentric model: According to this theory, the Sun is considered to be the central figure within the solar system, around which Earth and other planets revolve.

HTML: It is the abbreviation for hypertext markup language: a language that marks up documents for the World Wide Web. It can be used for text, art, sound, video, and hyperlinks.

Hydroxyl Ion: An ion made of an oxygen atom and a hydrogen atom, with a net negative charge, that is made by alkalis.

Image: The representation of an object formed by reflection from a mirror or refraction from a lens or prism.

Indigenous: It refers to a group of people who are native to an area.

Inductive Reasoning: A decision based on the memory of past actions.

Infrared (IR) Waves: Low energy electromagnetic waves with wavelengths smaller than visible light but longer than microwaves.

Internal Work: The work done within a system.

International Space Station (ISS): It was set up in low-Earth orbit mainly by the USA and Russia, with help and components from a multinational association.

Interstellar: It is the region between the stars that contains vast, diffuse clouds of gases and minute solid particles.

Ionising Radiation: Electronic waves that can remove electrons when they hit an atom and turn them into positively charged ions.

Ions: They are atoms with extra electrons or missing electrons.

Isthmus: It is a narrow strip of land surrounded by water on two sides.

Kinetic Energy: The energy a system possesses because of its motion.

Kinsay: It is a city that was captured by the Mongols in 1279. It helped them control all of China. With more than a million people, it was the world's largest city at the time—many times larger than the cities of Europe.

Lander: It is a space module that lands on celestial bodies such as asteroids, comets, planets, and natural satellites.

Language: A set of sounds whose meanings are shared by a group of people, organised into words and sentences.

Lattice: The pattern of arrangements of atoms, ions or molecules in a crystalline solid.

Light year: It is the distance travelled by light in one year, at a speed of 300,000 kilometres per second.

Light year: It is the distance travelled by light moving in a vacuum in the course of one year.

Mach: It is a relative measurement of high speed, usually compared with the speed of sound.

Marooned: It means to abandon a person on a deserted island.

Mechanical Energy: The energy that we see in the movement of objects.

Mechanical Waves: Non-electromagnetic waves made by the movement of atoms and molecules.

Mechanics: The science of motion and forces.

Mesopotamia: It is a Greek word for 'two rivers'. This name refers to the historical area between the rivers Tigris and Euphrates. It was dominated by the Sumerian, Akkadian, Assyrian, and Babylonian civilisations.

Microchip: It is a tiny silicon chip that can be found in many computers. It has electronic circuits that enable the chip to hold information.

Microgravity: It is a measure of the degree to which an object in space is subjected to acceleration. It is more commonly used synonymously with zero gravity and weightlessness.

Momentum: The amount of inertia in a body due to its mass and velocity.

Mutiny: It is a revolt against a superior officer.

N-dope: A non-metallic dope added to a semiconductor to make it relatively negatively charged.

Non-ionising Radiation: Electronic waves that cannot remove electrons when they hit an atom.

Normal Force: The force exerted by a solid resisting a substance pushing against it.

Optical Magnification: The ratio of the size of an image to the size of the object creating it.

Optical Resolution: The smallest distance between two objects that can make them appear as separate images through a lens.

Ore: A mineral from which metal can be extracted on a large scale.

Paramagnetic: Materials that can be magnetised for a short while

P-dope: A metallic dope added to a semiconductor to make it relatively positively charged.

Periscope: A device to make an image of an object that cannot be seen directly.

Photons: These are particles of light, and a type of electromagnetic radiation.

Plasma: It is the fourth state of matter (after solid, liquid, and gas); it is an ionized gas.

Pneumatic: In mechanics, this refers to an object that can be filled with air, or a system that works using air pressure.

P-n junction: A diode made by putting together small crystals of p-doped and n-doped semiconductors together.

Possession: The physical attributes innate to an object.

Potential Energy: The energy available in a system for conversion to work.

Precession: It describes the motion of a body spinning in such a way that it wobbles, so that the axis of rotation sweeps out a cone.

Proto humans: They are also called archaic humans. This phrase describes closely-related human species that lived on earth thousands of years ago. This includes *Homo neanderthalensis* (Neanderthals) and *Australopithecus afarensis.* All of them are now extinct, except for *Homo sapiens*, the modern humans.

Quadricycle: It is a cycle with four wheels.

Quantised: The property of all energy to be made of tiny units called quanta

Radio Waves: Very low energy electromagnetic waves with wavelengths longer than microwaves.

Radio waves: When electricity and magnetism interact, they produce a variety of wave-like effects called electromagnetic radiation. Many of these waves—radio waves, X-rays, microwaves, infrared rays, ultraviolet rays, gamma rays—are invisible to our eyes. Visible light, that is, all the colours of the rainbow, also consists of electromagnetic waves.

Relative Density: The ratio of the density of a substance to the density of a reference substance.

Sampans: They are narrow wooden boats used in East Asia.

Scalar: A physical measure with magnitude but no direction.

Semiconductor: A material that allows only some electricity to pass through it.

Semiconductor: It is a solid substance that is used in electrical devices, as it allows electrical energy and heat to move through it.

Sextant: It is an instrument used to determine the angle between the horizon and a celestial object like a star, the Sun, or the Moon.

Singularity: In reference to a black hole, when a star dies, the crushing weight of constituent matter falling in from all sides compresses the dying star to a point of zero volume and infinite density called the singularity

Solar wind: A continuous outflow of solar subatomic particles from the outer regions of the Sun into the solar system

Solvent: A substance that dissolves another substance.

Spark plug: It is a battery-operated gadget that sparks when a current runs through it. This provides the combustion for the engine.

Specific Gravity: The ratio of the density of a substance to the density of water.

Sphygmomanometer: A device that measures blood pressure.

Strait: It is a narrow strip of water surrounded by land on two sides.

Super hot water: Water that has been heated above 100°C, but has not turned to steam because of extreme pressure.

Supersaturation: A solution which has crossed the maximum amount a substance will dissolve in it.

Transistor: It is a device that uses semiconductors to control the flow of electricity in a machine.

Trigonometry: It is a field of mathematics concerned with functions of angles and their application to calculations.

Tutankhamun: He is possibly the most famous Pharaoh since 1922, when British archaeologist Howard Carter unearthed his treasure-filled tomb in Egypt's Valley of the Kings.

Vacuum: It is an empty space that is free of all matter, even air. It is not possible to have a true and complete vacuum, but you can get very close to it.

Vacuum tube: Also called a valve, this electronic device looks like a light bulb, but works like a switch. When the tube is heated up, it allows electricity to flow through. When the tube is cold, the current stops.

Van der Waals Force: The attraction between atoms and molecules of a substance due to minor electric charges on them (electric dipole).

Variolation: It is an obsolete technique of immunising a patient.

Vector: A physical measure with magnitude and direction.

Velocipede: It is a vehicle that runs on land with the force or effort exerted by human beings. The modern bicycle is a common example of a velocipede.

Velocity: The rate at which a body moves in one direction.

Victorian: It refers to an event, person, or invention from the Victorian Era or the period during which Queen Victoria ruled over the United Kingdom.

Viscosity: The resistance a substance offers to flowing.

Volcanism: Release of energy, mostly as heat, from within the earth.

Adhesion: The forces that pull atoms or molecules of two substances together.

Water radiator: It is a cooling system that keeps the engine from overheating.

Wavelength: The distance a photon moves while completing a single vibration.

X-rays: High energy electromagnetic waves with wavelengths smaller than ultraviolet light but more than gamma rays.

Cover

From left to right

Shutterstock: Front: Axel Alvarez; BlueRingMedia; Nathapol Kongseang; tr/Yellow Cat; vladsilver; panor156; wacomka; GraphicsRF.com; Sarunyu_foto; Alex Staroseltsev; Andrew Burgess; Eric Isselee; DM7; Sebastian Janicki; New Africa; Jiang Zhongyan; Grigorev Mikhail; Kletr; Vac1; robert_s; Inachis Projekt; **Back:** Romolo Tavani; Bonita R. Cheshier; Tatyana Mi; Radek Borovka; Dennis W Donohue; Vibe Images; Sunti; Anan Kaewkhammul; FrentaN; Hintau Aliaksei; Smit; Anton-Burakov; Eric Isselee; lusia83; Rattachon Angmanee; Eric Isselee; Quang Ho; Eric Isselee; design36

a: above, **b:** below/ bottom, **c:** centre, **f:** far, **l:** left, **r:** right, **t:** top, **bg:** background

Inventions and Discoveries

Shutterstock: 7c/Uncle Leo; 7b/Procy; 8tc/WH_Pics; 9tc/Mark Sheridan-Johnson; 9tr/Abeselom Zerit; 8&9/Nataliya Stolyar; 11tr/Kamira; 10&11/Homo Cosmicos; 12&13/Tartila; 13br/Cindy Xiong; 14tr/ecstk22; 14br/CRS PHOTO; 15tl/givaga; 15tr/dagherrotipo; 15bl/zawisak; 15br/C.J. Everhardt; 17tr/Milagli; 18cr/matrioshka; 18bc/Kokhanchikov; 19br/ChameleonsEye; 20cl/Halit Sadik; 21cr/Marko5; 20&21c/Seita; 23tr/Everett Collection; 23bl/Yevgenia Gorbulsky; 22&23bg/Magenta10; 25c/sisqopote; 26tr/TierneyMJ; 28tl/JuliusKielaitis; 28cl/buteo; 29tl/Tomas Kotouc; 29tr/FOTOGRIN; 30cl/GUDKOV ANDREY; 32br/Diego Grandi; 32br2/Don Mammoser; 34bl/Stefano Buttafoco; 35tr/Szasz-Fabian Jozsef; 35cr/Macrovector; 36tr/Marynchenko Oleksandr; 36cr/mekcar; 36cr2/Ground Picture; 36br/wichayada suwanachun; 37tr/Marzolino; 37cr/mipan; 37bl/Everett Collection; 37br/Sergey Kohl; 38crDmitry Kalinovsky; 38bl/BrAt82; 39cl/Skylines; 39c/Krishnadas; 39br/BCFC; 39r/DenisNata; 39bl/Everett Collection; 40tl/PitukTV; 40br/Andrey_Popov; 41tl/padu_foto; 41bl/RAY-BON&Everett Collection; 42b/emkaplin; 43tl/Everett Collection; 43bl/Artsplav; 43br/File:Sholes typewriter.jpg; 44tr/A_stockphoto; 44b/gyn9037; 45tl/Sashkin; 45cr/sdecoret; 47cr/HodagMedia; 49tl/fuyu liu; 50cl/J J Osuna Caballero; 52tr/T photography; 52cl/olrat; 52cr/Josemon_Vazhayil; 52c/Claudio Divizia; 52cr2/Q'ju Creative; 52b/Hit1912; 54&55/Magenta10; 54bl/Nejron Photo; 54c2/atticandtales; 55tr/antoniradso; 55c/Aigars Reinholds; 56tl/Hoika Mikhail; 56br/Everett Collection; 59c/muratart; 60c/clearviewstock; 60cl/Andrey_Popov; 60c2/wavebreakmedia; 60cr/Andrey_Popov; 60l/Aptyp_koK; 60bl/sirtravelalot; 60br/catshila; 61tl/sumire8; 61cr/Charles Brutlag; 61b/vchal; 62tc/create jobs 51; 62cl/create jobs 51; 62cr/Everett Collection; 62&63t/KaliAntye; 63b/Thomas Andreas; 64tl/Monkey Business Images; 64bl/Everett Collection; 64br/Oleg Golovnev; 64&65c/Apostle; 65br/luanateutzi; 66cr/Kateryna Kon; 66cl/Satirus; 66bl/nobeastsofierce; 67bl/Aleksandrs Bondars; 68t/Diego Cervo; 69bl/irinabdw; 70c/Sandra Foyt; 70br/Elnur; 70&71t/Jacob Lund; 72tr/Sergey Nivens; 72cr/vitstudio; 73bl/501room; 76bc/Asetta; 76br/Gilberto Souza; 77cl/svic; 79tr/FreshPaint; 83tr/3DMI;

Wikimedia Commons: 9bl/File:Venus of Dolni Vestonice 2014-09-30.jpg/wikimediacommons; 10tl/File:Bell Beaker, Copper Age, City of Prague Museum, 175585.jpg/wikimediacommons; 10br/File:DO-2346-VognserupEnge.jpg/wikimediacommons; 11tl/File:Gold bracelet bull head Transylvania.jpg/wikimediacommons; 11cl/File:Alaca Hüyük dagger.jpg/wikimediacommons; 11cr/File:Bronze age weapons Romania.jpg/wikimediacommons; 12c/File:Solvognen-00100.jpg/wikimediacommons; 12bc/File:Attic Black-Figure Amphora (HARGM3804) showing A side decoration.JPG/wikimediacommons; 12&13bc/File:1600 Himmelsscheibe von Nebra sky disk anagoria.jpg/wikimediacommons; 13tl/File:BMC 06.jpg/wikimediacommons; 13tr/File:Ironie pile Bagdad.jpg/wikimediacommons; 14cr/File:Exekias Dionysos Staatliche Antikensammlungen 2044.jpg/wikimediacommons; 16bl/File:Drop spindle from Egypt.jpg/wikimediacommons; 17c/File:South-pointing chariot (Science Museum model).jpg/wikimediacommons; 17bl/File:Model Si Nan of Han Dynasty.jpg/wikimediacommons; 18tl/File:Xerxes Cuneiform Van.JPG/wikimediacommons; 18tr/File:Sin-kashid cone (sikkatu), c. 1850 BC - Oriental Institute Museum, University of Chicago - DSC07176.JPG/wikimediacommons; 18bl/File:Shang dynasty inscribed tortoise plastron.jpg/ wikimediacommons; 18br/File:Tablet V of the Epic of Gilgamesh.jpg/wikimediacommons; 19cl/File:Odyssey manuscript.jpg/wikimediacommons; 19cr/File:Cheshm manuscript.jpg/wikimediacommons; 19bl/File:P1050763 Louvre code Hammurabi face rwk.JPG/wikimediacommons; 21tl/File:Hama-3 norias.jpg/wikimediacommons; 21cl/File:Chadouf égyptien, dessin de voyageur de 1890.jpg/wikimediacommons; 21bFile:PSM V38 D177 A trip hammer.jpg/wikimediacommons; 20&21b/File:The dawn of civilization-Egypt and Chaldaea (1897) (14577028168).jpg/wikimediacommons; 22tr/File:Marco Polo Mosaic from Palazzo Tursi.jpg/wikimediacommons; 22b/File:Route of Marco Polo.png/wikimediacommons; 23cr/File:YuanEmperorAlbumKhubilaiPortrait.jpg/wikimediacommons; 23br/FraMauroDetailedMapInverted/wikimediacommons; 24tl/File:Vasco da Gama Leaving Portugal.jpg/wikimediacommons; 24tr/File:A steel engraving from the 1850's, with modern hand coloring.jpg/wikimediacommons; 24bl/File:Pillar of Vasco da Gama.jpg/wikimediacommons; 25tl/File:Retrato de Vasco Nuñez de Balboa (1475-1517) – Anónimo.jpg/wikimediacommons; 25cl/File:Landing of Columbus (2).jpg/wikimediacommons; 25br/File:Monumento a Vasco Núñez de Balboa - Flickr - Chito (3).jpg/wikimediacommons; 26cl/File:Halve Maen front.jpg/wikimediacommons; 26br/File:Henry Hudson column jeh.JPG/wikimediacommons; 26c/File:John Collier - The Last Voyage of Henry Hudson - Google Art Project.jpg/wikimediacommons; 26bl/File:Hudson Arrives in New York Harbor.jpg/wikimediacommons; 27cl/File:Gilsemans 1642.jpg/wikimediacommons; 28tr/File:Charles Darwin seated crop.jpg/wikimediacommons; 28&29b/File:PSM V57 D097 Hms beagle in the straits of magellan.png/wikimediacommons; 30tl/File:Portrait of David Livingstone (4671614).jpg/wikimediacommons; 30cr/File:Congobasinmap.png/wikimediacommons; 31tr/File:Richard Francis Burton by Rischgitz, 1864.jpg/wikimediacommons; 31cl/File:1001-nights-burton-v3-p010.jpg/wikimediacommons; 31cr/File:The Romance of Isabel, Lady Burton - Richard Burton in native dress.jpg/wikimediacommons; 31bl/File:Sir Richard Burton's Tomb.jpg/wikimediacommons; 31b/File:2010-09-14 08-30-11 Tanzania Mwanza Mwanza.jpg/wikimediacommons; 33bl/File:Captain Roald Amundsen and crew aboard the GJOA, Nome, September 1, 1906 (NOWELL 252).jpeg/wikimediacommons; 33br/File:At the South Pole, December 1911.jpg/wikimediacommons; 33tl/File:GeographicSouthpolecrop.jpg/wikimediacommons; 33c/File:Gjøa.jpg/wikimediacommons; 34tr/File:John Ambrose Fleming 1890.png/wikimediacommons; 34br/File:SE-300B-70W.jpg/wikimediacommons; 35b/File:Classic shot of the ENIAC.jpg/wikimediacommons; 36tr/File:Volta battery-MHS 373-IMG 3840-gradient.jpg/wikimediacommons; 38tr/File:Reginald Fessenden, probably 1906.jpg/wikimediacommons; 39tl/File:Antonio Meucci.jpg/wikimediacommons; 40cl/File:John Logie Baird and television receiver.jpg/wikimediacommons; 42tr/File:Charles Babbage by Samuel Laurence.jpg/wikimediacommons; 42cl/File:Ada Lovelace portrait.jpg/wikimediacommons; 43tr/File:Museum of Science, Boston, MA - IMG 3163.JPG/wikimediacommons; 45bl/File:Charles K. Kao cropped 2.jpg/wikimediacommons; 46c/File:Omnibus vélocipédique Securitas, 1889.jpg/wikimediacommons; 46br/File:Bicycle two 1886.jpg/wikimediacommons; 47cl/File:Michaux boneshaker.jpg/wikimediacommons; 47b/File:1886 Starley 'Rover' Safety Cycle British Motor Museum 09-2016 (29928044262).jpg/wikimediacommons; 48tr/File:Aeolipile.jpg/wikimediacommons; 48bl/File:TrevithicksEngine.jpg/wikimediacommons; 48brFile:The Fulton ferry boat, (Brooklyn, N.Y.) LCCN97505116.jpg/wikimediacommons; 48bFile:Moving Rocket 2.jpg/wikimediacommons; 49cr/File:Daimler Maybach Grandfather Clock Engine.jpg/

INVENTIONS & DISCOVERIES | SCIENCE | SPACE — IMAGE CREDITS

wikimediacommons; 50tr/File:La Jamais Contente.JPG/wikimediacommons; 50b/File:Benz 1894 4HP Victoria on London to Brighton VCR 2010.jpg/wikimediacommons; 51tl/File:Leonardo Amboise Automobile.jpg/wikimediacommons; 51tr/File:Women2drive by Latuff.gif/wikimediacommons; 51cr/File:Paris (75), musée des Arts et métiers, Ford model T, 1908 1.jpg/wikimediacommons; 51b/File:Stand Peugeot au Salon de l'Automobile de Paris, janvier 1901 (Grand Palais).jpg/wikimediacommons; 53tl/File:Butler's Patent Velocycle.jpg/wikimediacommons; 53cl/File:Bat 1910 80kmh 01.jpg/wikimediacommons; 53cr/File:Soichiro Honda in 1963.jpg/wikimediacommons; 53bl/File:2016 Yamaha XV1600 Wild Star.jpg/wikimediacommons; 54tlFile:Model of a greek trireme.jpg/wikimediacommons; 54c/File:Wugongchuan - centipede ship.png/wikimediacommons; 54br/File:Mayflower in Plymouth Harbor, by William Halsall.jpg/wikimediacommons; 54cr/File:Queen Anne's Revenge.JPG/wikimediacommons; 55cl/File:Isle of Man Steam Packet Company paddle steamer Queen Victoria..JPG/wikimediacommons; 55c/File:SS Great Britain by Talbot.jpg/wikimediacommons; 55cr/File:USS Birmingham (CL-62) underway in Hampton Roads on 20 February 1943 (NH 90021).jpg /wikimediacommons; 55b/File:Supertanker AbQaiq.jpg/wikimediacommons; 56cr/File:Muenchen Deutsches Museum Fokker DrI.jpg/wikimediacommons; 57cl/File:Heinkel He 178 050602-F-1234P-002.jpg/wikimediacommons; 57cr/File:Concorde on Bristol.jpg/wikimediacommons; 57cFile:Rutan Voyager at the National Air and Space Museum, Dec 2017.jpg/wikimediacommons; 57br/File:Barack Obama leaving Air Force One by night.jpg/wikimediacommons; 58tr/File:Isaac Newton, English School, 1715-20.jpg/wikimediacommons; 58cr/File:Tipu Sultan, Indian warrior Emperor of Mysore.gif/wikimediacommons; 59tr/File:Yuri Gagarin 140-190 for collage.jpg/wikimediacommons; 59cl/File:Sputnik asm.jpg/wikimediacommons; 59b/File:International Space Station after undocking of STS-132.jpg/wikimediacommons; 61tr/File:Laennecs stethoscope, c 1820. (9660576833).jpg/wikimediacommons; 64bc/File:Portrait of Elisa Bonaparte.jpg/wikimediacommons; 65tlFile:Mary Mallon (Typhoid Mary).jpg/wikimediacommons; 65tr/File:Portrait of the Kangxi Emperor in Court Dress.jpg/wikimediacommons; 65bl/File:Ambulance 1905 Yellow Fever New Orleans.jpg/wikimediacommons; 67tr/File:Paul Ehrlich, c. 1910.jpg/wikimediacommons; 67bl/File:Albert Edelfelt - Louis Pasteur - 1885.jpg/wikimediacommons; 68br/File:Old Package of Aspirin.jpg/wikimediacommons; 69cl/Dr._Thomas_Starzl_after_surgery,_Pittsburgh,_Pennsylvania,_c._1990.jpg/wikimediacommons; 69cr/File:Christiaan Barnard 1969.jpg/wikimediacommons; 69br/File:Alexis Carrel 02.jpg/wikimediacommons; 70bc/File:Ambulance of the French Army.jpg/wikimediacommons; 71tc/File:A wealthy patient falling over because of having a tooth ext Wellcome V0012058.jpg/wikimediacommons; 72bl/File:Francis Crick crop.jpg/wikimediacommons; 72bc1/File:James D Watson.jpg/wikimediacommons; 72bc2/File:Maurice H F Wilkins.jpg /wikimediacommons; 72brFile:Rosalind Franklin.jpg/wikimediacommons; 73tr/File:Juan de Miranda Carreno002.jpg/wikimediacommons; 73bl/File:Allan Ramsay - King George III in coronation robes - Google Art Project.jpg/wikimediacommons; 74cl/File:Anaximander Mosaic (cropped, with sundial).jpg/wikimediacommons; 74tr/File:Hendrik ter Brugghen - Democritus.jpg/wikimediacommons; 74bl/File:Aristarchos von Samos (Denkmal).jpeg/wikimediacommons; 74br/File:Nikolaus Kopernikus 2.jpg/wikimediacommons; 75tr/File:Astronomer Edward Charles Pickering's Harvard computers.jpg/wikimediacommons; 75cr/File:AS12-52-7745.jpg/wikimediacommons; 75cl/File:At the Tomb of Omar Khayyam - by Jay Hambidge.jpg/wikimediacommons; 75bl/File:GodfreyKneller-IsaacNewton-1689.jpg/wikimediacommons; 75br/File:Julia Margaret Cameron - John Herschel (Metropolitan Museum of Art copy, restored) levels.jpg/wikimediacommons; 76clFile:RIAN archive 159271 Nikita Khrushchev, Valentina Tereshkova, Pavel Popovich and Yury Gagarin at Lenin Mausoleum.jpg/wikimediacommons; 76cr/File:VAB and SLS.jpg/wikimediacommons; 76bl/File:Nikita-Khrushchev-TIME-1958.jpg/wikimediacommons; 77tl/File:Gagarin in Sweden.jpg/wikimediacommons; 77tr/File:Kennedy Giving Historic Speech to Congress - GPN-2000-001658.jpg/wikimediacommons; 77cl/Photo: RIAN archive 837790 Valentina Tereshkova and Neil Armstrong.jpg/wikimediacommons; 77cr/File:Katherine Johnson at NASA, in 1966.jpg/wikimediacommons; 77br/File:Aldrin Apollo 11 original.jpg/wikimediacommons; 78c/File:Explorer I 02.jpg/wikimediacommons; 78r/File:PSLV C-35 at the launch pad (cropped).jpg/wikimediacommons; 79c/File:Albert II V2 launch.jpg/wikimediacommons; 79cr/File:Arabella web aboard second Skylab mission.jpg /wikimediacommons; 79bl/File:Vostok spacecraft.jpg/wikimediacommons; 80cl/File:Surveyor NASA lunar lander.jpg/wikimediacommons; 80br/File:NASA-Apollo8-Dec24-Earthrise.jpg/wikimediacommons; 81tr/File:Apollo 11 Lunar Module Eagle in landing configuration in lunar orbit from the Command and Service Module Columbia.jpg/wikimediacommons; 81br/File:LRO 2006.jpg/wikimediacommons; 82tr/File:AEHF 1.jpg/wikimediacommons; 82b/File:Canberra Deep Space Communication Complex - general view (2174403243).jpg/wikimediacommons; 82br/File:TIROS-1-Earth.png/wikimediacommons; 83c/File:Crab Nebula NGC 1952 (composite from Chandra, Hubble and Spitzer).jpg/wikimediacommons; 83b/File:Grantelescopio.jpg/wikimediacommons

Science

Shutterstock: 85b/Romolo Tavani; 86cr/Vadim Sadovski; 87br/Rick Partington; 88cr/magnetix & Vector FX; 88b/Szasz-Fabian Ilka Erika; 89tr/everything possible; 89b/pro500; 90&91c/ollomy; 92cr/tony mills;92cl/PHIL LENOIR; 92br/Standret; 93tr/ppart; 93cr/loggy; 93br/ilozavr 94tl/Okrasiuk 94cr/ Steve Cymro 95cr/Designua 95br/MilanB, 95bl/Alhovik, 96tr/fokusgood, 96cr/ ShadeDesign, 96bl/ MDL80; 97tr/zhengzaishuru; 97bl/gui jun peng; 97br/tornadoflight; 98t/DestinaDesign, 98cl/Aleksandr Pobedimskiy, 98br/ Francescomoufotografo; 99cl/BlurryMe, 99br/zentilia, 100tr/13_Phunkod,100bl/VectorShow,100br/Designua101cr/Sashkin, 101blNor Gal, 102cr/Fouad A. Saad, 102-103c/mipan, 102br/Photo smile103tr/Drp8, 103cr/papa studio,103brDesignua 104c/VectorMine, 104bl/yaruna, 105 julie deshaies 105cr/Designua, 105bl/Golubovy, 106-107b/lovelyday12, 106cr/Andrei Armiagov, 107cl/Puripat Lertpunyaroj, 107cr/Breedfoto 108cl/Mopic, 108cr/haryigit, 108bc/OSweetNature, 109tl/Khakimullin Aleksandr, 109cr/DedOK Studio, 109br/Lunja, 110tl/482592334, 110cr/solarseven, 110-111/petovarga, 111tr/Dragon Images, 111br/Gelia,112tr/Taras Kushnir, 112bl/Outer Space, 112br/ VectorMine, 113tr/Master1305 113b/Tom Wang, 114tr/JasminkaM, 114cl/Africa Studio, 114br/Malachy666, 115tr/VectorMine, 115bl/Nejron Photo,115br/isarescheewin ; 116br/Rost9; 116&117/Mauricio Graiki; 117cr/Andrey VP; 118tr/Georgy Shafeev; 118b/gui jun peng; 119tr&cr/Sergey Merkulov; 119br/ArtWell; 120bl/udaix; 120br/Vdovichenko Denis; 121cr/Unkas Photo; 121cl/Heide Pinkall; 121cr/Dmitry_Tsvetkov; 121bl/OlegD; 121br/Vladyslav Starozhylov; 122tr/Crevis; 122r/apiguide; 123cr/Jim Barber; 123bl/Nieuwland Photography; 124tl/3DStach; 124br/Prostock-studio; 125tl/Meletios Verras; 125cr/Dimarion; 125br/Momentum studio; 126cr/Viktoriia_M; 126bl/Yuganov Konstantin; 126br/Phonlamai Photo; 127tr/MarinaGrigorivna; 127cl/sspopov; 127br/AlexxAn; 128tr/Andrey Suslov; 128cl/Africa Studio; 129tr/MVIDEOMEDIA; 129cr/Volodymyr Horbovyy; 128&129 bc/Jenson; 130tl/Alf Ribeiro; 130cr/Soleil Nordic; 131l/ImageFlow; 131cr/Nathan Devery; 132t/Color4260; 132cr/Vasily Deyneka; 132br&bl/udaix; 134bl/udaix; 135cr/Designua; 135br/Fancy Tapis; 134&135c/Petar An; 136bl/varuna, 136r/Racheal Grazias; 136br/Olha1981; 137tc/haryigit; 137cl/Nattawat Kaewjirasit; 137cr/Anna Shepulova; 137bl/TTstudio; 137br/JaySi; 138bl/Fouad A. Saad; 138cr/RenataOs; 138br/Jorge A. Russell; 139cr/Pat_Hastings; 139br/Studio 37; 138&139c/Roman Juchimcuk; 140tr/REDPIXEL.PL; 140bl/Milagli; 140br/Alila Medical Media; 141tr/Volodymyr Nikitenko; 141cl/Billion Photos;

141br/MAV Drone/Fouad A. Saad; 142tr/VladisChern; 142bl/Robyn Mackenzie; 143tr/Edward Westmacott; 143br/feedbackstudio; 142&143b/Fouad A. Saad;

Wikimedia Commons: 86tl/File:The Soviet Union 1971 CPA 4060 stamp (Cosmonauts Georgy Dobrovolsky, Vladislav Volkov and Viktor Patsayev) cancelled.jpg/wikimediacommons; 86bl/File:STS-116 spacewalk 1.jpg/wikimediacommons; 87tr/File:Meal STS127.jpg/wikimediacommons; 86&87/File:SKYLAB I - view from a distance.jpg/wikimediacommons; 90br/File:Biographies of Scientific Men 167 Mendeleev.jpg/wikimediacommons; 117br/File:Sir Isaac Newton by Sir Godfrey Kneller, Bt.jpg/wikimediacommons; 119bl/File:Berthabenzportrait.jpg/wikimediacommons; 123t/File:Uss los angeles airship over Manhattan.jpg/wikimediacommons; 128br/File:R.U.R. by Karel Čapek 1939.jpg/wikimediacommons; 129br/File:Rube Goldberg's "Self-Operating Napkin" (cropped).gif/wikimediacommons; 131br/File:Barbara McClintock (1902-1992) shown in her laboratory in 1947.jpg/wikimediacommons; File:Nernst, Einstein, Planck, Millikan, Laue in 1931.jpg/wikimediacommons; 139tr/File:Fraunhofer lines.svg/wikimediacommons;

Space

Shutterstock: 145b/pixelparticle; 146bl/MaraQu;146bc/Zakharchuk; 146br/Vadim Sadovski; 147c/Designua; 148cr/vectortatu; 148bl/NASA images; 149tl/AZSTARMAN; 149tr/NASA images; 150cr/MU YEE TING; 150br/Nerthuz; 152tl/Dotted Yeti; 152cl/Orla; 152b/i7pu3pak;152cl/Dotted Yeti; 152bl/Orla; 152b/i7pu3pak; 153t/Vadim Sadovski; 153br/Maximillian cabinet; 154cl/Claudio Divizia; 155tr/snapgalleria; 155cr/Jurik Peter; 156bl/Vadim Sadovski; 156br/Jurik Peter; 156&157c/VectorMine; 157tr/yurchak; 157cr/Alpha Footage; 157bl/muratart; 158c/SRStudio; 159tl/Outer Space; 159cl&cr/NASA images; 160tr/NASA images; 160cl/Vadim Sadovskil; 161tr/Petr Malyshev; 162&163/Vadim Sadovski; 164tr/angelinast; 164br/Iron Mary; 165tl/Marzolino; 165br/posteriori&EreborMountain; 166tl/Marzolino; 166bl/Mykola Mazuryk; 166bc/Valeriya Fott; 167tl/Yganko; 167cr/Pozdeyev Vitaly; 166&167c/shooarts; 168c/angelinast; 168b/Foxyliam; 169tl/pecorb; 169cr/Jazziel; 169br/Miceking&N.Vector Design; 170cl/PTZ Pictures; 174tl/3DMI; 174cl/Morphart Creation; 174cr/Everett Collection; 174&175/muratart; 177cr/Vadim Sadovski; 177bl/Everett Collection; 178tl/Andrei Armiagov; 177cr/ Vadim Sadovski; 177bl/Everett Collection; 178tl/Andrei Armiagov; 178bl/Frontpage; 178br/DenPhotos; 180b/NikoNomad;

Wikimedia Commons: 146cr/File:Aleksandr Fridman.png/wikimediacommons/File:Georges_Lemaître_1930s.jpg/wikimediacommons; 148br/File:Messier59 - SDSS DR14.jpg/wikimediacommons; 149cl/File:Irregular galaxy NGC 1427A (captured by the Hubble Space Telescope).jpg/wikimediacommons; 150tr/File:Black hole - Messier 87 crop max res.jpg/wikimediacommons; 151tr/File:Eros - PIA02923 (color).jpg/wikimediacommons; 150cr/File:Eros, Vesta and Ceres size comparison.jpg/wikimediacommons; 151b/File:OSIRIS-REx artist concept.jpg/wikimediacommons; 153bl/File:Leonid Meteor.jpg/wikimediacommons; 154b/File:Moons of the Solar System.jpg/wikimediacommons; 155br/File:Globe of Science and Innovation, Cern.jpg/wikimediacommons; 157br/File:Stephen Hawking.StarChild.jpg/wikimediacommons; 158&159b/File:P200 Dome Open.jpg/wikimediacommons; 160bl/File:Accretion Disk Binary System.jpg/wikimediacommons; 161bl/File:NuSTAR spacecraft model.png /wikimediacommons; 162cl/File:Brahe.jpg/wikimediacommons; 162c/File:Charles Messier.jpg/wikimediacommons; 162cr/File:William Herschel01.jpg/wikimediacommons; 163tl/File:EdwardEmersonBarnard.jpg/wikimediacommons; 163tc/File:Hans Bethe.jpg /wikimediacommons; 163cr/File:Subrahmanyan Chandrasekhar.gif/wikimediacommons; 163bc/File:Cecilia Helena Payne-Gaposchkin (1900-1979) - Science Service.jpg/wikimediacommons; 170tr/File:1600 Himmelsscheibe von Nebra sky disk anagoria.jpg/wikimediacommons; 170bc/File:Madrid rosny bb 0033.jpg/wikimediacommons; 170br/File:Anaxagoras Lebiedzki Rahl.jpg/wikimediacommons; 171tl/File:Sanzio 01 Plato Aristotle.jpg/wikimediacommons; 171tr/File:Francesco Hayez 001.jpg/wikimediacommons; 171cl/File:Aristarchus working.jpg/wikimediacommons; 171cr/File:Heraclides Ponticus - Illustrium philosophorum et sapientum effigies ab eorum numistatibus extractae.png/wikimediacommons; 171br/File:Retrato de Julio César (26724093101) (cropped).jpg/wikimediacommons; 172tc/File:Jan Matejko-Astronomer Copernicus-Conversation with God.jpg/wikimediacommons; 172cl/File:Tycho Brahe.JPG/wikimediacommons; 172br/File:Portrait Confused With Johannes Kepler 1610.jpg/wikimediacommons; 173tr/File:Galileo Donato.jpg/wikimediacommons; 173tl/File:Galileo moon phases.jpg/wikimediacommons; 173cr/File:Justus Sustermans - Portrait of Galileo Galilei, 1636.jpg/wikimediacommons; 173b/File:Galileo Galilei; Galileo Galilei at his trial at the Inquisi Wellcome V0018716.jpg/wikimediacommons; 175cl/File:Edmund Halley. Mezzotint by J. Faber, 1722, after T. Murray, Wellcome V0002531.jpg/wikimediacommons; 175c/Pierre-Simon_marquis_de_Laplace_(1745-1827)_Guérin/wikimediacommons; File:Joseph Louis Lagrange.jpg/wikimediacommons; 176cr/File:STS-128 ISS-20 Destiny.jpg/wikimediacommons; 176b/File:ISSpoststs131.jpg/wikimediacommons; 177tr/File:1990 s31 IMAX view of HST release.jpg/wikimediacommons; 178&179tc/File:Half moon over The Hague (Unsplash).jpg/wikimediacommons; 179b/File:Falcon Heavy Side Boosters landing on LZ1 and LZ2 - 2018 (25254688767).jpg/wikimediacommons; 179br/File:Falcon Heavy Demo Mission (40126461851).jpg/wikimediacommons; 181c/File:AstronautsEatingBurgers.jpg/wikimediacommons; 181br/File:Worden w czasie przygotowa do misji Apollo 15 71pc0488-m.jpg/wikimediacommons; 182bl/File:RIAN archive 612748 Valentina Tereshkova.jpg/wikimediacommons; 182br/File:Sally Ride, First U.S. Woman in Space - GPN-2004-00019.jpg/wikimediacommons; 183cr/File:Astronaut Neil A. Armstrong (1964).jpg/wikimediacommons; 183br/File:Buzz Aldrin black and white dress uniform photo portrait.jpg/wikimediacommons; 184c/File:Apollo 8 crew training.jpg & File:Apollo8 Prime Crew (landscape crop).jpg/wikimediacommons; 184bc/File:Luna-9 model.jpg/wikimediacommons; 184tr/File:Prior to launch in May 1973, the Skylab space station.jpg/wikimediacommons; 184br/File:Crew of STS-107, official photo.jpg/wikimediacommons; 185tr/File:Space Shuttle Endeavour landing.jpg/wikimediacommons; 185cr/File:Eileen Collins on STS-93.jpg/wikimediacommons; 185cl/File:ISS-02 Soyuz TM-32 Taxi crewmembers in the Zvezda Service Module.jpg/wikimediacommons